"Stephen Bolt is a man who loves God and knows how to make money. This wisdom comes from his knowing the real priorities in life, in this case honoring the Lord Jesus Christ first, and then understanding how to invest His money. There are numerous books on investing and financial planning, but the uniqueness of Stephen's book is that it is a template to help people develop an academically sound yet personally based financial plan. Stephen Bolt boldly states that the number one asset in his life is Jesus Christ. As you get into the book you will find it interspersed with scriptures and solid financial tips. Stephen's book will help you to invest your money wisely if you own 401(k)s, IRAs, Mutual Funds, Insurance, and other money assets. Stephen's counsel will also provide a needed balance in your personal Spiritual life values. I recommend that you let Stephen's book help you make the most positive financial and Spiritual decisions in life with all your most coveted investments."

— DAVID B. WARDELL PHD.
Co-Founder of Promise Keepers

"Stephen Bolt hits a homerun with this book. His premise is basic and indisputable—all that we have belongs to God and we are only stewards. In a practical approach to investing, Stephen helps Christians learn how to manage their fiscal resources in a way that not only reflects Christian values but also bears witness that Christian moral principles are essential to any civilized society. This is a critical resource for the person who wants to be sure his investments are not supporting abortion, pornography, the gay agenda or other unbiblical values."

— TIM WILDMON
President, American Family Association

"Money on Loan from God is an exciting ride. Where others fear to tread, Stephen Bolt pulls no punches in his call to a more specific life in Christ that involves the management of personal finances. He weaves together the important threads of a life in Christ, a financial plan that supports it, and values-based investing. This book is both a beacon for the Christian community to enable its members to be truly good stewards of the money that God has given, and a wake-up call to those who have not realized the important role that they play in the war for our country's soul."

— JAMES H. MUKOYAMA, JR.
U.S. Army Major General (Retired)
Executive Vice President of Regal Securities, Inc.
A ten-year Promise Keeper

"The idea of aligning one's money with his or her faith and values is of paramount importance to not only each person, but also to our country. *Money On Loan From God* is a bold challenge to every reader to choose the path for managing their money that glorifies God and nurtures the foundational principles that have shaped America's greatness."

— PAUL DIETRICH
Managing Director, Foxhall Capital Management, Inc.

"Other so-called financial experts write feverishly on historical market trends in the hopes that quixotic investors will fall victim to the flawed theories of the stock market . . . but not Stephen Bolt. Bolt actively embraces solid biblical principles and the concepts of active management to clearly define what it is Christians are called to do as stewards of God's blessings."

— RICHARD LACKEY
Executive Director, ETS Capital Management, LLC
Author, *Cashing in on Wall Street's Ten Greatest Myths*

Money on Loan from God

STEPHEN R. BOLT

Rearden Publishing, Inc.
Franklin, Tennessee

Published by Rearden Publishing, Inc.
801 Crescent Centre Drive, Suite 450
Franklin, Tennessee 37067

Scripture quotations are taken from the New International Version, Copyright © 1973, 1978, 1984 by International Bible Society. Used by permission of Zondervan Bible Publishers.

ISBN-10:   0-9722183-1-9
ISBN-13: 978-0-9722183-1-3

Cover and Interior Design: Desktop Miracles, Inc.

Stephen Bolt is a registered representative of Capital Financial Services, Inc., member NASD/SIPC/MSRB. The views expressed herein are solely those of the author and may not necessarily be supported by Capital Financial Services, Inc., its officers, directors or any other company or organization except for Faith Financial Planners, Inc.

The information contained in this book is intended for general education purposes only and should not be considered as specific investment advice.

Publisher's Cataloging-in-Publication Data
(Prepared by the Donohue Group, Inc.)

Bolt, Stephen R.
   Money on loan from God / Stephen R. Bolt.
      p. : charts ; cm.
   ISBN : 0-9722183-1-9
   Includes index.

   1. Finance, Personal—Religious aspects—Christianity.
   2. Investments—Religious aspects—Christianity.
   3. Saving and investment—Religious aspects—Christianity.
   4. Investments—Moral and ethical aspects.   I. Title.

HG179 .B65   2006

                                          332.024

Printed in the United States of America

To my dearest, sweet mother,
Lenora Darling Bolt,
who gave her all in everything she did,
that Christ might be glorified.
I so terribly miss being able to wrap my arms
around her in a warm hug. Yet,
I nevertheless find joy in knowing that
she is now eternally fulfilled,
basking in the glory of her Father.

TABLE OF CONTENTS

SECTION THREE

INSURING YOUR FAMILY

SECTION FOUR

WHAT DO YOU WANT YOUR MONEY TO DO?

SECTION FIVE

INVESTING IN THE STOCK MARKET

SECTION TEN

VICTORY, AT LAST!

ACKNOWLEDGEMENTS

Money on Loan from God is my fourth book. The task of writing a book is certainly exhilarating, but it is also consuming in many ways. It could not be accomplished without the help of many people.

In that regard, there are a number of people I wish to thank. David Prentice with Lightning Source gave me his insights into how best to make this book available. The raw creativity that is the foundation for any book needs some serious editing help, and for that I thank the true professionals at Desktop Miracles. My very good friends, Reverend James Livengood, Ron Lively, and—in particular—Gary Wood, forced me to bring clarity to certain points.

I also want to thank James W. Bolt, RICA Researcher, for his help in documenting certain historical elements, and Austin Burrows for his help with statistical research. I especially want to thank Thomas H. Redmond for his unwavering support and encouragement in a "mighty, mighty way" throughout this 15-month project. Tom is truly someone who gives his all in the battles that he chooses to fight, whether as an accomplished NCAA wide receiver, the father of four wonderful girls, or fearless warrior in the battle for America's soul.

I also want to thank Kay Kay Ray for being that "available vessel" through which so much of God's guidance and blessing has come.

Finally, I wish to thank God for blessing me with a most supportive, encouraging, wonderful, intelligent, and (my favorite!) very spirited wife, whose outer beauty is surpassed only by that which fuels her from within. My children and I are truly blessed.

STEPHEN R. BOLT

ABOUT THE AUTHOR

Stephen R. Bolt graduated from the University of Alabama as a full-scholarship track athlete with a degree in political science and a minor in Russian and business. After college, the three-time NCAA All-American and sub-four-minute-miler ran at a world-class level on Nike's elite team, Athletics West, until the mid–1980s. In 1981, he joined a Lutheran financial services company and quickly became the top producer out of 2,000 agents. In 1987, he joined a competing Lutheran financial services company to establish a distribution system in the southeast U.S. After earning his Certified Financial Planner credentials in 1993, Stephen developed a highly successful financial planning firm in Nashville, Tennessee, where he also earned *Financial Planner of The Year in 1995* from one of the largest independent financial services firms in the United States. From 1994 to 1997, he served as host of "Financial Point" for a Nashville Christian radio station. In 1999, he developed MoneyAndValues.com, the first Internet-based technology that allowed investors to see what issues and values were being supported by investors' money in mutual funds and variable product sub-accounts. In 2001, Stephen and his brother Andy formed what is today Faith Financial Planners, Inc., a growing network of financial advisors committed to integrating personal faith into the financial planning process.

Along the way, Stephen also helped syndicate oil and gas investment programs, launched a values-based family of mutual funds, helped develop and syndicate a number of private offerings, served as chief manager of hedge funds investing in charged-off receivables, developed the industry's first values-based online stock trading platform (www.PKValuesTrade.com) and wrote four books.

Stephen and his wife Libby live with their four young children, Ruby, Ann-Rachel, Reagan, and Faith in Williamson County, just south of Nashville, Tennessee.

INTRODUCTION

I approached the first class line at the Delta Airlines counter in the Denver airport hurriedly, as always. Being a Platinum Level customer, although confirming too many days and nights away, also meant not having to wait in line and being able to arrive "just in time." This was pre–9/11, so security was not the bottleneck that it is today.

As I came closer, towing my bags across the marble floor, my eyes took in the lighted flight notices. I was relieved to find that there was only one passenger in front of me in line. Then I did a double take: Wow! That was *him*—my intellectual hero, William F. Buckley. I had watched him in awe, over many years, on everything from Sunday morning talk shows to PBS-sponsored debates. This was the champion of debate who so skillfully engaged his opponents with his unique combination of unmatched political genius, his grasp of the English language, and his display of classical etiquette and wit. His opponents were completely unaware that when he had finished, they stood in front of the audience completely naked . . . and *smiling*.

I was so close to *this master of intellect* that I could have touched him, or at least shook his hand and told him how grateful I was for his wisdom, for carrying the conservative torch through the most difficult period in American political history. But I didn't. Instead, I decided to let him simply enjoy being alone and "unnoticed."

In this book, I share my thoughts on issues of grave importance, such as our ability to sustain these great United States so that free citizens will continue to be able to live and prosper in a culture laden with the heritage of Christian values. William F. Buckley has had a profound influence on my thoughts. I remember something I read in an unauthorized biography about him.

The setting was a press conference in 1965 in New York City. Buckley was running for mayor as the Conservative Party candidate. The press wanted to know if Buckley truly wanted to be Mayor of New York City.

"I have never considered it," Buckley responded.

The bewildered reporter then asked, "Do you think that is something that at present should be considered?"

Buckley's answer belies the difference between statesmen and politicians, and between people of principle versus self-promoters who simply manipulate popular ignorance to their personal advantage. "Not necessarily. What is important is that certain points of view should prevail. Whether you or I administer those points of view is immaterial to me, assuming you are a good administrator."

I love that guy.

Can you imagine most any politician saying something so selfless and value laden? Picture a recent president (I do not want to get politically biased here, so I will not name the person from Arkansas that I am specifically referring to), or many senators, congressmen, and governors saying such a thing. How about pastors? Or financial advisors? Or... dare I say, *authors?*

There are numerous books on investing, on financial planning, on investing with liberal values, and on life planning available to the interested reader. But there is not one book that I am aware of that approaches the idea of establishing an academically sound financial plan for the specific purpose of advancing the Kingdom of God through each believer's life plan, so that the result of such stewardship on a mass scale could ultimately change the political culture of our precious country. *That* is why was I determined to write this book.

I wish that I were not the author of a book that could incite controversy against the politically correct status quo. But since I find no others advancing this idea in such a public manner, and from the perspective of an experienced financial services professional, and since I have only one life to live, I will step forward as that standard bearer.

And yet, as I write this book, I feel exactly the same way William F. Buckley must have felt running for mayor of New York City in 1965.

By the way, I am aware that Buckley lost the mayoral election by a significant margin, so you can suppose that my motives, like his, were something other than an attempt to engender popularity.

At that same press conference, the reporter kept quizzing Buckley about how many votes he thought he would get. The reporter reminded Buckley of the vote totals for the last election, just after the Party had been founded, and how the Conservative Party had come up short. He then asked his final question: "How many votes do you expect to get, conservatively speaking?"

Buckley, being Buckley, responded with, "Conservatively speaking, *one.*"

Principle, honor, duty, and moral virtue are becoming more and more rare as an integrated part of the tapestry of our great country. Over the years, I have heard, or read, many wise and virtuous sayings, some of which I have even framed and placed in my home, my study, and my office. One such saying that I find appropriate is from Groucho Marx, who once said firmly, "These are my principles. So, if you don't like them, I have others."

Very funny as a joke, but very sad as a political commentary on our American culture today. It is the antithesis to what Martin Luther said to the papal court in 1521, where he was told to recant his revolutionary theology or face execution. Instead of saying, "I have other principles, how about these? Will they suffice?" He said, "Here I stand. I can do no other."[1] Let the chips fall where they may. Today, millions of Christians thank God that Luther took that stand 500 years ago!

Still, there are those who say that the battle is too far gone, that we are already too outnumbered. Nothing we can do can get our culture back. You can't go against the tide. For them, I have another favorite, a poem from Shel Silverstein which is framed and on a wall in our home for my children to see everyday:

"Listen to the mustn'ts child,
Listen to the don'ts,
Listen to the shouldn'ts,
The impossibles, the won'ts,
Listen to the never haves,
Then listen close to me:
Anything can happen child, anything can be."

Shel Silverstein is right, but only to the extent that someone, the child, is willing to put principle before self.

This book is different.

"Some people like to tiptoe through life,
so that they can arrive at death safely."

If that is your mantra, then let me save you the trouble of reading this book. *Money on Loan from God* will challenge you in many ways, and it will, in fact, cause you to begin to question much of what you may have accepted previously as *truth*.

This book is not intended for those who wish to simply follow the crowd, be part of the current consensus, or who want to live life in such a way that they make as few waves as possible.

This is not a book for those who want to live a legalistic, cookie-cutter life following simple advice devoid of intellectual integrity.

Money on Loan from God is not for those who have been so brainwashed by our politically correct culture that they see anyone who questions the "truth" as being a racist, a male chauvinist, or a zealot.

It is not for those who want to live a formulistic life, following the newest version of the "Ten Rules of Investing Success."

It is not for those who want to be entertained and emotionally manipulated.

This book *is*, however, an important and timely resource for anyone who is intelligently searching for a template to help them develop an academically based financial plan. It is for those who want a plan that encompasses all of the elements of investing, including the dynamic which will help them use their money in such a manner that it will literally impact the course of the American cultural war we are engaged in today.

Finally, although I have total conviction about this book, I am also well aware that I am nothing more than a complete, disastrous sinner, unworthy of a reunion with my Creator, except for the redemption that I have through my savior, Jesus Christ. I am a faulty, sinful, broken clay pot. But I pray that through the Potter's merciful and loving perfect hands, I am able to be used through this book for His glory.

Martin Luther once said, "There is no pure motive for anything." I'm sure that if the onion that is my "motive" for this book is peeled back far enough, some sin will be visible. That, as Luther said, is inevitable. As a vessel, an author, I am imperfect, even in motive. But our recognition of that imperfection is not supposed to stop us from giving the battle our best. The grotesque sin of killing Christians did not stop the redeemed Apostle Paul from evangelizing, nor did sin stop the doubting Thomas or the liar Peter from ultimately giving everything they had for the glory of God.

With that said, I will paraphrase another of Luther's great posits: since we cannot help but sin, and since it is the grace of God that saves us and not our own righteousness, sin boldly.[2]

"Therefore, sin, and sin boldly, knowing that by the grace of God you are saved."

So, here goes!

Important Questions That Need Answers

Do you have money invested in mutual funds, stocks, bonds, or a retirement plan? If you do, you might be shocked to learn that the amount of money you give to your church and ministries each year likely pales by comparison to the amount you have invested on behalf of the radical gay and lesbian political movement, the abortion rights campaign, and the marketing of pornography. Yes, you read that correctly the first time, but go ahead and read it again.

That is absurd and horrible. How can that be?

Would you like to be sure that the money you invest in your 401(k), IRA, mutual funds, and so on is not only helping you attain your personal financial objectives, but is also invested in a way that reflects *your* core personal values? For example, is it important to you as a parent to know that your child's college education account is not being funded by mutual funds that are invested in the pornography, tobacco, or alcoholic beverage industries? If you are pro-life, you might sleep better at night knowing that your IRA is not invested in companies involved in the abortion industry. And if you are outraged at the blatant gay and lesbian shows on television, you might welcome the knowledge that your retirement fund is not invested in companies producing, distributing, or promoting those programs.

But how can you know?

Are you sick and tired of the stock market's rollercoaster ride? First you're up, then you're reeling from what feels like an out-of-control downward spiral. Would you like to find investments that offer the same kind of double-digit return potential as the stock market, but without the wild ride associated with market volatility?

Do such investments really exist?

If you are going to be invested in the stock market, wouldn't you feel better if you could add some form of a guarantee so that you don't lose your retirement income just when you need it?

Is it possible to have a guarantee on a stock market investment?

Have you ever wondered which mutual fund strategy works best? In your wildest imaginings, have you ever thought how great it would be to actually have a mutual fund manager oversee your private account, kind of like your own little private mutual fund?

Hire a mutual fund manager for my account?

Finally, have you ever looked at the stars at night, alone, with nothing but quiet space all around you, and wondered, "What's this thing called *life* really about, anyway? Why am I here? Where am I going? Does it matter?"

Can anyone really know those answers?

If you answered "yes" to any of these questions, sit back, relax, and enjoy the journey that is titled *Money on Loan from God*. This book is intended to present information that you likely won't find easily elsewhere. This knowledge will help you make educated decisions about your life and financial plan. In fact, by the time you are through reading this book, you will likely have more of an education than many of the so-called *financial advisors* that you have known or heard on the radio. That is simply because most financial advisors are very limited in their scope of knowledge. Sometimes this has to do with their particular licensing or their business model, and other times it is the result of limitations placed on them by their employers.

You would not believe the conversations we have with financial advisors who hear about Faith Financial Planners, Inc. and want to consider us as a career choice. *"You can do that?"* some say incredulously, when we talk about certain investments that their well-known employers do not allow them to offer their clients. They not only are prohibited from discussing certain categories of investments with their clients, but they may not even know those categories exist! I have worked with clients with a net worth in the hundred-million-dollar range who were totally insulated by their *financial advisors* from expecting anything other than that the stock market is the only answer. They went from one money manager to another, from one mutual fund to another, only to find the same lack of predictability. Up down, up down, up down.

Ever heard of alternative investments? Looking for double-digit returns with no stock market risk? Interested in predictable returns from business models that make sense—some with long track records? This book can help you learn about all of these options.

My Background

In 24 years in this industry, I have had the opportunity to consult for high-profile NCAA coaches, professional athletes, multi-million dollar pensions, and successful business owners, but also the struggling young single father or mother who has only $50 a month to invest.

Money on Loan from God is written to give you, the reader, the information you need to build the best, most effective, and personal financial plan you can possibly obtain, regardless of your current level of investment experience or net worth.

I have been blessed with an unusually broad and successful career in the financial services industry. So that you have a context within which to consider the validity of my comments throughout this book, below are some of the highlights of my career:

- Award-winning top producer at three national financial services firms.
- Launched one of the first mutual fund families that considered conservative values as part of the investment decision-making process.
- Founded MoneyAndValues.com, a leading Internet-based values screening company that allows financial advisors to see what values are represented by the holdings of as many as 14,000 mutual funds, as well as variable annuities.
- Co-founder of Faith Financial Planners, Inc., a national network of financial advisors with a focus toward values-based investing.
- Chief Manager of two hedge funds that focus on the charged-off receivables asset class.
- Helped syndicate an oil and gas program.
- Authored three previous books on financial planning.
- Interviewed on CNNfn, Bloomberg TV, regional Fox, over two hundred radio programs, and numerous periodicals.

Once again, however, I need to give you a note of caution: This book will challenge you. It's not like anything you've read before. You may have to think through some of the concepts, and some of your paradigms may be challenged. It is not a "bandwagon" or "me too" book. If all I do is tell you what you expect to hear and meet you in your comfort zone, then I am wasting time for both of us. Instead, I am using the following three principles as my guideline:

Is it relevant?

Is it interesting?

Is it true?

You'll have to be the judge of whether I accomplish the second guideline.

The Role of Money in Life

There is a movement of historic proportion that is tearing us away from the fundamental Judeo-Christian principles that this country was built on. And there is a revolt of similar proportion taking place within Christendom, as the landscape shifts. George Barna in his book *Revolution* quantifies this movement and says that we are being forced to choose sides.

I do not mean to offend anyone and if I do, I ask for your forgiveness. My intent is to teach critical thinking as a necessary dynamic in both financial planning and "choosing sides."

If you are tired of looking for answers by watching television programs that focus on the stock market, reading the financial section of newspapers, listening to your stockbroker's newest "great stock pick," fearing a life insurance salesman's pitch, or attending another profoundly boring financial seminar, then this book is for you. I am excited to help you free yourself from a lack of information, a lack of objectivity, and what must feel like an overwhelming complexity involved in the investment decision-making process. You, my friend, are about to find out what you have been missing.

Life, Purpose, Plan, Money. The order that you place these four simple words will determine whether your life has meaning, or is simply an interlude between birth and death. I am not being overly dramatic when I make that statement.

Most people unintentionally place so much emphasis on money—its abundance or deficiency—that their entire life revolves around it. Scripture tells us that the "love of money is the root of all kinds of evil." The love of money in order to get that new house, furniture, boat, Ivy League education, or country club membership is a symptom of warped priorities. And adding money to that will only exacerbate problems. Do you ever think that money could somehow miraculously solve all of your problems? If you could just win some sweepstakes, or the lottery, that life would be perfect? Not so, says Jesus. Not so, says real life. Consider the following real life story.

"For Mack W. Metcalf and his estranged second wife, Virginia G. Merida, sharing a $34 million jackpot in 2000 meant escaping poverty at breakneck speed. Years of blue-collar struggle and ramshackle apartment life gave way almost overnight to limitless leisure, big houses and lavish toys. Metcalf bought a Mount Vernon-like estate in southern Kentucky, stocking it with horses and vintage cars. Merida bought a Mercedes-Benz and a modernistic mansion overlooking the Ohio River, surrounding herself with stray cats.

"But trouble came almost as fast. They were divorced in 2001. Metcalf's first wife sued him for $31,000 in unpaid child support, a former girlfriend wheedled $500,000 out of him while he was drunk, and alcoholism increasingly paralyzed him.

"Merida's boyfriend died of a drug overdose in her hilltop house, a brother began harassing her, she said, and neighbors came to believe that her once welcoming home had turned into a drug den.

"It was as if their lives as rich people had taken on an eerie symmetry. So did their deaths. In 2003, just three years after cashing in his winning ticket, Metcalf died of complications relating to alcoholism at the age of 45. On the day before Thanksgiving, Merida's partly decomposed body was found in her bed. Authorities are looking into the possibility of a drug overdose. She was 51.

"Some friends and relatives said the moral of the story was clear. 'Any problems people have, money magnifies it so much, it's unbelievable,' said Robert Merida, one of Merida's three brothers." (James Dao, *New York Times* News Service, 12/05/05)

Placing too much emphasis on the advantages that money can bring is akin to idolatry, in that it displaces God as the focus of our life. That is somewhat self-evident. But what about the flip side? What about the people who are so committed to getting out of debt that they let life—and God's calling—pass them by in the process?

I once did a seminar in Clarkesville, Tennessee which covered a broad range of financial issues. After it ended and most of the attendees were saying their farewells, one lady, who looked to be about 50, approached me. "Mr. Bolt," she said, "I need your help. After almost 18 years, I will finally be completely out of debt when I make my next month's house payment." Instead of with a big smile normally associated with the achievement of a difficult and admirable objective, she spoke matter-of-factly. "I've worked three jobs and thought of nothing else except getting out of debt for so long, that I never really gave much consideration to what I should do when I finally reached that goal.

"Now that I have paid everything off, I will have some money and I want to know what I should do with it," she asked with a countenance that suggested she was in uncomfortable, uncharted waters. This bewildered lady was completely lost and without any life compass.

I wanted to hug her and cry. She had completely missed the point of life because she was so caught up in the idea of getting out of debt. How many relationships did she compromise by working three jobs? How many hugs with her children did she forgo, over eighteen formative years, just so that she could achieve her financial goal? How many times did she ignore a call from her heavenly father because she was so preoccupied? And now, since she literally had no real life—since her purpose in life, to get out of debt, was now in her rear-view mirror—she was completely lost, and her countenance confirmed it.

God's Role

This book is about money and also the values that it supports, regardless of whether you choose to pay attention to that dynamic or not. I will attempt to take you places you have never been and give you insights on investing that, to my knowledge, don't exist in any other text. But more importantly, I want to help you *make educated decisions about how to invest, so that you are in a better position to fulfill the calling that is God's purpose for breathing life into you— unique and special you—and placing you at this pre-appointed place and time in all of history.* Without that context, frankly, money is completely irrelevant. Whether you are able to reduce your income tax burden, achieve a better rate of return on your retirement assets, or otherwise achieve your financial goals is nothing but a huge waste of time at best, and quite possibly a path to selfishness and narcissism at worst, if the goal is anything other than glorifying God.

One final note: This book is written from a decidedly Christian point of view. I do not mean to offend anyone, nor do I mean to try to force my faith on anyone. Each person is accountable to God for his or her own faith and actions. Each one of us is on our own very personal spiritual journey. My faith has developed over 50 years, and—God willing—it will continue to take me deeper and ever closer in communion with my God. Please know that just as I sincerely encourage you to invite my God, the father of Jesus of Nazareth, the Triune God, into your life, I also respect that you have a right not to do so.

I am honored that you are allowing me to share the insights I have learned over my career with you. What you do with this information is entirely up to you.

Okay, now you have been sufficiently warned. Let's go exploring!

The Meaning of Life

Chapter I

Life

It was September 30, 1971. We were joking around and cutting up, as 16-year-old high school students will do, while performing the mundane task of filing 3"x 5" index cards in drawers that listed contact information for each student's family. In 1971 there were no computers, so a handful of students were selected by the office to help with the chore. It was early in the day, about 8:15 A.M., and we were in the spacious lunch room. Each of us was responsible for certain parts of the alphabet. The easy work was made much better by telling jokes and kidding around. It was fun for the hour each day that it lasted.

Out of the corner of my eye, I saw Ray Reynolds, Assistant Principal of Virgil I. Grissom High School, burst into the room. Mr. Reynolds had a couple of very unflattering names that he was known by in student vernacular. Mr. Reynolds was not, shall we say, fun to be around. Like a Nazi SS trooper, he stalked the halls daily, looking for trouble. He was always scowling, but as he ran into the lunch room heading directly for us, he seemed particularly agitated.

"What are you doing?" he yelled at us, his eyebrows furled, his face showing rage, and his animated body movements reinforcing the unfolding drama. "You should be done by now!" He began rifling through random drawers, seemingly searching for a specific card. He jerked his head up and yelled, "We have an emergency situation and I need to find the parents!"

I'll never forget those words as long as I live. At that instant, my world literally stopped. I froze. Everything became foggy. The room took on a surrealistic look, as if a heavy New England fog had suddenly moved in. An unworldly, out-of-body experience unfolded. I remember dropping the cards that were in my hand onto the table, standing up very slowly and backing away. Ray Reynolds was still in the midst of his frantic search, but I was already at the end. I knew.

I remember walking ghost-like out of the lunch room and into the hallway, heading to the gym where the coaches' office was located. I was a star track athlete, so the athletics department was my second home. Something in my head told me to go there. I had to get to a phone, and I knew there was one in Coach Robinson's office. My emotions were out of control, screaming and bouncing off the walls inside my head. "Phone. Need to get to a phone." Outwardly, I felt as if I had the movements and appearance of a zombie. I had no idea if anyone saw me, nor did I care. Nothing mattered *at all*—except the phone.

Finally, I arrived in the bright orange locker room of the Grissom Tigers and pushed through the door that separated the coaches' office from the entrance hall. No one was there, thank God, because I literally could not talk. How would I be able to explain my unexcused absence from the lunch room filing party, or why I needed a phone? I didn't care. Nothing mattered at all—except the phone. God's grace carried me, uninterrupted, to the wooden chair at the coach's desk, where a black rotary phone sat waiting for me.

I picked up the receiver slowly and, with fingers shaking, dialed my home number and prayed that my mother would answer. She said, "Hello?" Sounding soft as a whisper, but with the pain of pulling myself across shards of broken glass, I said "Mom, come get me. Joel's dead." As I very slowly took the receiver from my ear, I heard my rescuer say, "I'll be right there."

I didn't know if it was from drugs, carbon monoxide, or a bullet fired at very close range, but I did know that it was suicide. Joel and I were close friends. In fact, as we later found out, I was the last person he spoke with before he pulled the trigger.

Joel was a very intelligent kid and we enjoyed intellectually challenging each other and everything about the established world. But whereas I had a solid Christian and family foundation from which to exercise my developing intellectual aptitude, Joel's world foundation was fluid. I was aware of that difference between us. In fact, he often said that the only reason he considered me his friend was because I was "different" than the other jocks and honor society students of the "establishment." Joel had been an excellent wrestler, but he gravitated increasingly toward the siren song of the drug, anti-establishment, and rock culture of the 1970s. He soon jettisoned his involvement with organized *anything*—especially sports.

"No, you won't, Joel," I had counseled late the night before on the phone, in what turned out to be our last conversation. "You are always saying that you're going to 'go out' this way or that, but you're not going to do it. That's a lurid fantasy. I'll see you in home room tomorrow morning and we'll talk about it then." I tried—as I had in every similar conversation for the past several months—to keep him engaged, looking forward to the next something—anything. I had prayed that this suicide thing would just go away. Joel was a very good-looking guy, with dark brown hair, a tall, slim athletic build, and very bright. He had absolutely nothing to gain by committing suicide. It *had* to be a phase. It had to be. Right?

"This time is different. The walrus, man. I am the walrus, kookoo kuchoo. Come together," Joel softly said, with what I guessed was a coy smiling face on the other end of the phone. I could hear The Beatles playing in the background and guessed that his attempt at quoting a few lines from a couple of random Beatles tunes was drug-induced. Pills or marijuana, I didn't know—didn't care. I often talked with Joel about drugs and how he needed to stop using. I never even considered using. I had no interest.

Before dawn the next morning, Joel would take his father's hunting shotgun, sit on the floor, put the barrel in his mouth . . . and pull the trigger.

I was a pallbearer at his funeral. I remember wanting to scream at his parents for the unimaginable injustice of their son's suicide, which I blamed on them. I was seething. How else does a 16-year-old make sense of it? The other person I held accountable was . . . me. After all, though I certainly wasn't the cause, I saw myself as a failed solution.

The Aftermath

I remember, a couple of weeks later, driving down Four Mile Post Road, a narrow two-lane road in Huntsville, Alabama, where we lived. The speed limit was 40 mph, but I had the 1967 yellow Plymouth Belvedere station wagon up to 60 mph, and the telephone posts on the side of the road were flying by remarkably close to the right side of my parents' car. I remember looking at my hand gripping the steering wheel so hard that it was almost white. As usual, I was thinking that I had no right to life for having failed Joel. At that moment, at 60 mph and climbing, I could do something about it. The only solution to this cosmic black hole that would forever haunt me was to pull that brown steering wheel ever so slightly to the right, just before the next telephone pole. My heart was racing, my breathing heavy. Just a couple of inches to turn the wheel. The telephone poles were flying by now. I had only about 800 yards of opportunity left before the road widened. Just a little more to the right, that's it. Here it comes, yes . . . now! *WHAM!*

But I didn't.

Instead, I did my penance by finding clever ways of buying vodka and taking it with me to Joel's grave. There I would sit for long periods of time on nights when I could get away from home. *Why? Why? Why?* I would look up at the black night sky, with stars brightly twinkling in God's incomprehensible universe, and rage that question at Him. Ultimately, I would give in to the silent reply and simply break down and sob until I was exhausted.

No one really knew about my grief. I hid it well. I was tough, smart, and well on my way to becoming the best high school miler in the nation. *Get over it.* But I didn't. For many years I secretly kept a copy of Joel's obituary in a recess of my wallet as a reminder of September 30, 1971.

I had been raised in a Christian home with strong Missouri Synod Lutheran parents. I was baptized and later confirmed publicly at age 13. I held my Christian faith as the core of my essence and relied on its compass to guide my decisions. So I accepted Joel's death in the context of my faith . . . sort of. But I did not understand the *why* part of it. Couldn't God, the God of love and mercy, do something to intervene? Why did He allow Joel to sink so low and pull the trigger? Where was my God, the God of the Bible, of Christmas and Easter and miracles?

Life Goes On

Life, as they say, goes on. I did, in fact, go on to become the best high school miler in the nation in 1973, according to *Track & Field News*. Recruited by every major college in the country, I finally decided to stay home and run for the Crimson Tide of the University of Alabama. While there, I was a ten-time Southeastern Conference (SEC) champion, and became the first person to break the four-minute mile in SEC history (the record still stands as I write this book). I finished my collegiate career with three NCAA All-American titles. After college, I continued my competitive running as one of Nike's elite runners, winning 10K races and marathons around the country and in England. Throughout the years, though, the *why* never left me.

I made the transition from competitive world-class running to business in a surprise move, but also with greater success than I would have imagined. In 1984, with no prior thoughts about retirement, I crossed the finish line of the Stockport (England) Daffodil International Marathon a full minute ahead of second place. I was barely able to stand up, and still gasping for sufficient oxygen, when I turned to my wife and the gaggle of people around me with cameras and flowers and champagne and said, "I'm finished."

"Of course you are", came my wife's response as she held me upright. "And you won!"

"No", I protested. "You don't understand, "I'm done. It's over." I spat the words out at the cost of more oxygen.

"Yes, 42 kilometers, and now you're done. Congratulations!" came the reply again, this time from someone with the news crew.

I said, "I quit. I'm not racing again. I'm not going to run any more races—I'm ending my career with this race." (In retrospect, I think it was oxygen deprivation that made me do it—*just kidding!*)

Turning to business, I quickly became the top producer of a large Lutheran financial services company. After seven years in sales, I resigned and moved to that company's competitor as a general manager, charged with developing a distribution system in the southeastern United States.

I was very intellectually engaged in the study of the Christian faith. I owned a small library of reference books, including *What Luther Says*, various concordances, books by Josephus, the disciples, apologetics, and the occult. I enjoyed reading Billy Graham, Josh McDowell, and Robert Schuller. My best friends were ministers. My most enjoyable times were spent over coffee in some pastor's kitchen, or on horseback with a pastor traversing the incredible beauty that is the Colorado Rockies, or even at a Lutheran Octoberfest with a German brew in hand—*always* engaged in a serious polemic conversation about some aspect of Christian faith. Intellectually, *I was there.*

But whether involved in competitive running or competitive business, the *why* of September 30, 1971 never left me: at midnight when I suddenly woke up, or during a run when my mind wandered. And especially at church.

No one could explain the *why* of September 30, 1971 to me. It took a revelation from God Himself on August 12, 1998, some 27 years later, to answer *why*. Set in an intellectual knowledge of my faith, satisfied with my business success, having achieved most of what I had set out to do in my athletic career, and with a very stable marriage and a daughter that we had adopted at age 10, life was quite comfortable. Little did I know that my life was about to get rocked and that the worst—and best—was about to come.

The Rocky Years

The years of unimaginable chaos in our daughter's life that had preceded our adoption of her had sewn intractable fear and distrust in our little girl. That combination, mixed with the complexities of teenage development, ignited. What we experienced as parents was a life we had never known before and were entirely unequipped to handle. For nine years we struggled painfully. The events we found ourselves immersed in seemed surreal, like something out of a nightmare. Up was down, and down was up. And then, at the age of majority, our daughter Linita disappeared.

My wife and I separated, and eventually were divorced. It was unimaginable: no infidelity, no financial problems, no greed. Just two Christians who got divorced.

My world was no longer solid. I was on fluid ground. I knew what my values were, and I knew who my God was, but now to the *why* of September 30, 1971, I could add two more whys. I was wandering in a spiritual wilderness.

Eventually, I met Elizabeth (Libby) Monette. One Sunday I took her to a church I had been visiting in my home city of Nashville, Tennessee. The senior pastor at the time, Charles McGowen, delivered a particularly insightful and inspiring message that day on the prodigal son. With tears in her eyes, Libby looked over at me and said, "If I ever get married again, I want a church like this to be the center of my family." (That did it. *Ring, please!*)

Libby and I were married in 1997. She had a beautiful eighteen-month-old little girl from a previous marriage that I fell immediately in love with. Then, it happened. We got pregnant. *I was going to be a father of my very own baby!* This baby even had a name: Forrest Stephen William Bolt. There is no word in the English language to describe how exhilarated I was. At every visit to the doctor, every kick of the baby, every sonogram, I was there. This was the event of my life!

Flying across the country and arriving home late one night from a business trip, I was met in the kitchen by Libby. This would be my last trip until Forrest's birth—only a few days away now. We chit-chatted about the day's events, and then moved to the bedroom. It was late and we were both tired. I asked if Forrest was being his usual energetic self, kicking and trying to arrive as early as possible in his new world. At that question, Libby's countenance showed some concern. She had not felt Forrest move for quite some time, when she thought about it.

We began considering information and options. We finally called the doctor, who told us that she would meet us at the hospital and to come as quickly as we could. We did. In fact, we beat her. The doctor on the floor interviewed us and then called for a sonogram. Having seen a number of these in the previous months, I knew what to look for. But it was not there.

Instead, the listless, still, silent little body of Forrest Bolt lay there—totally motionless and with no heartbeat. *WHY?* I wanted to scream. *Why, why, why?*

Oh, the pain I felt, Libby felt, and our parents and friends experienced. What an astounding tragedy. *Why?*

Revelation

After the c-section the next morning to deliver our beautiful baby, I needed some fresh air. I had not eaten in about twenty hours, nor did I want to. Nonetheless, I knew that I needed something.

My phone rang, and it was Linita, my daughter! In God's phenomenal mercy and grace, she had, in the last two years, gotten her life together and blossomed into one of the most outstanding, emotionally and spiritually grounded people I know.

"Dad, I am so, so sorry", she said. "I don't know what to say, but I also don't understand why God did this to you."

WHAM! All of a sudden, I felt something I had never experienced, and may never again experience. It was as if in one nanosecond I was presented with the story of God and man. I saw the spontaneous creation of Adam, the perfection of the Garden of Eden, the horror of the Fall, the prophets, the birth of Jesus, his ministry, the pain of the resurrection and his father turning away from him in the final sacrifice. Then I saw Jesus' triumphant resurrection and, finally, his charge to his people to minister to his creation until he returns in glory. All of that in the same span of time it took to flip a light switch. That is the only way I can describe the revelation that I received at that moment.

Immediately, I found myself replying forcefully to my daughter. "No, Linita! Forrest's death was *NOT* God's plan. His death is the result of a broken world where sin and chaos and destruction reign. No, this is not the world that God created for us. That world is now long gone, destroyed when Adam and Eve decided that they wanted to be like God and ate from the forbidden tree. They chose to renounce God's paradise in favor of their own authority. And in so doing, they accepted Satan as their partner. Forrest's death was not what God intended, it is what *Satan* intended. Destruction and chaos is what *Satan* wreaks, not God."

Finally, the answer to the great *why* of the painful events in my life. The unspeakable joy that now filled my heart at this most painful hour percolated from the knowledge that instead of God simply allowing us to rot in a terminal world of Satan's destruction, God has, throughout the ages, pursued us with his incalculable love, even to the point of providing the sacrificial means of taking our sin from us and placing it on his one and only perfect son. And because of that cosmic act, my beloved Forrest and I will be reunited in heaven, together in the paradise that God had intended from the beginning.

No, the question is not *why did this have to happen*, but rather *why doesn't more of this happen*? How can it be that there is any good in this world at all? That, my friends, is the true question post-Fall. If God were like us, he'd have said something like, "To hell with you, then. After all I've done for you. I even *created* you! And now, you throw it all away to partner with Lucifer, the angel of death, with whom I am at war, who seeks to destroy everything I have created, including you! You are not worthy of me. I'm moving on. You're on your own!"

The revelation I had I wish I could give to everyone. It gives life purpose and meaning. Everywhere we turn, people are asking *why*. No one gets to skate through life unscathed. Everyone has their Joels, their divorces, their problem teenagers, and their grief. Everyone. But moving from *why* to *praise God for His mercy* will literally change your life.

God as Anchor

The balance of this book will traverse a tremendous geography of financial information intended to help you truly understand the world of investing like you never have before. But before we leave this first, most important chapter, I want to do everything I can to set an anchor that you can hold onto when the roaring waves come crashing in—and they will. Satan has seen to that!

Understand that the extent to which you truly understand the Fall directly correlates to the extent to which you know the true God. A shallow understanding of the story of the Garden of Eden and God's intended relationship with man will set the state for a very shallow appreciation for, understanding of, and relationship with God, your incredible redeemer. Know the Fall and you will know your God.

One final, poignant example of how universal, transcending, and debilitating the *why* questions are. This one you will remember. On January 5, 2005, MSNBC, like every other news outlet and human interest program, was covering every angle and nuance of the recent devastating tsunami in southeast Asia. The death toll was up to 200,000 people, and it was climbing as new reports came in daily from remote locations. Death had come swiftly and unexpectedly to sunbathers, vacationers, taxi drivers, hotel workers, and worst of all—to children. Tens of thousands of little children had been swallowed up in a raging aquatic horror.

And now, the world's eyes were turned to God, the Father, the Creator, the God of love and peace and mercy, and with palms open and outstretched His children begged, *Why?* This time though, some 34 years later, I knew the answer.

Now, watching *Scarborough Country* on MSNBC, I was mortified to hear how a distinguished panel of Christian leaders (along with a Jewish rabbi and an atheist) responded to host and former Congressman Joe Scarborough's provocative question regarding God and the tsunami, *"Why did God allow this tragic event to occur?"*

One of the most prominent Christian female leaders today had a fantastic opportunity to answer the question for many unbelievers and troubled faithful. But, in my opinion, she missed the target.

"I know that God is a loving God. I don't look at the tsunami and what has happened at Asia. I look at the cross. And when I look at the cross of Jesus Christ, when God sent his own son to die to take away my sin, I know that God loves me . . . Why he has allowed this to happen, I don't know. I can't answer that question," she said. This author, speaker, and teacher went on to extol the nature of the love of our God and ended with, "So, this is a tragedy and it's a disaster, but it's not a reflection on the fact that God doesn't love us, because God loves us and the proof of that is the cross."

Her answer was true enough, but it had nothing to do with the question and left the audience to think that this icon of Christian faith did not have the answer (which, of course, she did)! In her defense, I'll say that it's easy being a "Monday-morning quarterback" in my cozy study, watching her on the hot seat while I sip a cold drink in front of my big-screen TV, dog snoring soundly on the leather couch next to me. I've been on live national TV (CNNfn, Bloomberg, regional Fox, etc.) and I'll just say . . . *it ain't as easy as it looks.*

The other defense I'll give her is a systemic problem that a lot of us who know our subject fall prey to. This was illustrated by something (then) House Speaker Newt Gingrich said to about 30 Republican campaign executives at the RNC's Campaign Management College outside Washington, DC in 1995. I was sitting about five feet from him when he said, "You know, we Republicans have the right message. We just don't know how to articulate it so that the average person can understand it." In other words, instead of answering the question, "What time is it?" with a simple "nine-thirty," we feel the need to explain how the darn clock *works.* This particular evangelist is so filled with faith and knowledge of God that she—and many of us—may miss the simplicity of the answer at times.

Next up on the TV show was Jennifer Giroux, Director of Women Influencing the Nation. Her response to *"Why did God allow the tsunami to kill 200,000 men, women and children in such a horrific natural disaster?"* made me cringe. Where the earlier guest had only missed an opportunity to be more on target for the unbelievers in the audience, Ms. Giroux left me with the impression that her God was a blind and raging God of wrath.

"Throughout history and as reported early in the Bible, God has always used plagues, floods and natural disasters as a source of punishment," she scolded. I was stunned. I'm imagining an Indonesian father with outstretched arms holding the bloody remains of his three-year-old son. Stricken with unimaginable grief, he is able to mouth the word "*why?*" through unstoppable sobs while looking with mind-numbing sadness into the MSNBC camera. And *this* is the response he gets? That his son died a horrible, painful death because . . . "throughout history . . . God has used plagues, etc. as a source of *punishment?*" And this is the God of love that we are supposed to want to be with for all eternity? No thank you!

But the worst was yet to come. The pompous and arrogant Rabbi Shmuley Boteach, author of *Face Your Fear,* responded with, "I think Jennifer Giroux is guilty of colossal blasphemy and even more colossal arrogance, because even Jesus on the cross says in Matthew 27 and Mark 15, 'My God, my God, why have you forsaken me?' He wanted to live. He was challenging God. He was saying life is precious, unlike (the evangelist) who just said only the afterlife matters. Jesus challenged God.

"How dare one say that 150,000 people, that you have never met, who are probably more righteous than you, more innocent than you, poor people who just worked hard to feed their kids, how dare you say they were punished by God? You don't know those people."

Man, I had never heard such blasphemy in all my life. We are supposed to challenge God, remind him that life is precious? Are you kidding? He is the *creator,* for heaven's sake. How can I possibly tell Him something about *His* creation that He doesn't know?

Finally, the atheist responded. She actually made a lot of (logical) sense. The combination of the panelists not having any commonality about their answers, and the tragedy having not been supernaturally stopped, is all she needed as confirmation that God does not exist. Too bad.

God *is* love. Read His story, the Bible. Not what you think God's story should be, or what some other explanation says God is all about, but rather His story as He has recorded it for us to know. The first chapter opens with us looking in on God creating the universe, the earth, and ultimately man and woman. Then evil enters the story in the form of Satan, the very real fallen angel who is on a mission to defeat God and destroy His creation. Man and woman succumb to the temptation of God's nemesis, and immediately ruin the paradise that God had created specifically for us. But instead of letting us be destroyed by the evil that we bring into God's custom-designed world, God *pursues* us with passionate, unconditional, and everlasting love, to the point of sacrificing His only son to take the burden of sin off of us. We are therefore redeemed, made right in our relationship with our true father and creator, through nothing that we did for ourselves—*nothing*—but rather through Jesus' death on the cross and subsequent resurrection.

The end of the story, as written in the final chapter of the Bible, shows us what God already knows: that evil and its destruction and death are defeated, and God renews His paradise for our benefit for all eternity.

In between the beginning and the end is our own individual story. Understand that you—yes, *you*—were chosen by this same God to be born even before your parents ever thought about conceiving you. *You* were created as a unique individual, profoundly unique, to play *your* role in God's cosmic plan to redeem His creation. Though Satan is wreaking havoc all around us, *you* are partnered with the Creator Himself through this fight to ultimate victory and an eternity where there is no Satan, and therefore no more *why*. He is remaking this sinful world through his Spirit moving in people like you, showing love where there is none, compassion when it is uncalled for, and the joy and peace of being redeemed even in the midst of utter personal failure, global moral decay, and tragedy. To the world, this is total nonsense, but to those who have been reunited with God, this is their very reason for living!

If you don't know how and why greed, murder, cancer, and tragedy, and all of the other evidences of sin entered the perfect world that God created for us, then you will never appreciate who God really is, and what unfathomable love he has for you. My prayer is that this chapter has provoked a serious and lifelong personal quest in you to find the answer to *why*. Once you find that answer, your world will then forever always make sense. It won't make it any less dangerous, or tragic, or painful, but the turmoil and suffering you will meet along the road that is your life will be matched by God's unending and unchanging power, love, forgiveness, and joy.

Life: this chapter explains who *you* are as a uniquely designed and valuable part of creation, a child of God Almighty who is set in this specific time and place to literally bring transformation to your world by being the personification of God's love. *That* is life. Nothing else can substitute.

With this life as our foundation, we move on to explore the second word in our sequential journey examining **Life, Purpose, Plan, Money.**

Chapter 2

Purpose

It was a clear but cold day as I hiked briskly up the back side of a small New Mexico mountain on a snow-covered trail. My heart was pounding not so much from the rather fast climb in altitude, but from the knowledge of what I would be confronted with at the top.

Sure enough, I had no sooner taken the last step of the summit trail than I saw two young men with ropes moving quickly toward me. "Grab on to this while I fasten the belt," the one with the black ski cap on his blonde head told me. While he fastened me, the other one pulled ropes toward me. Here was my great fear of the weekend executive management retreat. Rappelling down cliffs, scaling a 70-foot wall, and standing on a pie plate loosely fitted (and I mean *very* loosely fitted) to the top of a telephone pole in the woods was nothing. Piece of cake. No problem. But a zip line off of a rock that jutted out over rocky stream far below? No way! Heck, I could barely even see my "partners" on the other side, standing ready to pull me down from my death-defying flight across the deep canyon.

Are those ants over there? No, wait, I see a head. I think it's a human head. And that movement. I think those specks over there are humans. Waiting for me! Ohhhhhh, I really, really don't want to do this. Someone get me outa here!

I had no choice. I was a leader, a general manager for Lutheran Brotherhood Financial Services, and my entire agency was waiting for me. The zip line was inevitable, but I had a plan. It had taken me awhile to come up with a way to overcome—or sidestep—my fear, since I didn't see any hallucinogenic mushrooms, illegal drugs, or strong alcoholic beverages around. Not that I would have used any of those—*probably.*

My plan was simple, and also quite legal and in line with my Christian principles. I would almost run to the top, barely stopping for the requisite ropes and attachments, before I simply jumped off. I didn't want the time to realize what I was really doing. Bingo. It would be over and I would survive to enjoy another day.

"Ready?" the black-capped man asked his partner in this evil exercise.

"Yep. Go when ready," the mean-spirited partner said to me as he stepped back. (Lucky *him.)*

Without another thought, I took a quick step to the ledge and began my space flight in gravity.

"Wait!" I heard. My momentum was stopped and I felt myself pulled back to the edge. Both partners in this crime had all four hands on my ropes, holding me literally on the edge of this cliff, which now appeared to be ten miles high. "Before we will let you go, you must first slowly, and I mean slowly, look to your right." I did. "Now slowly, slowly, look all the way to your left." I did. "Now, look down. Notice the clear water and the jagged rocks and how high this ledge is." Oh, yes, I surely did. Time stood still. Thanks guys. *Jerks.*

"Now, go whenever you're ready." *Great, thanks.*

After what seemed like ten minutes, but was probably all of 60 seconds, I did—intentionally and with full knowledge of the implications involved—step off the ledge. "Ahhhhhhhhhhh, I knew it! I'm freefalling to my very painful death!" My thoughts raced as the zip line had enough slack to make me experience a true, but only initial, fall. Then, just as quickly, the rope became taught and I zipped to the other side, totally exhilarated. *Hey, that was really fun!*

Of course, my helpers were neither jerks nor mean, and the exercise was not evil. To the contrary, the two instructors knew that there was nothing to be gained by me simply going through the motions. No, the gain came from me knowing *exactly* what I was doing and choosing to do it anyway, despite what appeared to be the danger inherent in the unknown of the zip line.

What Is My Purpose?

My zip line experience is a metaphor for what so many people do with their lives. They rush through each phase almost blindly, without true knowledge of what they are involved in. They stumble through what they refer to as their *life*.

Diapers to walking. Pre-school through college. First job to retirement. Marriage, children and then grandchildren. Retirement home to total care facility. Hospital to morgue. It's over. *What the heck was that all about, anyway?*

Here's a poignant exercise on life mortality. Stop reading and grab something to write with and a piece of blank paper. Any size will do. Now, draw a straight line one inch from the bottom of the page ending at one inch below the top. At the bottom of the page, centered just below the beginning of the line, write the word "birth." Now go to the top of the page, and centered just above the end of the line, write the word "death."

Take the point of your pencil and, starting at the bottom of the line where you wrote the word birth, begin slowly tracing over the line you drew toward the top. Stop at that point on the line between the bottom and the top that best represents where you are in your life between your birth and your death. Place an "x" at that spot on the line. Observe. *How much time do you have left?*

Do you suddenly feel a greater awareness of your own mortality? And with that new sense of urgency about your life on earth, can you now look in the rearview mirror and honestly say that you know what *purpose* your life has served up to this point? What the underlying reason is that you have to get out of bed every morning? Most people mistake "going to work," or "taking care of the kids," or "being a better wife/husband" as their *purpose* in life. Goodness, if that were the case, life would simply be a monotonous and thankless journey through a never-ending series of chores, tasks, vocations, and goals. No, the *acts* of life are not in themselves the *purpose* of life. What I am referring to is *eternal purpose,* which is the driver of all we do in this life and, yes, the next one. To really understand that kind of purpose, we need to peel the onion back a bit more.

Look at it this way: Life is the *who*. Purpose is the *why*. Plan is the *what*. Money is the *how*.

Every spirit-filled believer knows *who* he is. There is no difference among us, whether white, yellow, red, black, or brown, whether male or female, young or old, rich or poor. There is no difference in Christ. We are all the same in sin and the same in redemption.

From this universal foundation develops our common *purpose*, our foundational motivation behind all that we do. It is the spiritual *why* behind everything that you do. However you choose to actualize your own unique life, as individual as that might be, living a life of purpose means that *you live to bring God to this fallen and broken world. That* is your true *purpose*. Every decision you make, whether financial, relational, behavioral, or vocational, will be—at the most fundamental level—motivated by that purpose. Though the ways in which we each live out our purpose will be unique, the underlying motive for living that life will be the same for all of us.

Now, let's go back and revisit "going to work," "taking care of the kids," and "being a better wife/husband" with that motivation in mind. Through the lens of our kaleidoscope, we turn the lens and picture those same life acts, but they look different now. All of a sudden those acts of life become purposeful, because in "going to work" we are able to convey the God of love, mercy, truth, and righteousness, to what we do vocationally. No longer do we just "take care of the kids," but rather use that season in life to share the unbreakable and everlasting love of our children's heavenly father with our offspring. "Being a better wife/husband" changes from simply learning more about the differences between Mars and Venus to becoming a unique opportunity to be an earthly example of the divinely inspired notion of unconditional love and a true unending covenant relationship.

The word that applies here is *transform*. To get from simply an existence to a purposeful life, we each first need to be transformed.

What Does the Bible Say?

The Apostle Paul talks about this concept of transformation a great deal. He makes the distinction that we are called to be *in* this world, but not of it.

> "Therefore, I urge you brothers, in view of God's mercy, to offer your bodies as living sacrifices, holy and pleasing to God—this is your spiritual act of worship. Do not conform any longer to the pattern of this world, but be *transformed* by the renewing of your mind."
>
> ROMANS 12:2

Jesus uses the words "born again" to describe this change:

> "I tell you the truth, no one can see the kingdom of God unless he is born again."
>
> JOHN 3:3

This simple declarative sentence is probably the most important sentence in this book. Unless you are "born again," it will literally be impossible for you to live a life of everlasting purpose, bringing God to your fallen and broken world. Sure, you can set out to accomplish a goal, but that is not the definition of purpose as I am using it. Simply accomplishing a goal does not make either the objective or the process truly meaningful. It is only in transforming the motivation behind both the process and the objective that they become meaningful. It is then that the purpose becomes the point. The act is only the means of manifesting it.

> *"I want to be a father who gives his kids the best life possible"* is transformed into *"I want to be a father who expresses the glory of the God of the universe through the relationships and events of my family life."*

> *"I stay at home with my children, so that they know their mother really cares about them"* becomes *"I am a stay-at-home mother, and doing so allows me to model the love, grace, and character of God to my children."*

> *"My work allows me to express my creativity and use my degree"* changes to *"My work affords me the opportunity to personify the integrity and ethic of my heavenly father."*

> *"I passed a number of securities exams and am now taking on new clients"* turns into *"Being a financial advisor gives me the opportunity to share my faith through the work I do with my clients."*

> "So whether you eat, or drink, or whatever you do, do it all for the glory of God," Paul tells us.

The Roman centurion who approached Jesus to ask for His help in saving his seriously ill servant likely continued to be a Roman soldier after Jesus performed his requested miracle, but he no doubt was transformed, never to be the same again.

If Matthew, the former tax collector-turned-disciple of Jesus, ever did return to collecting taxes for the government, I think it is safe to say that he did so in a way that reflected his transformed nature.

Again, what we are discerning here is the difference in motivation. Genesis contains a story about two brothers, Cain and Abel. Both delivered sacrifices to God as was customary, but because the motivation behind Cain's sacrifice was sinful, God did not accept it. Angry at God and jealous of Abel, Cain killed his brother. As a result, God cursed Cain and sent him out as a wanderer. Eventually, Cain and his growing tribe settled and built a city. In fact, his descendents, though still living in sin, are credited as being the first "cowboys," herding livestock and living in tents, the first to "play the harp and flute," and the first to "forge all kinds of tools out of bronze and iron." All of these agricultural, cultural, and technological developments became important dynamics in the development of the human race. However, in and of themselves, they meant nothing. The developers benefited from their creations only in a one-dimensional, temporal way. Eventually, every inventor died. And eventually, every invention returned to dust.

Fast forward a few thousand years. Watch the television commercials about fast, technologically-advanced new cars, the latest fashions from New York, and never-ending variations of cosmetics. Watch the ads for services that promise to help you find a better paying job. Watch the commercials touting mutual funds, insurance products, and online brokerage platforms. Now, let me summarize what the combination of all of these is really saying:

> To get the car of your dreams, look like you are a runway model,
> to enjoy the optimum lifestyle, you need to earn more money
> and make more money on what you invest.

There it is. Cain and his tribe would be very comfortable with this message. I want to scream out from the top of a mountain in reply, "Who cares what you look like, or what you drive, or how much money you make, or whether you are able to achieve a world-record return on your mutual funds if you have no clue what the point of life is? A hundred, or fifty, or five, or one year from now you will be dead and none of that will have mattered one little bit!"

Don't think that I am saying that to truly know real purpose in your life you have to forgo all of life's pleasures. To the contrary. Jesus tells us,

> ". . . I have come that they may have life, and have it to the full."

JOHN 10:10

What Jesus means is that you *can* have it all. Not just a job, but a job that allows you to express your faith. Not just a family, but a family that knows the Father and that will not die when the body gives out. Not just a portfolio of good investments, but one that reflects the morality of God and can be used to support a life in Christ.

Life in "full," as Jesus describes, begins with transformation, from sinner to a redeemed child of God. That change creates a wellspring of unstoppable love and joy for the Father, who gave His only son to die for us, that we might be reunited with Him both now and through eternity. And that realization causes us to want to express that love and joy and appreciation for God in all that we do.

A Real Transformation

Let me give you an example of someone whose life was transformed and who lives a life of eternal purpose. I had the privilege of meeting a wonderful man who attended a Promise Keepers' conference in Atlanta and stopped by the Faith Financial exhibit to pick up some information.[3] After a couple of unsuccessful after-hours attempts to contact the home office, he became frustrated and decided to leave a voice mail with the president of the company, who happened to be me.

I retrieved the following message one morning, which had been left a few hours earlier at 2:30 A.M. "I know you must be busy, but I would really like to talk with one of your advisors about my retirement funds and how I can invest them in a way that reflects my values. I work nights, so I know it's hard to get in touch with me, but I'll give you my cell phone number."

I felt so badly for this gentleman who was so earnestly wanting to be a good steward of his money that I decided I would call him myself. Dennis Gruba was thrilled and surprised that the president of the company would call him, but as it turned out, he was much more a blessing to me than I could ever be to him.

I met him in the nicely decorated, spacious lobby of the hotel where he was staying near Knoxville, Tennessee, while he was attending a ministry conference. I immediately liked him. His physique and mannerisms suggested a big teddy bear, and his robust voice indicated a hearty man. His quick wit, coupled with a deep devotion to Christ, was an intoxicating combination. That word, *intoxicating*, came up often as Dennis told me his life story. An abusive wife, who several times threatened to kill him and their young boys, committed suicide, and left him with serious debt that took years of long hours of work to pay. He had wrestled with his own struggle against drug and alcohol addiction and severe, debilitating depression. He had developed, not surprisingly, resentment against God, whoever that was. Dennis was a man who had every reason to be angry at the world and live only for himself. Then he told me how God had pursued him until he opened his heart, accepted Him in, and *transformed* his life.

Dennis Gruba is a remarkable man with an almost unbelievable story. But that is only the beginning. He has taken his *purpose*—to bring God to his fallen world—very seriously and in many and varied ways, beginning with his vocation as an aeronautical grease mechanic, as he refers to himself. (In actuality he is an airplane mechanic supervisor.) In his humorous way, he related how he tries to bring God to every situation, regardless of the circumstances. I remember one such story that made me laugh.

"This beautiful private jet flew in, and I waited for the 'rare air' people to climb down the stairs before I went to work. You know what 'rare air' people are, don't you? They're the ones who think the air they breathe is a good bit more important than the air you and I breathe," Dennis said. "By the way, I figured you initially for a rare air type, but you're not," he mused, much to my relief. "Anyway, sure enough, down the stairs come these two runway model-type gals with their noses so high that they'd drown in a rain storm." He was holding his nose up in the air, mimicking the young ladies in his story.

"Even though I suspected that they wouldn't want to talk with a grease mechanic like me, I went up to them and offered the comforts of the private lounge and some coffee while they waited for the plane to be worked on. I was right—they ignored me. Oh well. Then I saw the pilot and made the same offer, and found out that he was not only a regular guy, but a man of faith, too. It turned out to be a conversation that uplifted us both," Dennis said. "Regardless of who I come in contact with, I want to do what I can to show them the love that redeemed me."

In addition to his regular job, Dennis has also developed a house painting business to benefit single moms, seniors, and widows who otherwise could not afford the color and uplift that comes with a fresh coat of paint. And as a former drug addict, he'll drop what he is doing to be a listener, mentor, or leader to anyone wrestling with addiction. Dennis' upbeat, positive personality naturally percolates into sharing his joy in Christ with anyone who will listen, whether in his home town in Georgia, or as far away as his new ministry in Nicaragua. He shares the story of his life and faith with so much learned wisdom, self-deprecating humor, and passion for Christ that it catches you off guard. So human, so refreshing, so real.

Dennis Gruba has purpose in all that is his life. He went on to tell me all sorts of funny and meaningful anecdotes about how he tries to live his faith through his relationships with people. Whether as an aeronautical grease mechanic, missionary, father, mentor, or house painter, Dennis Gruba lives life with the specific purpose of bringing God to his fallen and broken world.

Living a Life of Purpose

Living life with purpose transforms a mere existence into one that is an important and meaningful part of the tapestry that God is weaving as He brings redemption and renewal to his fallen creation. And here is a phenomenal bonus to living a life of purpose. As incredible as it seems, this bonus is also often overlooked.

> Living a life of purpose means that it is literally impossible to fail!

Imagine that. You simply can't fail at life, regardless of the difficulty or challenge of life's circumstances that you might find yourself in. By subordinating our will to God's, we are able to continually bask in the security of victory in life, regardless of circumstances. If your true purpose for marriage, career choice, having children, buying a home, or anything else is to glorify God, you are *promised* in Scripture that the outcome will be an eternal victory.

No, that doesn't mean that your marriage will be perfect, but it does mean that God will bring you to a closer relationship with Him through it, regardless of how rocky (or smooth) your marriage is.

No, that doesn't mean that your career will always blossom, but it does mean that God will be present and manifest Himself throughout the twists and turns so that you come to know Him more clearly.

How about that big decision to buy a home? Can you be sure that this huge purchase will be to your financial benefit? Is the home guaranteed to appreciate in value? Nope. However, I can guarantee that God will be with you and your family in that home and you will be blessed according to His purposes by it.

Remember what the Holy Spirit promises us through Paul's words:

"And we know that in ALL things God works for the good of those who love Him, who have been called according to His purpose."

ROMANS 8:28

God's purposes will not be thwarted. God's love cannot be separated from us, regardless of the mistakes we make, the wrong turns we take, or the destruction that Satan and sin throw at us.

My first-born son died before he had a chance to take his first breath outside his mother's womb. *How can that be a victory?* Ah, let me count the ways:

- In the midst of this devastating tragedy, I was touched by a remarkable revelation from God giving me a glimpse of His power, love, and purpose. I received His joy and His peace. I will never be the same again.

- My son was carried to heaven to enjoy eternity with his Father, where we all will meet again one day. I experienced in the most extreme way, spiritually, what I had only known intellectually before.
- My faith grew overnight by incalculable dimensions.
- I was inspired to write a book (*Money for Life*) about faith and money that has ended up in tens of thousands of homes. I would have otherwise never had any interest in such an undertaking.
- Countless people who also have gone through the death of a baby have come forward and shared with my wife and me. God's grace flowed through them to us, and through us to them.
- The divine love that *saved* my first-born is so etched in my soul that I get teary-eyed often as I consider each of my other children and know that they, too, are heirs of that same divine, everlasting love.

Live your life to bring God to your fallen and broken world and you will live a life of purpose. Regardless of circumstances, your life will be meaningful in the most eternal sense. When your head hits the pillow at night, you can rest in the joy that God's will is being accomplished through your purposeful life. When life's events turn against you and the money runs out, your spouse brings you pain, or your boss gives you that pink slip, remember that you will never, never be alone. God will never leave you and nothing can separate you from His purpose. His grace will surround you, renew you, and lift you up—to a higher place.

When you take your last breath as your earthly body fails you, and all of your possessions in that instant become worthless, you can smile the eternal smile of having lived a life of such purpose that the God of the universe was able to manifest Himself through you and has now called you home. He will say,

"Well done, good and faithful servant."

MATTHEW 25:21

What Does the Bible Say?

If you follow God's call in your life, don't expect that everything will work out according to *your* plans. Not financially, relationally, or vocationally. The litmus test for whether you are living a life of purpose is not how simple, smooth, or successful you are. In fact, quite likely, it will be the exact opposite. But "fear not," because God has made provision for those mistakes and failures. He already knows they will happen. He is not concerned with that, because—after all—He is God and He will work it all out according to His purposes, regardless of the number or depth of your failures. The only thing He will not do is *force* you to live your life on purpose.

One of my favorite sayings is, "Some people want to tiptoe through life so that they can arrive at death safely." Think about that. Is living a *safe* life what God has called us to? If so, why were 11 of the 12 disciples killed for their ministry? Did Jesus live a safe life? Hardly. And maybe the greatest example of a man who lived a purposeful life is the Apostle Paul. How many times was he imprisoned, tortured, starved, beaten, and whipped?

Just suppose we go for it: follow our calling, grit our teeth, and jump right into a life of purpose, doing our part to bring God into our fallen and broken world. What if the mistakes mount, bad decisions haunt us, and failure seems our destiny? Or does living a life of purpose mean that we will always make the right decisions and bask in the bounty of having done so?

Living a life of purpose means living a life of passion, regardless of obstacles. Facing challenges head on, the life of purpose is overflowing with God to the point that it cannot be contained. It is fearless: reliant not on its own abilities, but rather on God himself. As Paul wrote to Timothy almost 2000 years ago:

> "For God did not give us a spirit of timidity . . ."
>
> 2 TIMOTHY 1:7

You are not called to live a self-consumed life, simply filling your time on earth with the stuff of daily existence. Neither are you called to be a sheep, or to have your rough edges chipped off so that you, too, can conform to some arbitrary universal image shaped by a giant Christian cookie cutter, stamping out perfectly congruent little Christians. Rather, you are uniquely hard-wired by God your father, the creator of the universe, to play a very different role from anyone else in the mosaic that is God's comprehensive plan and *your* unique life. In this way, the God of the universe brings His character, His love, and His glory to this fallen and broken world.

Think of it this way. What were Jesus' final words, as recorded by Matthew? Were they:

> "All authority in heaven and on earth has been given to me. Therefore go and make disciples of all nations, being sure that you always have plenty of money, never get into debt, only wear very conservative clothes, drive cars that look like they are part of the government's fleet, and—above all—always be nice."

As my good friend and author/illustrator Bill Ross's book says, *"Hey, that's not what the Bible says!"*

No. Instead, Jesus says,

> "All authority in heaven and on earth has been given to me. Therefore go and make disciples of all nations, baptizing them in the name of the Father and of the Son, and of the Holy Spirit."

MATTHEW 28:19

There's your purpose. It could not be more clear.

By contrast, for those who prefer to sit tight and see how it goes, Jesus has words of condemnation and judgment. In Revelation, Jesus says to the Church in Laodicea,

> "I know your deeds, that you are neither cold nor hot. I wish you were either one or the other! So, because you are lukewarm I am about to spit you out of my mouth."

REVELATION 3:15–16

Even on a secular level, we see how creation requires purposeful action even if it is, at least initially, somewhat flawed. In the seminal business masterpiece of the mid–1980s, *In Search of Excellence,* authors Tom Peters and Robert Waterman report findings that clearly reflect Jesus' condemnation of lethargy and maintenance of the status quo. Regarding those companies that they consider "excellent," they find that they all live by a philosophy that could be summed up the following way:

> "Disorganized action is always preferable to organized inaction."

Jesus' fiery disciple Peter was anything but lethargic, and got himself into serious trouble on at least three occasions. The first occurred when he tried to convince Jesus not to go through with his walk to what would be his death on a cross. Jesus admonished him,

> "Get behind me, Satan! You are a stumbling block to me; you do not have in mind the things of God, but the things of men."
>
> MARK 8:33

Next, Peter tried to stop Jesus' arrest by the guards in the Garden of Gethsemane by whirling his sword. But the most devastating failure Peter is known for is his denying any knowledge or association with Jesus—not once, not twice, but three times on one important night.

Because Peter could not be trusted to always make the correct decision, Jesus expelled him as a disciple in favor of a short-haired, once-married, financially solvent, nice, soft-spoken accountant who was always right and whose wife and kids were perfect. Right? *I don't think so!*

Quite the contrary. When Peter tells Jesus that he knows Jesus is the son of God, Jesus is so moved by Peter's faith that he tells Peter that it will be on "this rock that I will build my church, and the gates of Hell will not prevail against it" (Matthew 16:18). By the way, that little incident where Jesus rebukes Peter ("Get behind me Satan!") happens shortly *after* Jesus is impressed with Peter's faithful insight. Even though we may be living a purposeful life, it does not mean that we won't continue to make mistakes.

It is not Peter's perfect judgment, mellow personality, or ability to always say and do the right thing that Jesus commends so powerfully, but rather Peter's *faith*. And faith is one very, very small step away from the purpose of bringing God to this sinful world.

As I have tried to live out my own unique life of purpose bringing God to my fallen and broken world, I have employed my resources, my relationships, and my own hard-wiring as a pioneer in financial services, particularly as a pioneer in the rapidly growing values-based investing niche. I have chosen a career path that focuses on the development of products and technology that allow Christians to better reflect their values in the way they invest. In this journey, I have experienced both the pleasure of bountiful success and the weight of substantial failure. I have experienced times when I had more wealth than I ever imagined, but also worse-than-lean times when I suffered financially. At times I had to choose between my personal financial comfort and support of my personal vision for bringing God to this world of sin.

The apostle Paul, who at times lived in luxury and at times lived in poverty, put it this way:

> " . . . for I have learned to be content whatever the circumstances. I know what it is to be in need, and I know what it is to have plenty. I have learned the secret of being content in any and every situation, whether well fed or hungry, whether living in plenty, or in want. I can do all things through (Christ) who gives me strength."
>
> PHILIPPIANS 4:11–13

Doing all things is Paul's actualizing his life of purpose, preaching, mentoring, comforting, and sometimes even tentmaking, bringing God to his fellow men. Paul's purpose was not his own financial gain, but rather his ministry to bring God to his fallen and broken world.

Living a Life of Purpose

Could I live very comfortably if all I did was consider my family's interests? Sure I could. My industry pays handsomely for good work. There is no doubt in my mind that I could now, as I have in my past, earn very serious compensation with a substantially less work load, stress, and liability if I simply attended to a select list of clients. Plenty of money, yes. Everything my family could want, yes. All the extra time to be at home or church, yes. Play on my ATV with all four kids in tow every day instead of just weekends, yes. Retire at an early age, yes. Certainly.

But is that really why God caused me to be born and hard-wired me the way that he did? Is that the best way for me to live my life of purpose? No. We are called to be "light and salt" to a decaying world.

I thoroughly enjoy my work. It can be exciting and rewarding, both spiritually and financially. I cannot imagine *not* being totally immersed in this attempt to transform the financial services industry so that investors have the opportunity to reflect their core values on important issues such as abortion, pornography, and the political agenda of the gay and lesbian movement. I have been given this opportunity by God to manifest my life of purpose, and in this way bring God to my fallen and broken world. And despite all the mistakes, failures, and challenges that have come with it, I am thankful that God has led me to this place.

What about *your* life of purpose? Are you afraid to "step out" of your comfort zone and follow your calling? Don't let your fear be your compass. Remember that life is a journey that is supposed to have both peaks and valleys along the way. Your reward will be commensurate with your risk. And the ultimate irony is that your success with God is already certain, literally guaranteed. Amazing, isn't it? I'll bet you never thought about it that way. Your ultimate safety net is God's promise to provide for you. Nowhere in Scripture is this more clear than in Paul's letter to the Church in Rome, especially in the eighth chapter:

> "And we know that in all things God works for the good of those who love him, who have been called according to his purpose.

If God is for us, who can be against us? He who did not spare his own son, but gave him up for us all—how will he not also, along with him, graciously give us all things?

For I am convinced that neither death nor life, neither angels nor demons, neither the present nor the future, nor any powers, neither height or depth, nor anything else in all creation, will be able to separate us from the love of God that is in Christ Jesus our Lord."

I think that about covers it. Can there be any adversaries Paul left out? You are hesitating to bring God to your fallen and broken world because of fear of . . . *what?*

Follow your God-inspired passion and watch God go to work. Problems? Sure. Failures? You bet! Challenges? Every day. But just as God sent dumb birds (ravens) to feed his prophet Elijah when there was no food, He will "work things for good" for you, too.

Ever hear of that famous President Abraham Lincoln? You know, he's the really, really smart one that never made a mistake, right? Wrong. Lincoln failed several times in business and was financially destitute before he learned the wisdom he needed to become president of the United States at a tremendously difficult time in our history.

More recently, Steven Covey, the author of the acclaimed book *The Seven Habits of Highly Successful People,* failed financially and filed for bankruptcy only a few years before he gave the world a most important piece of work. He is now an acclaimed speaker, mentor, and author whose advice benefits millions.

Even Promise Keepers, the phenomenally important Christian men's movement, has had its share of financial troubles. *Yet it has never wavered from its purpose, and never retreated.* Hopefully, the financial problems are all in its past, but even if they were to arise again, God will no doubt *work all things for good . . .*

What God wants is not a *perfect process,* but rather a *perfect purpose.*

At this point, you may be thinking, "Okay. I get it. I am supposed to understand who I am as a redeemed child of God. Got it. And from that wellspring, I am to direct my life, so that every decision I make reflects *my* unique way of living a life of purpose, bringing God to my fallen and broken world. Understood. I also see where God is not concerned about my potential failures or mistakes along the way, because he will always work whatever those challenges are into his plan. He will always provide and He will never leave me.

"But what if I decide to actualize my purpose one way today and an altogether different way next year? What if I choose to play in a Christian rock band today, but then five years from now decide to get my MBA and become a corporate CEO? Is that OK? Am I still living a life of purpose?"

Absolutely. It does not matter how you choose to bring God to your world, so long as whatever you choose to do, your motivation—your purpose—is God.

I like the way author and psychoanalyst Scott Peck, Ph.D., puts it. He says that every day when he wakes up, he asks God if this life he is living is still what he is being called to do. So long as the answer continues to come back "Yes," that's good enough for him. But if the answer ever changes, Dr. Peck will be ready and available to move on to the next mission.

What is *your* life of purpose? How are you, as Martin Luther admonishes us to be, a "little Christ" to your world? Whether bringing democracy to the world, defeating communism, or simply attempting to show undeserved kindness to people who think they breathe rare air like my friend does, your life is literally the extension of God at this moment, in this world. God has purposely called *you* into being and placed *you* at this precise time and place to live your unique life of purpose.

How you define that life of purpose is truly an exciting and never-ending process. It is in this context of purpose that we move ever closer to the question of money.

Chapter 3

Plan

My finger could barely feel the trigger of my Ruger Model 77 .270 caliber rifle. My hands were encased in a Thinsulate glove to ward off the bitter cold of the Colorado Rockies, at 8,500 feet altitude, in November. Between the last few steps of my ever-so-slow walk in the knee-deep snow, I heard the unmistakable *EEEEUUUUOOOO* of a cow elk. At this time of year, I knew that if there were cows around, there would be bulls as well. Maybe big bulls.

The sky was a translucent gray, one of those where you can't tell if the clouds are 5,000 feet above your head or just outside your reach. Snow was continuously swirling in front of my face, impeding my vision. I wasn't sure if it was falling from the sky or simply being whirled off the ground and branches of the beautiful, tall evergreens by the strong wind. Besides covering my eyelids, the snow filled the front eyepiece of my Leupold Vari XIII scope on my rifle, reminding me that even if I saw a bull elk, there was no assurance I could actually put the crosshairs on him.

There was a wide opening in the thick woods, about 50 yards in front of me, that I had been heading for over the last hour. Though the snow was too deep to allow for any elk to be grazing, the thought occurred to me that I might be able to at least pick up a trail. *One foot up—slowly—one foot down—slowly.* My right arm held my gun, and my left pushed snow-covered Douglas fir branches out of my way. *EEEEUUUUOOOO.* There it was again, probably coming from that field. A few more steps now and I'd be able to see for sure.

Just as I moved past the last snow-covered branch, I saw it. Or rather, them. All of them. Moving. In line. Lots of *EEEEUUUUOOOOs* now emanating from the herd. I pulled my scope up to my eye—darn! Couldn't see a thing, too much snow in the lens. I blew it away, then rubbed the finger of my glove around it to dislodge more snow, and put it back up to my eye. Now I could see. Still too much swirling snow. Was that a cow or a bull? How about those over there? And there? Lots of elk, all moving fairly rapidly into the woods now. Not much time before my window of opportunity would shut. Too much snow blowing in the wind, too little light. They'd see me if I moved closer. Had to make my stand right here. Find him. Find that bull. Where was he?

There! Standing still while the herd walked briskly by. Nice bull. I felt the trigger oh-so-lightly touch my gloved finger. The snow was still swirling, but I could make out the distinct image of the bull. I needed a frontal right shot, a good clean kill. *BANG!*

The crack and roar of my shot scattered the elk in a frenzy. There were elk racing everywhere, crashing through the Ponderosa pines, Douglas firs, and aspens like a train wreck. It was chaos, with snow blowing so hard that I could barely see, and virtually all the elk evaporated into the deep woods. Where was he? Where was my bull? I began walking quickly now, not caring about sound or motion that might be detected. Tracks. I had to find his tracks. There were plenty of tracks, but which ones were his?

There! A blood trail. I stopped and looked up through the thick coniferous forest and . . . there he was. Wow. My first bull elk. What a magnificent animal.

I have a color 8"x10" glossy of me next to both my first bull elk and another one shot by a friend from the same herd within ten minutes of my kill. In fact, I had a total of eight friends hunting that day, and our group enjoyed a remarkably successful elk hunt. The wide grin on my face in the photo indicated my buoyant disposition at that moment. Little did I know that within a couple of very short hours, my life would be in jeopardy.

Getting an elk is quite an accomplishment. Packing one out on horseback when you are miles deep in the mountains is even more challenging. Five of our hunting party headed back to the cabin with three kills and six horses. Three others stayed behind with me. We had four horses and they were all needed just to carry out the two elk. No riding that evening.

Horses don't like elk. They must have been quite the fiery enemies hundreds of years ago. They can become really agitated when in the proximity of one, regardless of whether the elk is alive or not. You have to find ways to "pretend" that the elk aren't really there. One such way is to put Vicks Formula 44 in the horse's nostrils to stifle the smell of nearby elk. I had to do that with two of the four we had.

The snow and wind had stopped. What a fantastic day it had turned out to be! When a couple of my fellow financial advisors, accounting buddies, and I had decided, a year earlier, to turn my cabin and acreage joining the National Forest into a part-time outfitting service to lure friends and acquaintances from "back east" to a great western hunting experience, we knew it would allow us to write off a lot of our equine and collateral capital, but we never imagined it would be this successful.

With the panniers over the saddles now on all four horses and full of elk, we began the long, two-and-a-half hour journey back to the warm cabin where we could relax, recover, and finish the day by telling our stories of success over and over again. It was late in the day and, as the only guide with knowledge of the geography, I wanted to get moving quickly. No sooner had I found the trail then it began to snow again. This time, it was a heavy snowfall. Really heavy. In fact, within five minutes the trail had disappeared.

Compounding our problem was the darkness that had crept in. In a heavy snowfall late in the day, darkness can sweep in without warning. And it did. The next thing I knew, there was not only no trail to follow, but I could not see a thing.

I stopped the horse train to re-gear myself for the new circumstances. I could not help but notice the banter, laughter, and conversation of the other three in my party. They were entirely clueless about our very dangerous situation. My job was to keep them like that for as long as possible. The last thing I needed at that moment was panic.

I replaced my hunting cap with a black felt Stetson to help keep the snow off my face, and grabbed my flashlight. We were experiencing heavy snowfall, pitch blackness, and a missing trail, and we were hours away from the nearest shelter. Then, Mother Nature decided to start her powerful wind again. *Thanks.*

We started the single-file horse train again, leaning forward against the wind, sheltering our eyes against the sharpness of the snow that hit our faces at mach-one force. We plodded along, each of us with the lead rope of a horse carrying backpacks, gear, guns, and elk. The wind became so strong that I could no longer even hear my heavy breathing. My friends were no longer talking, let alone laughing. Turns out they weren't as clueless as I thought they were.

There were two incidents that we encountered which nearly spelled disaster. The first occurred when I started down what turned out to be a steep ravine. Way too steep. I caught myself by grabbing an aspen, but my horse kept going, sliding. This was bad. The others were following my horse. "Turn around, *now!*" I yelled, and was able to get their attention in time do a U-turn back up toward where I thought the trail might be. They followed, horses and men, in disarray.

Back on level ground and realizing I had made a turn to the east way too soon, I returned to the direction I thought would take us home. About thirty minutes later, I heard a commotion behind me and stopped to look back. One of the horses had gone down and could not get back up. The snow was so heavy that it fully covered the horses, and all the gear and elk they were transporting. Against the wind, in high altitude and with all that weight, the horses couldn't take it. My friends were just about to panic now.

"No, don't try to get him up. Let him lie there a moment," I said. I hurried back to where Levi, my young sorrel, was on his side, eyes the size of a dinner plate and nostrils forcing air in and out like a leaf blower.

I took my gloves off and slowly walked up to the panicked horse, bent down, and untied his load. I let him regain his composure, and then gingerly coaxed him back to his feet and placed the lead rope back in his rider's hands. "Okay. Let's leave the gear and game and just take the horses," I said. We did. The horses very much liked that idea.

For two more hours we fought the panic, the blackness, wind, and driving snow. At last, I thought I saw light. Foggy, far away, but light it was. We reached the summit 500 feet above my cabin, and only then did we know that we would make it through this night alive. The sound of my generator turning gasoline into electricity was the most beautiful music I had ever heard. We were home. To this day, when I think about that sight, my eyes get moist.

(Did I mention that I now live in Tennessee? Our "blizzards" come at most once or twice a year, with a maximum punch of 6–8", and it all melts in 72 hours . . .)

Our purpose was sound enough. Take a handful of Christian financial advisors, add a couple of cabins, a dozen horses, and hundreds of miles of National Forest and develop a (very) part-time outfitting business. Peace Mountain Trails, Inc. would be our way to share what we loved about that part of God's creation called the Colorado Rockies with others, giving glory to God and honoring Him with our witness. Nothing was wrong with our purpose—but our *plan* needed a little tweaking.

In this chapter we are going to explore the nature of life plans, and why they are an essential part of God's design for this world. We are also going to see that God is not so interested in the plan being flawless, without mistake, or failure. Rather, He is interested in the process of bringing ideas into reality, which give opportunity to illuminate the glory of God, regardless of how rough the journey gets.

Our final chapter in this section focuses on money. The balance of this book explores the options for building a sound financial portfolio that reflects the character of God. However, like the contractor who needs to know what the house is to look like before he orders the lumber, cement, and bricks, we need to know what life plans we are going to need money for.

What Is a Life Plan?

Understanding what a life in Christ means is fundamental. It then naturally flows to giving purpose to every life choice we make. For example, a young married couple decides to honor God by creating a family. They need to purchase a home. But where? How big a house should they buy? What should the layout be? How much can they afford? How do they finance it?

Life plans are the stuff that make up our days on earth. Go to school? Where? Get married? To whom? Have children? How many? Arrange to have mommy stay at home? For how long? Take time off to teach, or study, or do ministry? When? These are the questions that help us formulate a life *plan* that puts our purpose into action.

And as you consider life plans, remember that they are not cemented in concrete, unchangeable once they are dedicated. Rather, life plans are—like you—*alive*. They are not etched in stone, but rather in erasable ink. Because we encountered an unexpected heavy blizzard at just the wrong time in our hunt, did that mean that we should abandon our plan to develop Peace Mountain Trails? Of course not. When the Apostle Paul was thrown into prison, or beaten for his attempts at establishing the first Christian churches on earth, should he have abandoned his plans altogether?

Don't ever confuse a failure of *tactics* with a failure of *objective*. Just because some part of your plan doesn't work out doesn't necessarily mean that your plan should be scrapped. Back to the analogy of the house for a moment. What if the house was built and all of a sudden the roof began to leak? Should the newlyweds abandon the idea of a home? How absurd! What if the house was appropriately financed, but the family income was interrupted because of a job lay-off, or a business failure? Should the owners consider that turn of events a "sign" that they should never have bought the house in the first place? Of course not!

I joke and say that I used to be somebody in a former life. I did have a successful competitive running career throughout high school, college, and into my young adult life. I kept a log of every workout I ever ran, along with a log of each race. Sometimes my races did not go so well, and because I was running at a world-class level, the defeats were traumatic. So, on the inside cover of my log book, I pasted the following words written by the Apostle Paul as he, too, considered his own deficiencies:

"Forgetting what is behind and straining toward what is ahead,
I press on toward the goal to win the prize for which God has
called me heavenward in Christ Jesus."

PHILIPPIANS 3:13-14

People who abandon their dreams, because of tactical failures in the execution of their plans, simultaneously bury their purpose and ultimately live irrelevant lives. By contrast, people who keep their purpose alive, continuously upgrading their plans by taking advantage of their tough lessons along the way, become warriors.

When I think of a warrior, I think of someone who has seen battle. Scarred, sometimes beaten but never defeated, a warrior knows why he gets out of bed every morning. His purpose is to bring life to his plans.

I am a student of history, particularly that of the United States through the end of the 19th century. My favorite example of a warrior is Confederate General Nathan Bedford Forrest[4], arguably the most creative and talented leader in American military history. His tactics were so superior that the English cavalry was required to study Forrest's battle movements as part of their preparation for World War I.

Forrest was wounded three times, and had 29 horses shot out from under him. He was one of the few officers of the Confederate high command who did not earn a diploma from West Point. In fact, he had to raise his own rag-tag army in his hometown of Memphis by placing ads in the newspaper that included the dictate "bring your own gun and horse, or mule." Forrest was not literate, not wealthy, and not even outfitted by the Confederate Army, yet he became by far the most feared commander by Union troops.

He never lost a battle, even though he was frequently outmanned 10 or 15 to 1. Nathan Bedford Forrest's plans involved repelling the invasion of the federal government's army. He designed and executed countless plans, most of which worked, but some of which did not. In the end, General Forrest surrendered his small army only after his government and its army ceded victory to the federals. Nathan Bedford Forrest was the epitome of a warrior.

So, what are your plans for the life God has given you? Thinking through the prism of what your purpose is as a child of the Lord God, what specifically will you do with your life?

This morning I was driving the 5-year-old love-of-my-life, Ann-Rachel Bolt, to preschool. She is a horse girl—one of those people who simply have that gene. As she was intensely studying the pictures in her horse book, she suddenly looked up at me in the rear view mirror and said, "Daddy, what do you think God wants me to be when I get bigger?"

How do I answer that? It's hard enough when the audience is adult and I have a book of about 300 pages to get my thoughts across. When there is only one-mile-to-go-before-the-preschool-car-line and the person asking is only five-years-old, it is even harder.

I told her that she would be free to do whatever she wanted to do, so long as she asked God for His guidance. I think I mumbled some additional words to make myself (and anyone else who happened to be hiding under the seats and hear our conversation) feel like I gave it a valiant effort.

The 5-year-old context is actually quite appropriate. Although I firmly believe that God puts in our hearts those purposes to which He has called us, I do not believe that He really cares whether we buy the black or the brown shoes. Or park on the right or left side of the road. Or take our vacation the second week in July instead of the third.

My father served as president of our church congregation years ago. I remember he got into it one time with a fellow member who said pompously, in a public forum that, as she approached a parking lot in her car, she always prayed for a parking place close to the door of the store—and voila!—one usually opened up. My dad, always 100% on theological target, replied to this middle class, very healthy 40-year-old lady, "Oh, that wasn't *God* answering your prayers, that was Satan giving you what your flesh wanted. You see, a human body benefits from walking. God would likely have opened up a spot quite farther away from the store in order to help you get some needed exercise and thereby keep you healthy and active." I love my dad!

I once heard what I think is a great metaphor for defining the dichotomy of our freedom and the Creator's design and purpose. Think for a moment of a very large park, created by God, in which He has placed all sorts of playground equipment including bicycles, teeter-totters, slides, swings and a sandbox. The metaphor suggests that God does not care which of the equipment we choose to play with, or in what order, but He does care about two things:

1. That we play in a way that reflects His glory.
2. That we not venture outside that park into murder, drug use, cheating, lying, stealing, sexual sin, or other anti-God behavior.

What a great way to set the stage for the freedom that we have to develop our individual life plans! What equipment are you going to play with and for how long? The choice is yours and completely within God's blessing. Don't worry about the cost right now. We'll deal with that later in this book. For now, simply let your imagination go. With only one life to live—there is no such thing in life as a dress rehearsal—consider what life plans you would like to make.

Life Choices as a Business Plan

The most natural context to examine my existence in terms of **Life, Purpose, Plan, Money** is within the universal structure of a business plan. I have had occasion to write quite a number of them. Though unique in purpose, they all have the same exact structure:

- Goal
- Objectives
- Strategies
- Tactics

In the context of life planning, we can change those words to:

- Life in Christ
- Purpose of my life
- Plans for manifesting that purpose
- How much money I will need and when I will need it

It has always seemed so peculiar to me that in the 24 years that I have been a financial advisor, the vast majority of people I have encountered have absolutely no concept of the first two bullet points, only a slight idea of the third, but want to spend a huge amount of time and energy on the last item. As I mentioned previously, *who cares how much money you make, or save, or earn, or profit if you have no clue why you need it in the first place?* Using our building contractor example, that's like building a house and telling the local concrete company, "Start dumping concrete, as much as you can make. Drop it anywhere you want, because I'm sure I'll need it at some point."

Please stop thinking that the quality of your life is correlated to the amount of money that you have. It is certainly true that the carnal and narcissistic dimensions of your life are directly correlated to your ability to make and spend the maximum amount of money for your pleasure. But a life in Christ? One with eternal purpose? No such correlation exists.

Let's do a quick review, so that you are truly free of any "carry-on baggage" you brought with you to this section. First, remember that *the battle* is already won, that Satan and sin and death are defeated. Not by anything you did, but by the beauty, love, and character of God, your Father. Therefore you will find yourself motivated by a deeper purpose, giving meaning to the plans that make up your life.

Consider your hard wiring. What are your talents, your likes and dislikes, your hopes and dreams? You are totally free to be what you want to be. Free to make whatever plans you choose for your life. Free to play wherever you want in God's park.

Next, prioritize your list of life choices. Are some options more important than others? Are you willing to work harder for some? How about risk? Will you take more risk to achieve certain objectives than others?

You will need to distill your options down to a plan for your life that has a high degree of specificity. Otherwise, your life plans will never become more than just dreams. A dream becomes a goal when it has a deadline.

Finally, how much will it cost? When will you need the money? In what increments and for how long? Money for a home, a car, an education, a family, a business, a ministry, and just maybe even a dream that you are passionate about.

A Passionate Plan

I was really tired. My legs ached. I had qualified for the mile final, won the two-mile, and anchored the winning two-mile relay, all the night before. The University of Alabama Crimson Tide was looking good on the scoreboard of the Southeastern Conference Championship indoor track meet at the LSU field house, but Stephen Bolt was tired. Really tired. And what was so sad was that I was in the best shape of my life.

After having been named High School Miler of the Year by *Track & Field News* and receiving full scholarship offers from every major university in the U.S., my freshman year in college had been a disaster. But I had come back with an unremitting determination to become the first person in the history of the SEC to break the four-minute mile. I had trained with a singular focus for over a year, twice a day, and averaging 100 tough miles a week in workouts. I had deprived myself of every empty calorie my body otherwise craved. (Actually, that's not entirely true. I still remember the morning I bought a Three Musketeers Bar and *ate it*. It was a clear day in January, about 45 degrees, no wind. That's how rare I allowed myself any culinary transgressions.)

"Last call mile run," the announcer blared. I didn't even get nervous. I just didn't care. It was over. Another year, an entire year, of running in the Tuscaloosa heat in August, in wind-blown sleet in January, sacrificing college life. Great.

Then, as I began taking off my warm-ups and heading toward the starting line, a thought flashed into my mind. Go for it! What difference does it make if you fail? No one will suspect that you would actually try to break four minutes after all you've been through. Just go for it!

By now my heart was racing. I could barely contain myself. I threw off my white jacket and stepped from the infield onto the track in front of the gathering competitors. I didn't even consider them. As far as I was concerned, they didn't exist. It was only . . .

The Distance
The Clock
And Me.

"Runners set . . ."
BANG!

I immediately jumped out front on the 220-yard rubberized track. It only took one lap for my teammates to figure out what was going on. They saw my split. "Look what Bolt's doing!" I heard, as I pushed into the second of eight laps. "He's going for it!" someone else said.

Then, as if the entire coliseum figured it out, all of the spectators began standing and pointing. The competitors waiting for their events in the infield stopped their stretching and turned their heads to follow the spectacle of what might be the first sub-four minute mile in SEC history.

"Ladies and gentlemen, that was a 57-second first quarter. Bolt from Alabama is on track to break four minutes," the excited announcer barked. At that, the standing crowd, together with all of the competitors from each of the SEC schools, began clapping in cadence with my stride. *Clap-step-clap-step-clap-step.* My legs ached like never before, my thighs wanting to burst. *Push, push. Focus. Push.*

One lap to go now. The bell sounded and people began spilling out of the stands and crowding onto the track. Adrenaline was rushing through my veins and I became oblivious to everything except extracting the very last drop of energy out of my muscles and burning every molecule of oxygen I could force down my lungs.

Fifty yards, twenty yards, five yards, lean! I crossed the finish line and immediately turned to my left to see the digital timer in the infield. 3:59.4! *Yes! Yes! Yes! I did it!*

What a race. Even as I write this some 29 years later, my pulse beats faster. I thank God for that feat, especially since as of the date of this book, that record still stands.

Passion Fuels Dreams

Passion. It is the fuel that energizes the dreams of life. And it is in the achievement of those dreams that God's creation reflects His vision for a better world.

President Kennedy gave America the dream of landing a man on the moon and returning to earth safely. President Reagan later gave this same country the goal of defeating communism. There are countless examples throughout history of men and women who dreamed great dreams and then acted on them. Our lives are far better because of them.

One of my favorite examples of passion fueling the advance of a life-long dream that changed the world for the better is the almost single-minded focus of Thomas Jefferson and John Adams to achieve democracy in America. Sewn into the tapestry of these two storied men of history is the juxtaposition of their distinct differences. Jefferson and Adams were as committed to the cause of democracy as they were at odds with each others' strategies and lifestyles. Each had his own unique perspective, but they both shared both a common goal and a fierce passion.

Arguably one of the most intelligent presidents we've ever had, Jefferson's impact on America is deep and wide, touching everything from the Declaration of Independence (which he penned and helped author) and the Constitution, to science, culture, law, education, agriculture, and architecture. Jefferson's contemporary, John Adams, the second president of the new republic, was a man of tremendous principle, a stickler for prudence in both moral and financial affairs. Adams and Jefferson quickly became very close friends and political partners, but then had a serious falling out which kept them bitter enemies for most of the rest of their lives.

Only in their twilight years did these two great men of purpose rekindle the friendship of their youth. As a student of history, I found David McCullough's nearly 1,000-page biography of John Adams, and his personal and political quarreling with Jefferson, quite fascinating, but, of course, one-sided. So, I also read Willard Sterne Randall's acclaimed biography of Thomas Jefferson to view the arguments from the other side.

In the end, I learned that both positions held elements of validity, and in combination were inextricably fundamental in creating what is today the unprecedented strength and vision of the United States of America. Without both arguments (federalism and decentralization) strenuously advanced by Adams and Jefferson, we could not be the great country that we are today.

Historians will argue to what extent Jefferson and Adams were true believers. Jefferson, in particular, offers us commentary from time to time in his life that suggests he was more a deist than a modern-day evangelical Christian. However, both Jefferson and Adams felt a clear calling to bring God to their fallen and broken world by forming a representative democracy. These two great Americans had an unequivocal purpose that manifested itself in their commitment to developing a free country comprised of the rule of law, individual liberty, and the freedom to live one's faith.

Nothing more exemplified this principle of their lives than the timing and manner in which each man died.

American independence came to be celebrated on the 4th day of the month of July. John Adams, fighting against old age and death by continuing to write and lecture on the American system of government, finally succumbed at the remarkable age of 91, dying on July 4th, 1826. Not July 5th, or July 6th, but July 4th. On the exact same Independence Day in 1826, John Adams' fellow warrior in the battle for American freedom, Thomas Jefferson, also died, at the age of 83.

Jefferson had been in and out of consciousness for weeks. As his strength began fading into what everyone knew would inevitably be his last breath, Jefferson would raise his perspiring head and with all the strength he could muster, ask one question in only a whisper: "What day is today?" Upon learning the date, he would then lie back down and eventually lose consciousness again.

When he finally heard the words, "Today is July fourth," Thomas Jefferson lay back down and breathed his last breath.

John Adams, the second president, and Thomas Jefferson, the third president, personified two very different perspectives within the debate over American democracy. They both died on not only the same day, but, most importantly, on Independence Day. *That* is an amazing example of living for a purpose. John Adams, the New Englander with almost puritanical principles of living, and Thomas Jefferson, the high-living plantation owner from Virginia: two very different human beings, two very different lives, but two men who lived life with a passion for purpose. They lived their lives fully and, in their unique ways, brought God to their fallen and broken world. What a remarkable legacy they left for us, who over 200 years later enjoy the bounty of living in the most prosperous country in the history of this planet, free to worship whenever and however we so choose!

Don't make the mistake of thinking that God is looking for conformity in His children. God is a god of creativity. Just look around you at the splendor of nature, or the uniqueness of humanity. There is nothing in God's creation to suggest that he wants us to conform to some specific personality, as if we were each cut from some giant cookie cutter in the sky. Jefferson advanced the argument of decentralization. Adams advanced the argument of a strong central government. Both perspectives continue to be an important part of America's continuing political debate.

Okay—enough philosophy. Let the fun begin. The next chapter is the beginning of the end of your lack of knowledge on financial matters. My goal is to give you enough information to make *you* able to educate the next stockbroker, life insurance salesman, or banker who tries to sell you something, and especially to be able to intellectually challenge every self-proclaimed financial guru you hear on radio, or see on television. (I won't name names, but you can. Yes, those are exactly the people I'm referring to.)

Think that's a tall order? Nah. It's really no big deal at all. You see, I don't have an ax to grind, or a television show to promote, or a radio show to hype. I just have information, and I think you are totally qualified to digest that information and turn it into something that propels your life plan.

That's all. But that's enough.

Chapter 4

Money

Well, here we are. The final step in the **Life, Purpose, Plan, Money** chronology. Money. What do we do with that word? How do we handle such a sharp-edged topic? I'm reminded of something a friend once said to me about my concern with having to be partnered with someone I considered a snake for a certain project. He thought a moment about my quandary and said thoughtfully, "There's really nothing wrong with handling a snake. Just never, ever forget that it is a snake."

The Apostle Paul instructs Timothy regarding the venomous nature of money:

> "For we brought nothing into this world, and we can take nothing out of it. But if we have food and clothing, we will be content with that. People who want to get rich fall into temptation and a trap and into many foolish and harmful desires that plunge men into ruin and destruction. For the love of money is a root of all kinds of evil. Some people, eager for money, have wandered from the faith and pierced themselves with many griefs."
>
> 1 TIMOTHY 6:7–10

There you have it: our model for how to apply money in our lives. Let's break it down.

1. There is nothing money can buy that will benefit us eternally, because we can't take anything with us when we leave this world.
2. Use money for those things that serve a true and necessary purpose, such as food and clothing.
3. Remember that seeking money is idolatry, turning your focus from Christ-centered to pleasure-centered. And in that change of focus lies a trap filled with destruction, pain, and grief.

We want to approach the question of money intellectually and not emotionally. That's what Paul's second principle is teaching us. Use money for good and necessary purposes. Doing so requires an intellectual consideration of the issues involved. Too often, people put emotions first. Let's look at two examples that are prevalent today, each at an opposite extreme.

On the one hand, as Paul points out, money can be viewed simply as a way to obtain carnal pleasure. From inappropriate cosmetic surgery to overuse of credit cards for improper luxuries, expensive vacations, and endless entertainment, money is very often a means to acquiring sensual pleasure. This is the "trap" that Paul is speaking of.

On the other hand, you have the *extremist reformers,* as I call them, who have had a terrible experience with overspending or a business failure. They now crusade against all debt, any personal luxuries, and all purchases that bring some form of pleasure. Neither extreme is appropriate, because both spring from emotion, not intellect.

Author Larry Crab warns against the natural instinct to engage in a situation or a relationship by either withdrawing altogether from it, or by totally manipulating it. Spending too much and making inappropriate purchases is a way to manipulate one's world (through money) to acquire the pleasures necessary to attempt to continuously fill the inevitable and insatiable vacuum that is life without God. On the other hand, withdrawing from any use of credit for purchases and using money only to gain the bare essentials for a simple existence is not looking at money through a Christ-centered prism, either.

Instead, Larry Crab suggests that living a Christ-centered life means not going to either extreme, but rather "stepping into chaos" in the real world in between. And that is exactly where I will take you with the rest of this book. I'll do that by forcing you into the middle, by asking questions and giving you information, so that you are in a position to make educated, intellectual decisions about money in your (Christ-centered) life. It would be arrogant of me to suggest that I know how you should build your life plan. I don't know, because I *can't* know. Only God knows. After all, He created you for His purposes, and He made you intentionally, by specific and unique design. I can only help by pointing to questions, stimulating your thinking, and giving you an education regarding your financial options.

Can you imagine what our world would look like if there was a presumption that all Christians should build the exact same house? The same frame, the same number and size of rooms, the same colors? Yet there are those who would have you believe that to please God, you must always buy a certain type of life insurance, or never invest in partnerships. How absurd! How intellectually demeaning that is. How sad the outcome can be, too.

Sometimes as I am changing radio stations I encounter a certain financial guru's program. It is hilarious as the callers, one by one, describe their "unique" circumstances, only to hear the host give answers that are anything *but* unique. The answer seems to always be the same, regardless of the individual circumstances of the caller. It goes something like this:

> "Well, get an extra job, buy an old used car with cash, cut up all of your credit cards, and if there is any money left, pay off your mortgage. And invest in mutual funds where you'll earn a 12% return. Now, let's hear from Jane."
>
> Jane calls in and says, "But, Mr. Host, here's my situation . . ."
>
> Answer: "Well, Jane, get an extra job, buy an old used car with cash, cut up all of your credit cards, and if there is any

money left, pay off your mortgage. And invest in mutual funds where you'll earn a 12% return. Now, let's hear from John."

John calls in and says, "But Mr. Host, here's my situation . . ."

Answer: "Well, John, get an extra job, buy an old used car with cash, cut up all of your credit cards, and if there is any money left, pay off your mortgage. And invest in mutual funds where you'll earn a 12% return. Now, let's hear from Greg."

On and on, day after day. Where's the intellectual honesty in that? Where is there room for the uniqueness that God created in each of us?

Be very careful of paying attention to anyone who uses the words *always* and *never*. The premise of that thought process implies that we must subordinate our God-created uniqueness to some arbitrary conformity. *Always buy term life insurance. Never invest aggressively.* Really? I certainly see the emotional component of these directives, but I see nothing developed from intelligent thought and analysis.

Remember what Larry Crab warns us: to stay diligent so that we don't fall prey to our natural instinct to gravitate toward one or the other extreme. Instead, he suggests that to allow God to practically use us in His plan, we must step out into the gray which is neither black, nor white, but is chaos, and let God be God in our lives, trusting only in Him.

The Apostle Paul, in his second letter to Timothy, warns us also against this natural urge to simply follow something that is easy and instinctive:

> "For the time will come when men will not put up with sound doctrine. Instead, to suit their own desires, they will gather around them a great number of teachers to say what their itching ears want to hear [such as *always* and *never*]. They will turn their ears away from the truth and turn aside to myths."

> 2 TIMOTHY 4:3–4

I got a good laugh from a story one of my fellow financial advisors, Tom, told me the other day about a famous self-proclaimed financial guru. Apparently, she—like so many in the pop culture of financial media—is an opponent of the use of variable annuities in most situations, and had just given another one of her typical this-is-why-you-should-never-invest-in-them emotional tirades. Then someone from the television audience called in to say that she was glad that her late husband had invested their retirement savings in a variable annuity. Apparently, some time after he had made the investment, the stock market fell substantially and during that low tide, he became ill and died. The caller went on to say that instead of receiving only the balance of the account which had taken a serious drop, the insurance company sent her a check for the entire amount of the original investment. My hearty laugh came when Tom then said that the financial guru sat there on national TV, virtually speechless, and finally just mumbled something and moved on.

Are variable annuities good instruments to invest in? Yes, sometimes. Are they the wrong investments for some people? Yes, sometimes. Are children an incredible blessing and joy to parents' lives? Yes. Are they also an enormous physical, emotional, and economic burden? Yes. Investments, like children—and virtually everything else in life—are neither always a pure pleasure, nor always a huge burden.

The key is to not look at investments as always good, or always bad, but rather *whether they are appropriate, or inappropriate, to a given situation.* Variable annuities typically have higher fees than, say, a mutual fund wrap program. Most variable annuities also carry higher surrender fees, and can have tax penalties for premature withdrawal, too. So, if you are a 35-year-old seeking an investment that you might want to redeem in just a few years, a variable annuity would not be a wise investment. On the other hand, if you are 65 years old and you want to participate in potential stock market gains, but have your retirement income protected regardless of what the market actually does, whether you die too soon, or live too long, a variable annuity might be the absolute best choice.

Here's one way to make sure that you are getting proper advice: Always have whoever it is dispensing the advice write it out and sign it. That way it is on record and there is accountability. Everything a licensed financial advisor recommends is put in writing in the form of an application. His or her supervisor has to agree with it, as does his or her broker dealer. There is a system of checks in place designed to do everything possible to control the quality of the advice. Advice without accountability is worthless.

Following are some of the attributes I recommend when looking for a financial advisor to help you build and manage a financial plan:

- **Experience Does Matter.** Look for someone who has a minimum of 3–5 years experience in the securities and insurance industries. This does not preclude working with young and inexperienced financial advisors, but I would make sure that they partner with someone who is experienced, so that between the two of them you end up with good advice.

  Recommendation: 3–5 years of full-time industry experience.

- **Career Only, Please!** You wouldn't think of going to a doctor who worked part-time in the medical profession and part-time at Wal-mart, would you? The financial services industry is so demanding in its professional requirements such as licensing, continuing education, staying abreast of tax law changes, and product innovations that someone who works part-time cannot possibly be up to date.

  Recommendation: Full-time financial advisor.

- **Independence Means Choice.** If you walked into a Ford dealership and described what type of car you were interested in and asked for the salesman's advice, what kind of car do you think he is going to recommend? A Toyota? Too many people don't stop to ask who pays the advisor's compensation. Is it an insurance company? A mutual fund company?

  Recommendation: Work with a registered representative who is licensed with an independent broker dealer.

- **Licensed to Sell What You Need.** Be wary of getting advice from someone who is not fully licensed to recommend both securities and insurance products. By law, a financial services salesperson can only discuss those products that they are licensed to sell.

Recommendation: Life insurance licensed *plus* either NASD series 63 (securities laws), 6 (mutual funds and variable products), 22 (limited partnerships), and 65 (investment advisors), or 63, 7 (general securities, limited partnerships, mutual funds, variable products), and 66 (investment advisors).

- **Shares Your Values**. Your personal values should be central to the question of how to invest your money. The vast majority of financial advisors have no idea what values-based investing is, and those that think they know will likely mistake you for someone who is interested in investing in socially responsible (SRI) mutual funds. SRI is the virtual polar opposite of values-based. You are either a values-based (socially conservative) investor, or a socially responsible (socially liberal) investor, but you cannot be both.

  Recommendation: Ask your financial advisor if he can make sure that the money you invest in the stock market, mutual funds, variable annuities, and privately managed accounts will reflect your values on issues such as abortion, pornography and the gay and lesbian political agenda. If he hesitates, move on. If he says, "Yes, no problem," make him prove it.

Life, Purpose, Plan, Money. The order of these fundamentally important words establishes the base upon which we can now begin to consider *how* to invest. The rest of this book is full of important and exciting information that can help you make more informed decisions about how, when, and where to invest. In fact, I'll go so far as to say that a lot of the information I present will be new and very challenging and unlike anything you've ever been presented before. As fun and advantageous as that might be, nothing is more important than truly understanding the meaning behind **Life, Purpose, Plan, Money.**

Now, let's go exploring the world of financial planning.

The Financial Planning Process

Chapter 5

The Importance of Preparation

Okay, by now you might be thinking, "Good heavens! How in the world do I figure out how to do all of this **Life, Purpose, Plan, Money** and put it into a financial plan?"

By the time you get done reading this book, you are going to be saying, "Yes, I want my money to reflect my values, and I want some of that alternative investment stuff, I want stock market investments to also have some guarantees, and I definitely want some of those tax credit things. But how in the world do I go about getting all of this stuff?"

Glad you asked. But before we go there, I want to develop a contrast to really drive home how important it is that everything in your financial plan be there for a very good reason. For starters, let me introduce you to Faithie, my three-year-old little fairy.

It doesn't snow that much in Tennessee, so when it does, it's a really fun event (well, at least for the kids). A few days ago, the skies blessed us with some of the white stuff. The three older kids ran around excitedly, grabbing gloves, hats, coats, boots, and all of the requisite paraphernalia necessary to play in the snow. I could tell they were heading out to the trampoline. For reasons that are beyond me, a trampoline with snow on it was the most exciting objective to be had. Left behind was poor little

Faithie who, at three years old, had no clue what was happening, but certainly knew enough to realize something very, very exciting was going on and that she wanted to be a part of it.

Faith Keyes Bolt (named in part for the most intelligent, morally grounded person Libby and I have ever had the honor of meeting, Dr. Allan Keyes, the former U.S. Ambassador to the United Nations), is in a leotard phase of life. She sleeps in one and changes versions all day long, and so it was really not a surprise when she came running to me in the kitchen wearing one as her siblings flew out the back door. She also had boots, gloves, and a hat—but no coat. That might detract from the leotard thing. Faithie was ready to head out to the icy trampoline party, arms and legs totally exposed, with her torso protected from the subfreezing temperature by only her trusty leotard.

Faith is only three years old. She doesn't yet understand the relationship between taking an analysis of the situation and preparing properly before attacking an objective.

Many people who know that they want the objective of financial independence do the "Faithie thing." They want it so badly, and there is so much excitement at times about this investment or that one, that they just start making investment decisions without first analyzing where they are in relation to where they want to go. They don't prepare a proper plan for getting there. They just grab some boots, gloves, and a hat, strap on that trusty leotard, and go!

Whoa. Let's slow down. There's a system that needs to be followed to make sure that everything has been seamlessly integrated, so let's get that engaged. We'll review exactly what needs to be considered and what to expect when you and your financial advisor work together in order to get you to the trampoline party! In fact, we'll use a three-step process. Let's look at each one.

Chapter 6

The First Interview

My assumption at this point is that you have already selected a financial advisor to work with, whether fee-only, commission only, or some form of hybrid (my favorite). You've checked his or her experience, licenses, discussed your shared values, and the chemistry works for both sides. Okay, you're good to go. What happens next?

The first session or initial interview is complimentary. I've never heard of a planner who charges for this introductory session. This session will provide you with an opportunity to know more about the planner. He or she will explain their planning process: How will it be accomplished? Will there be others on staff with whom you will interface in this process? How much time will it require? What will it cost? How will the fees be structured?

This is a get-acquainted session that lasts between thirty and sixty minutes. During that interview, the planner should ask why you are interested in financial planning and what specific things motivated you to do a financial plan. Is there a life event or personal issue that drives your motivation?

For example, a client may say, "I just moved into town," "I just changed jobs and got a big promotion," "I am thinking about buying a new house," or "I've received a large inheritance." Or it could be simply, "I'm not pleased with my current investment program." Any type of change in your personal life or your financial life may trigger a session with a planner. The planner will want to know about this motivation. You should not expect the planner to make specific recommendations—yet—but rather cover those issues in a broad conceptual manner.

At the end of the session, the planner will give you a homework assignment. You will need to complete a Personal Information Questionnaire (PIQ).

The financial analysis creates a complete picture. Your financial plan starts here. Don't be bashful—step right up and stare into what is metaphorically a mirror. Stare with the confidence that, regardless of your degree of comfort about what you might initially see, for the rest of your life, once you've completed the process, every time you see that mirror again you will be at peace with what is reflected.

The process needed to develop a financial analysis sounds complicated, but in reality it's straightforward. Two overriding dimensions need to be fully considered. One involves taking inventory of your financial resources; the other involves identifying your goals and objectives. As in the case of a vacation, if you fail to appropriately consider both dimensions, you'll either end up halfway through without any money, or you'll have money, but you'll not be enjoying it as much as you could be.

The questions you'll need to address when completing the PIQ require an honest look at your current financial situation. It is important to pay attention to accuracy, even if requires a bit of effort on your part to gather the necessary information.

Often this sort of information is located in a variety of places. The value of such information comes when you pull it into an integrated document for study. To help you become familiar with this process, I've included an example of this questionnaire in the appendix on page 267. A full-size blank version is available on our website, www.faithfinancialplanners.com

Some of this information isn't easily located and will cause some frustration in finding it, so be prepared. Some of the information will be in your bank checkbook, but it will need to be reconstructed. Some of it may need to come from your accountant or attorney. Some may come from the benefits administration department at work. Some of it might even be gathering dust on the top of your refrigerator. Yes, one of my clients actually stuck his life insurance policy on top of the refrigerator and forgot about it. If the information isn't readily available, then you'll have to get creative about how to recreate it.

Incidentally, don't make the process any more tedious than it has to be. For example, there are no grades given on the form for penmanship. In fact, sometimes you don't have to fill in every blank if you provide supplemental materials like copies of insurance policies, account statements, and retirement account reports. The point is to provide thorough information.

I always warn people in advance about this process. First, it isn't fun. You are not going to enjoy it, so be prepared for that from the beginning, although there is a certain amount of fulfillment in working toward a worthwhile goal. You will have to appropriate time from your life for the purpose, probably from one to two hours. The good news, though, is that once you complete this form, you will never have to complete it again. From that point forward, it is simply a matter of updating the records that we, or another financial planner, will keep electronically for you.

The first portion of the process involves objective information about your current financial situation. For example, you will need to list your various assets (separately for husband, wife, and jointly-held property), including:

- Retirement accounts
- Investments
- Insurance contracts
- Checking accounts
- Savings accounts
- Money market accounts
- Personal property, including residence and automobiles

The second portion is more subjective and deals with what you want the money to do for your life. This section includes such questions as:

- When do you want to retire? What will you do during retirement?
- How much money do you want to have when you retire?
- Do you want to help your children through college? How much money do you want to give them?
- Are you planning for a second home?
- Are you planning for a change in residence?
- Do you want to set aside appropriate funds for recreation, such as for a boat or horses or an avocation?
- Do you have any significant gifts that you want to make? To your church? To a mission?
- Is there a period of time in your life when you would like to not work in order to serve in the mission field, or to study some subject, go to school, or help an ailing family member?
- Do you have plans to begin your own business? For you or your spouse or both?
- Are you going to have children? Do you want one spouse to stay home and, if so, for how long?

These questions are not exhaustive, but they acquaint you with some of the possibilities for consideration in this process.

Each one of us has the freedom to pursue our own individual way through life. Goals vary in length, structure, specificity, and resources. There is no correct *Christian* standard for when to retire or for how much to help with your child's college education or for whether you should go into a second career. What a joy it is to live every day in the knowledge that God breathed life into us as individuals, knowing us even before we were born, and that nothing can separate us from the love of God! What a passion for life we have when we desire to live a life of purpose, reflecting God's creativity, love, and joy throughout our life plan as it evolves.

Don't be too demanding of yourself regarding hard and fast goals. Keep in mind that life is dynamic and that no matter what goals you establish, you will change and refine them over a period of time. The central purpose of goal setting is to establish a clear direction. Take a few moments to consider what you want to have in your future and when you want it to happen.

Your goals don't have to be singular. You can have four or five simultaneous goals—retirement, a second home, sending somebody through college, maybe taking four years off. Each of these goals might require a different time horizon and a different investment strategy. The key lies in flexibility and individualization. You should follow the plan and strategy that is right for you. One of the most critically important objectives for a financial planner is to free people from feeling the need to fit their life into someone else's preconceived idea of what that life should be.

As the saying goes, there is no such thing as a dress rehearsal for life. This is *it*. The life you are living now and planning for in the future is the only one you get. So, do it your way, as a natural outgrowth and reflection of your relationship with God, and make it exciting, dynamic and powerful!

Chapter 7

Mini-Marathon—
the Second Interview

The second session with your planner should last from two to two-and-a-half hours. During this session, the planner will review the details of your financial situation with you line by line and page by page.

All the effort you put in to filling out the PIQ will bear fruit in the form of a Comprehensive Financial Analysis. We refer to our version at Faith Financial as the *Money For Life Plan*. The Comprehensive Financial Analysis will be the basis for determining whether you are on track to reach your goals, or whether you'll need to make some changes. Your financial analysis should be comprehensive and unbiased. You need to be able to see the entire picture before you can make any decisions. And you need to keep in mind that any analysis that a salesperson uses specifically to market a particular financial product (such as life insurance, annuities, or stocks) might have a bias toward a particular product built into the result. So, watch for that.

Any Comprehensive Financial Analysis should include:

- Cash flow report
- Net worth statement
- Insurance analysis

- Income tax projection and analysis
- Investment portfolio analysis
- Retirement income projection
- Education funding report
- Estate transfer report
- Personal values analysis

As these reports are reviewed, the planner will be giving you suggestions, strategies, options, and solutions for you to consider.

This session requires a great deal of interaction between you and the planner. Typically, at the end of this session, you feel like the Gary Larson cartoon character who, sitting in a classroom, raises his hand and says, "Teacher, may I be excused? My brain is full." Hopefully, your planner will summarize the discussion and recommend a course of action.

One caution for this step in the process: Don't get caught up in "analysis paralysis." Fear of making a mistake can totally immobilize some people, rendering them unable to do *anything*. If this happens to you, remember the adage from the book *In Search of Excellence: "Disorganized action is always preferable to organized inaction."* The key is to do *something*.

At the end of this mini-marathon, you and your financial planner will have decided on a route for designing and implementing a financial plan. You'll also have had plenty of coffee!

Chapter 8

Plan Implementation— the Third Interview

Either during the second interview or in a conversation over the telephone, decisions have been made about such things as life insurance, investment portfolio, retirement strategies, tax-reduction techniques, and so forth. Each one of these decisions triggers some paperwork to implement the new strategy. This paperwork will probably be handled by one of the financial planner's staff at the office, through the mail, or by the fax machine.

At the third meeting, all the numbers from the initial financial analysis will have been reworked to include the recommended changes. For example, during this third session you will not find a gap between your retirement goals and the strategy to reach those goals (unlike your opening session when you didn't yet have a plan). You and your planner will have created the means to reach those goals.

At this time any contracts or policies or new account statements will be added to your financial organizer, which will become your one source for all your financial information. You will want to bring this organizer with you to each meeting; it not only organizes all the complex information regarding your plan, but it serves as a resource for you and your family.

For example, one of my long-term clients was a former Baptist minister who lived in the Midwest. When he reached age seventy-five, his health deteriorated. He grew concerned about his family's lack of knowledge regarding his financial plan. During the annual review of his financial plan, he asked, "What do I do about their lack of information?"

I said, "Just give them our phone number. We have copies of everything." When my client left the Church militant and joined the Church triumphant (that means he died), his children called our office, and we brought them up to date on his financial plan. As the financial planning firm for the deceased, we had a complete record of his information. That saved the grieving family countless hours of frustration and anxiety, and kept them from having to hire a lawyer to track down all the details of the pastor's financial life.

During this third session, you also review your overall financial plan. Does it still make sense? Are there other adjustments? Are there lingering questions? This interview usually lasts about an hour.

After this third interview, it now becomes simply a matter of monitoring the financial plan, generally at annual reviews.

It's unfortunate, but life is much too fluid to create a financial plan that lasts "once and for all." There are no rigid thirty-year decisions, and you will be fortunate if you are able to stay most of the course for five years. On the other hand, if you have created a good, well-thought-out plan with competent professional help, then your goals will be sufficiently elastic to easily accommodate the ups and downs of real life.

Life is dynamic—always changing, always moving, always evolving. "Dynamic" is an excellent word to apply to your financial plan. That is why your financial goals will also evolve and change. A financial plan is alive. It grows and matures. It incorporates many different changes along the way. Your goals will change if you change careers, get married, have children, watch them grow up and leave home, receive an inheritance, take time away from your career, or decide to start your own business. No matter what happens in your life, your financial plan must evolve with you.

Continual changes and innovations in financial products will also require that you have a fresh look at your plan. Another reason for an annual review—even if there are no life changes or the financial industry hasn't changed—is that more than likely the government has introduced new rules regarding financial matters. Congress is not stagnant about financial issues, and laws are constantly changing. The tax laws are continually being revised. During the nearly two decades that I have been in the financial planning industry, I can recall about thirteen significant changes regarding Individual Retirement Accounts alone—and that's not counting all of the other tax law changes that affected a host of other financial strategies and instruments.

A financial plan, like your life plan, is a reflection of you. And it is alive.

Insuring Your Family

Chapter 9

How Much Is Enough Insurance?

The title for this chapter is a critically important, very personal, and never-ending question that will be examined in depth through the financial planning process. In the next few pages I will explain the various types of insurance, and you can use this material to review your own situation. The apostle Paul wrote Timothy, "If anyone does not provide for his relatives, and especially for his own family, he has denied the faith and is worse than an unbeliever" (1 Timothy 5:8). Those are strong words. Translated, that means, "Buy enough life insurance!"

Before you can afford to invest a dollar, you must first protect that dollar. Insurance is the wonderful financial instrument that allows us to exchange a potentially profound and unlimited risk for a reasonable cost (i.e., the premium). Because we can transfer this unlimited liability to an insurance company, we are able to live with confidence. We have the assurance that if something tragic happens, then at least we will be financially protected.

Insurance is sometimes maligned as a confusing financial tool. How much do we need? What type should we purchase? How long should we hold a particular type of insurance? What benefits are included in the insurance?

Why Should You Have Insurance?

Before I cover the specifics of insurance, let me first say that life insurance is one of the most intimate and personal decisions a family can make. However, because of the new American cultural dynamic of "entitlement," it has become a fuzzy blur of an idea. One of the main reasons why our country has so many cultural, political, and economic problems today is precisely because the government is doing so many things for its citizens that the founding fathers never intended. As individual citizens, we have failed to take responsibility for accumulating sufficient assets to cover our retirement, and we have failed to protect ourselves from the high cost of healthcare with adequate, self-paid insurance protection.

Many people believe they are entitled to healthcare and retirement benefits through government-created programs. Not only is there a cultural cost to shifting responsibility for our financial welfare to the government, but there is also a huge monetary drain. If these entitlement programs were eliminated from the budget of the United States, our country would not only be able to significantly reduce taxes, but it could also run a continual surplus. Over 50% of the federal annual budget is earmarked for social welfare programs, and that percentage continues to increase.

In a free society, each person has an individual responsibility to appropriately manage his own insurance and financial plans. That is not the responsibility of the government. If we fail to take individual responsibility, we contribute to the fiscal (and social) decay of our nation. This phenomenon is almost never discussed in the mainstream media, but the truth of the matter is that each of us bears our own personal responsibility, whether we retire and live to 125 (like I hope to do!), become disabled, or die prematurely. That is our individual privilege and also our responsibility.

Regarding insurance, remember two key points. First, be responsible and buy the appropriate insurance that will cover your needs. Second, remember that insurance must be purchased *before* you need it. You have to buy insurance before the risk it is designed to cover actually *occurs*. You can't wait until you have an auto accident to buy insurance to cover the accident. Nor can you wait until your health deteriorates before you purchase health insurance. If you are ill, no insurance company will reasonably accept you.

The lesson is clear: Apply for insurance before you need it and while you are eligible.

A Special Message for Families

I am now going to ask one of the most important questions anyone will ever ask you. What do you consider to be the most important financial instrument? I'll give you a hint. It is neither a retirement plan, nor a college savings plan. No, the answer is related to a much more fundamental aspect of family survival. Follow me as I paint a picture from real life experiences.

I barely recognized the ring of the phone, having been in such a deep sleep. I slowly opened my eyes and looked at the red glow from the digital clock next to my bed. It read 1:21 A.M. Emphasis on the "A.M." part. I reached for the phone, cleared my throat, and put the receiver to my ear. "Hello," came out of my mouth.

I heard a woman on the other end say my name slowly and tentatively. "Stephen." Then complete silence for what seemed an eternity, and then the words, "Wayne's dead." Those words entered my ears, but they were so incomprehensible that they did not register. Again, I heard her say, "He's dead."

Helen was in shock. Her wonderful husband of thirty-two years had collapsed from a major heart attack and died. He left behind his adoring wife and eight, e-i-g-h-t, 8, children between the ages of 4 and 18.

Wayne was my most mature, productive financial advisor in my new agency in Tennessee.

It was July 1987, some five months since I had left my home in Colorado to take on the responsibility of developing a distribution system for a large Lutheran financial services company, and it had been a rough time for us. I had been on top of the world in Colorado. I had owned nine horses, a 250-acre ranch, and 40 acres and a cabin in the mountains where we rode horses, hunted, and fished non-stop. Did I mention that I was also the top producer for a large financial services company? I had plenty of both of life's most pleasant elixirs: time and money. Yet something was not right. I did not feel that I was using the gifts that God had endowed me with to their fullest, so I made the very challenging move to our competing company. I left my wonderful life to develop a new agency for Lutheran Brotherhood in the south, where none had previously existed. Now, my best financial advisor was dead, leaving behind eight lovely children and a grief-stricken wife.

We made it through that tough period and went back to work. About three months later, while on vacation back at my mountain cabin in Colorado, the heavenly peace that is the breaking of the morning sun across the Rockies was shattered by the sound of a vehicle attempting to work its way up the slope to the cabin as fast as it could. At 5:35 A.M., the sound of a grinding engine in low gear, pushed to its maximum output and getting louder by the second, was well past my ability to compute. I lay in bed, still. Suddenly, the engine stopped and I could hear someone running on the wooden deck to the front door. Then I heard the cabin door burst open and someone running up the stairs to the bedroom.

Totally out of breath, gasping for elusive oxygen at 8000 feet altitude, was my close friend from Boulder, John Gunter. His body shook from his ordeal to get to me as fast as possible. He stopped at the top of the stairs and exclaimed, "There's been an accident! Greg Barret is dead and so is his wife. The two children are in the hospital in intensive care. It was a head-on collision near their home in Chattanooga. Since he was a friend and one of your financial advisors, I knew you'd want to know as soon as possible. I'm sorry." And with that, he turned slowly, headed back down the stairs and left as quickly as he came. I lay there in bed, breathless and stunned.

That was a tough one. A beautiful young family destroyed. Two little boys without parents. *Good God, when will Jesus return and be done with this kind of horrific destruction?*

But we got through it. We moved on. Then, about a month later, another tragedy. This time it was a good friend from church. Again, a car wreck and a young family. Wow, that is tough to watch. A funeral with the surviving wife and three small children. No human being should have to go through that.

Three good friends, all in the prime of their lives, dead. All in a span of five months. It hit me hard. I came very close to resigning from my position with Lutheran Brotherhood and just crawling in a hole somewhere for awhile. But I didn't.

I did learn, though, that life insurance is THE most important financial instrument a family can have. I learned that in a very dramatic, and permanent, way.

We can't stop Satan's attack on God's creation. That's a war beyond us that God has won and will finish in His time. In the meantime, though, there are very specific actions we can take to protect our families, and the very first one is to provide an adequate amount of life insurance in the event that one of the breadwinners is removed from the equation.

Life Insurance

Most people are substantially underinsured. They are underinsured for two basic reasons: (1) They don't know how to calculate their true insurance need, and (2) they think that even if they did know their true need, they couldn't afford that amount of insurance. You can solve these two problems easily, but only after getting rid of your biases. Simply determine your need and then shop for the least expensive way to fulfill this need. Here's a good rule of thumb: Your life insurance coverage should be between five and ten times your annual earnings. To meet this need, begin to consider annual renewable term insurance. You will be amazed how inexpensively you can provide the amount of financial security that your family deserves.

There are two additional considerations before you actually purchase the insurance. The first consideration relates to love and the second relates to taxes.

1. *Life insurance might be considered the greatest love letter you could ever write to your family.* If the most traumatic event did occur, if a wage-earning spouse/parent died, the emotional toll on the family would be incalculable. There is no earthly way to mitigate this loss. However, we can substantially eliminate the accompanying financial loss. In fact, I will say that a Christian has a responsibility to make adequate provision for the care of his family even in the event of his death.

   Many times I've discussed the responsibility of life insurance with a couple and I hear, "Oh, she'd get remarried," or "He could get a better job." These kinds of responses project unrealistic expectations in the face of a most tragic event. Instead, I've developed a rule about the decision-making process: Before you decide on how much insurance to purchase, assume that you are . . . *already dead.* Picture yourself sitting in heaven and peering down through the clouds, with a checkbook in hand. As the clouds part, you see your family in your home. If you could simply, magically, write a check and deposit it into your family's bank account at that moment to make sure that the emotional loss was not compounded by economic depravity, what would be the amount of that check? Whatever your answer, that is the amount of insurance you should own. *That* is the purpose of life insurance.

2. You might be thinking that buying a big life insurance policy to provide for your family is going to be an expensive proposition, particularly if you outlive the point where you need it. True enough. But consider this interesting tidbit, especially if you are in a high tax bracket: *Life insurance enjoys very special tax treatment.* To the extent that your life insurance has a cash value (savings)

portion to it such as universal life, or (my preference) variable universal life, that savings element of the contract will grow tax-deferred. In other words, you will not have to pay income tax on the investment gain inside the contract while it accumulates. In fact, depending on the type of policy and the method used for accessing the cash value, it is possible to *never* pay any tax on the earnings. Because of the unique tax advantages associated with cash value life insurance, flexible-premium options, and the opportunity to access the cash value virtually on demand, a state-of-the-art cash value insurance policy, such as variable universal life, can be an excellent cornerstone to a developing financial plan.

Let's illustrate the power of the tax-deferral benefit of a variable universal life policy. You determine to save $300 each month for the next twenty years. Investment A is currently taxable, but investment B is tax-deferred. In this hypothetical example, we'll assume that both investments receive the same rate of return—say 12% annually. If you are in a 28% tax bracket, at the end of twenty years, investment A would be worth $191,443—but investment B would be worth $296,777. The difference amounts to $105,334. Of course in the case of life insurance we would also have to take into consideration the cost of the insurance. In most cases, however, particularly where the intent is to invest the maximum into the policy that tax law allows, even after considering the yearly cost of the policy, the difference in savings associated with tax deferral makes the variable universal life insurance contract an attractive investment option. If you defer the income tax on your investment gain, it can make a tremendous difference in the ending net value.

Whether to use cash value insurance instead of term, or which type of cash value insurance to use and how much to invest, are issues well beyond the scope of this chapter. I strongly suggest that you and your financial planner consider this special tax treatment for your life insurance before you determine how to solve your insurance need. Tax-deferred insurance can also be a factor in addressing your long-term savings program.

Life Insurance as a Financial-Planning Tool

Here are some general principles that I use in the area of life insurance planning with my clients. I see whole life insurance as an expensive, inflexible, and obsolete type of insurance. I recommend some form of straight term insurance or universal life insurance, especially if you are considering it as part of your overall investment plan, and especially if you are in a higher tax bracket.

To really give you some insight into what you can do with life insurance as a financial planning tool, I'll give you a peek at what I personally own. I have a variable universal life policy, which offers multiple mutual fund investment choices (referred to as separate accounts). These funds represent multiple asset classes, which I have managed by a values-based money management firm. The policy allows me to access the profit from my investment without ever paying any income tax. This is accomplished through a "wash loan" provision, allowing me to access my invested dollars in the policy on a tax-favored basis through borrowing. And because the policy guarantees that I will never be charged more for the loan than I earn in interest on the borrowed funds, I may be able to keep the money and never make any payments—*principal or interest*—on the loan. Now *that's* a life insurance policy. You should know that certain situations could occur to cause the loss of these tax benefits—again underscoring the importance of relying on professional financial planning assistance.

Several years ago I was involved in one of the most interesting applications of this concept. One day a young, single doctor in his mid-thirties came into my office for some financial assistance. By most people's standards, this doctor was well-to-do. His investment portfolio approached $1 million, but his income taxes were so high that he felt as if he were spinning his wheels. By the time his loss of personal exemptions and deductions were accounted for, and then both the highest state and federal income tax rates were applied, he was only able to keep about 55 cents of every dollar he made (whether from his investments or wages). I proposed that this doctor fund a variable universal life policy. The tax laws calculate the maximum contribution allowable to a VUL in any year without reducing or eliminating the income tax advantages. In his case, we set up the VUL so that he contributed $90,000 a year. With that amount going in, the death benefit of the policy turned out to be $2,791,574.

Obviously this young, single professional with a million-dollar investment portfolio didn't need that much life insurance. In fact, you could argue that he didn't need any life insurance at all. But he did need income tax help, and the VUL policy gave him such assistance. He did well on the earnings over the next five years, averaging about 12%. And he didn't have to pay a dime in taxes.

At the end of the fifth year, he had accumulated over $472,000 in his cash value. If you subtract out the $364,000 in premiums he paid in this period, he still gained about $108,000. Now if the same dollars that were invested in the variable universal life policy had been invested instead in, say, a taxable investment averaging the same 12%, the gain would have only been $55,119. And keep in mind that not only did the young doctor gain an extra $52,000 over the taxable equivalent, but he also had the advantage of a $2.7 million insurance benefit!

This example is for illustrative purposes only. To determine whether a variable universal life policy is in your best interest, you and your financial advisor should carefully review the pros and cons of such a policy.

Here's the bottom line regarding insurance: Commit to purchasing enough life insurance so that if you die prematurely, your family will be financially secure. Don't be afraid of the premiums. If you buy the policy when you are healthy, term insurance is very inexpensive. If you choose the more expensive method of providing life insurance benefits through a cash value product such as variable universal life, recognize that there are many creative ways of paying for it that can have a very positive impact on your overall financial plan.

Children and Life Insurance

Before I leave the section on life insurance I want to address one more issue, and that is the question of whether children should have life insurance. I'll give you my answer with a story of an incident that happened a few years ago. Early in my career, my employer developed a program that allowed its insureds to convert their whole life policy for the more state-of-the-art universal life policy. In most cases, this was definitely in their best interest. I was contacting all the insureds in my territory about the program.

One of these families consisted of two parents and three little girls. They lived on a farm in rural eastern Colorado, and were, by community standards, of moderate income. I also knew them as members of our church. They considered the program and decided it was something they wanted to do. In the process, I provided each of them with increases in coverage, including the girls. In fact, the small $5,000 policies for the children were converted to $25,000 policies. I remember thinking that amount would be something they could take with them into their new families in the years to come.

One Sunday about four months later, our pastor began praying for one of the little girls who had just been diagnosed with leukemia. Startled, I made a mental note to check on the policy to make sure it was issued and in order. Thankfully, everything was in order. The little girl's condition deteriorated, and the prognosis was not good. The parents made continuous visits to Denver for the little girl's chemotherapy. Each trip took all day. The driving time alone was five hours, plus hours at the hospital for treatment and recovery. Eventually, the situation got so bad that people in the community and church began helping do the farm chores, including the arduous irrigating by hand that had to be done in that dry climate.

One day, I stopped by their house to check on them. When I knocked on the white-frame farmhouse door, the mother greeted me and asked me to come inside. As the three little girls played outside on the trampoline, she began to give me an update, and her eyes filled with tears. Suddenly, we heard a scream and ran to the door, only to see the sick five-year-old girl jumping on the trampoline and crying at the top of her lungs, "I'm going to die, I'm going to die, I'm going to die!"

The two sisters just watched, and the mother bolted out the door to wrap the poor girl in her comforting arms. As I silently walked to my car, I saw all four of them in one big family hug, crying and holding on to each other.

About six months later, the little girl died. Again, I made my way out to that white farmhouse and knocked on the door. The mother and father both came to greet me, but no words were spoken. They knew why I was there. I handed them the check for $25,000 and whispered, "I'm so, so sorry."

The mother, with tears streaming down her face, hugged me and I departed. Later I found out that because the cancer treatment was considered experimental, their health insurance did not cover over $100,000 of their bills. And with the enormous costs of running a farm as an absentee owner, the family was in debt well beyond anything that $25,000 could begin to cover.

Do I believe children should have insurance? You bet! How much insurance? Enough coverage to pay for their funeral and to cover any expenses associated with the parents turning away from their occupation and focusing on the physical health of their sick child. The insurance should also cover the emotional health of the family—for a long time to come.

Don't skimp on this important area of life insurance. The potential cost of bypassing this coverage is much higher than you can imagine.

Chapter **II**

The Other Important Insurances

Although life insurance is generally the most underinsured and misunderstood aspect of a family's total insurance portfolio, there are several other important insurance policies that need to be well thought through as well. These include:

1. liability insurance
2. homeowner and renter insurance
3. automobile insurance
4. disability insurance
5. long-term care insurance
6. health insurance

1. Liability Insurance

Lawsuits with heavy financial consequences and personal liability are rampant in the United States. Whether someone trips and falls in your yard, accuses you of slander, gets bitten by your dog, or gets hit by your child, you'd better be prepared to suffer through a lawsuit. All too quickly a simple mishap can turn into a nightmare. Television commercials that feature attorneys who advertise their legal prowess remind us that each of us is vulnerable to such lawsuits. At present, our best option is to protect ourselves with a personal liability policy. As the book *The ABCs of Managing Your Money* points out, "a personal liability umbrella policy will protect you and your family from claims arising out of nonprofessional activities." The author, Jonathan Pond, CPA, says, "A good umbrella policy will protect you, your family members living in you home, children attending school away from home, and even pets. In addition, the policy should cover legal defense costs, critically important since even the successful defense of a lawsuit can be very costly. The best protection against the threat of a lawsuit is to purchase a personal liability umbrella insurance policy."

This liability insurance policy can be purchased at a reasonable cost, depending on the amount of exposure and coverage. This type of policy should give you peace of mind when you watch those video blooper shows that replay a neighbor's car rolling down the sidewalk without a driver—headed toward the swimming pool across the street.

2. Homeowner and Renter Insurance

Your property insurance should cover unexpected loss to your property. Most policyholders tend to be underinsured. Here are some suggested coverage guidelines:

- Homeowner or renter insurance should cover at least 80% of the replacement value of your home, allowing for annual inflation. This coverage will add additional cost to the policy, but it represents a necessary value.
- Your policy should also include replacement-cost coverage for your household contents so that you avoid having to haggle with the insurer over the actual cash value of any losses.
- If you have a special collection such as jewelry, guns, or paintings, you'll want to add a floater policy to your basic contract. This

floater policy will cover the value of the collection that exceeds the minimum allowed through the basic plan.

- Be aware that computer equipment and other material used to operate any business inside the home will necessitate additional coverage.

3. Automobile Insurance

Most automobile insurance policies cover a standard, which meets the minimum needs of most motorists. The following list includes five types of coverage that you will want to make sure are included in your policy:

Bodily Injury Property Liability

This insurance covers injury to pedestrians and occupants of other vehicles, and damage that you have done to the property of others. Discuss with your insurance agent the proper amount of coverage, being aware that as you accumulate more assets, you should increase the amount of your insurance.

Medical Payments Insurance

This insurance will cover medical payments on behalf of the policyholder and family members, as well as other passengers in the vehicle. Ask your agent to compare the need for this insurance with what your health insurance policy will cover.

Uninsured Motorist Coverage

Although many states require a minimum amount of liability coverage for any vehicle, some motorists disobey this law. Additionally, the minimum required insurance may be less than what is needed to compensate for actual loss. By purchasing this insurance, the policyholder will be covered for both uninsured and underinsured risks from other drivers.

Collision Insurance

This insurance is usually required on any vehicle with a mortgage or lease. It covers damage to the vehicle regardless of who actually caused the loss. If your vehicle is not financed, you may find it more economical to reduce or eliminate this coverage—particularly if your vehicle has little monetary value.

Comprehensive Insurance

This insurance covers your vehicle from virtually all risks including theft, vandalism, collision with animals, and so forth.

4. Disability Insurance

For most working people, the greatest risk they have probably comes from the loss of income due to a protracted disability. Yet unless there is a comprehensive policy available through an employer, most people will not have a sufficient amount of disability insurance on their own to protect against such a long-term loss.

Disability insurance is designed to replace your lost future wages in the event of an illness or injury. For example, if you are currently earning $40,000 a year and expect to work for another twenty years, adjusting for inflation at 4%, even without any real increase in your salary, you will earn $1,191,123 during this time period. You and your family will expect at least $1.1 million from your wages over the next twenty years to accomplish your dreams. So if you suddenly became disabled and could not work any longer, your dreams would evaporate. And because you can typically expect an increase in expenses to accompany a disability, those dreams can be transformed into nightmares for the entire family.

Having some amount of disability insurance, but not the right kind, can also be devastating. I had this fact forever ingrained in my mind with a story I heard shortly after I moved to Nashville. Gary, a thirty-five-year-old husband and father of two, was involved in an accident that paralyzed him from the waist down. Instead of working as a construction foreman, Gary had to sit in a wheelchair. On the one hand, Gary was lucky because he survived the accident. And because he had earlier purchased enough disability insurance, his economic lifestyle did not have to change. On the other hand, however, he wasn't so lucky. His benefit period capped out at five years. Gary was already wrestling with a loss of self-worth; as he faced the termination of his benefits, he grew increasingly distraught. Finally, in the last year of his benefit period, unable to cope with the loss of both his physical abilities and his income, Gary resorted to suicide. He left a note telling his family that he could not bear to watch them suffer the effects of both his physical inability to be a father and husband, and his economic inability to provide for his family.

Disability insurance protects wage earners from adding financial tragedy on top of personal tragedy. Here are some guidelines when shopping for this type of insurance:

- Cover at least 65% of your earnings. If you purchase the policy, any of your benefits from the policy will be tax-free.
- Extend the period of time between when the disability begins and when you can start receiving benefits for as long as your assets will provide for your needs. This coverage will result in reduced premium rates.
- Be sure to add some kind of inflation protection, and update your coverage annually.
- If you are in a specialized field, you may want to add your "own occupation" to the definition of disability. This type of policy will increase your disability insurance expenses, but it will allow you to collect benefits if you cannot perform the primary duties of the job you are working.

5. Long-Term Care Insurance

Like disability insurance, long-term care insurance is designed to protect assets. As the United States population grows increasingly older, the need will increase for long-term care (LTC) insurance. You cannot depend on Medicare to cover these expenses. Medicare will not cover the costs associated with long-term convalescent care. Unless you intend to pay upward of $40,000 to $80,000 a year for that care from your own assets, you'll need a well-thought-through LTC insurance policy.

Until the late 1980s, insurance companies had scant actuarial information to establish the baselines for benefits and premiums. This situation has changed drastically today. A number of excellent plans are available from reputable and established insurance companies. In fact, today a long-term insurance plan should be purchased through a "building process." There are numerous benefits that can be built into a plan in order to develop just the right package for any insured. For example, some individuals are quite firm that they never want to enter or be treated in a convalescent home. For these individuals, an LTC plan with the primary benefits weighted toward home healthcare will not only allow them to remain in their home while receiving care, but it will also give them increased peace of mind as they enter their twilight years.

An LTC insurance plan can be customized with many benefits. Because there are too many to address here, I'll instead suggest that you use the following guidelines when considering LTC insurance:

- Be sure you have a sufficient home healthcare provision.
- Extend the coverage for life, not for a period of years.
- Include as few ADL triggers (activities of daily living) benefits as possible.
- Buy LTC insurance early (when you are in your early sixties).

Here is a primary profile of someone who needs this type of insurance. He or she would be approaching retirement with a net worth between $200,000 and $1,000,000. If your net worth is below $200,000, the premiums might be prohibitively expensive when compared to your income. If your net worth is above $1,000,000, it might make more sense to pocket the premium and self-insure. Your individual situation may be different. Seek professional counsel, and involve your children in the decision-making process.

Always remember that you are in the driver's seat. There are almost limitless ways you can arrange benefits to fit your needs. When a salesperson suggests a particular type of LTC policy, don't buy it immediately without some additional research. Contact your state insurance commissioner's office and ask for information about LTC insurance. They will provide you with a pamphlet that details the various features of a LTC policy.

Finally, don't be penny-wise and pound-foolish. What do you need in LTC? Determine this first, and then add benefits that meet your particular goals. For example, let's say you want your insurance to cover your costs for any extended convalescent care. If the average cost for that care in your area is running about $110 per day, don't buy a policy that covers only $75 per day. Additionally, make sure you add an inflation adjustment feature to the policy. In the final analysis, you should shop for what you need, not for what you want to pay in premium.

6. Health Insurance

Most Americans have health insurance through their employer. Self-employed workers and those workers who are not covered by a group plan will need to buy an individual policy. There are three types of plans on today's market: HMOs (health maintenance organizations), PPOs (preferred provider organizations), and traditional health plans. HMOs and PPOs will be less expensive than a traditional plan, but the policy will not usually be as flexible or as portable as a traditional plan.

The following are some features that you should make sure are part of your health insurance plan:

- Comprehensive coverage that will cover you wherever you need treatment and for whatever ails you. Stay away from the cheaper policies, which cover only certain types of illnesses or injuries.
- Acceptable and definite maximum out-of-pocket costs. Know the amount of your maximum portion for any catastrophic claim.
- Guaranteed renewable. Reputable insurers have a long history in the industry and sell comprehensive policies. Almost always these

comprehensive policies include the provision to be guaranteed renewable.

Never buy solely according to the premium! Health insurance is like everything else in a free market—you get what you pay for. Don't shop for the lowest premium until you (a) have the policy provisions that you want, (b) know you are dealing with a financially secure insurer that has been in the healthcare business for many years, and (c) know that you can be approved medically for the policy.

Here's one final thought about health insurance: If you are self-employed, I strongly encourage you to look into a medical savings account (MSA). The government authorized 750,000 of these as an experiment. An MSA has a high deductible ($2,500 to $15,000), which initially sounds like a disadvantage. However, that high deductible is complemented by a tax-deductible contribution to your medical savings account, so that you have the money to make up for the deductible if you need it. And here's the great part. If in any year you don't need to use the money you put into the MSA, you get to keep it! And keep in mind that it was already a tax-deductible contribution. The bottom line is that you could end up saving thousands of dollars (toward your retirement or other financial goal) that would have otherwise gone to an insurance company to pay the higher premium associated with low-deductible plans. Now that is more typical of the American way to address high healthcare costs!

What Do You Want Your Money To Do?

Chapter 12

New Choices

When I first started in this industry in 1981, there were less than 500 mutual funds available to investors. There was no such thing as a variable annuity. Annuities were all fixed and guaranteed. Then, about mid–1980, everything began to change. The impetus was a combination of dynamics that collided:

- High interest rates
- Higher life expectancies
- Advances in technology
- An increasingly sophisticated public

These were all very good things, in my opinion. We never looked back. A couple hundred years ago, the primary prescription doctors administered to patients was, disgustingly, a practice referred to as blood-letting. Whatever your illness, the doctor's answer was to get rid of some of your blood. Yuk!

In 1981, we financial "doctors" had very few prescriptions, and very little ability to develop any kind of true customization. Today, however, nothing could be farther from the truth. Instead of your financial advisor telling you what he or she has to offer, we are able to turn it completely around and ask, "What do you want your money to do?"

Stock market? Okay. Bonds? Okay. Mutual funds selected from over 14,000 options? Okay. Customized life insurance? Okay. So far, no surprises, right? Well, consider these:

- An expected double-digit return with no stock market risk? Okay.
- An investment in the stock market with a guaranteed income, regardless of what the market might do? Okay.
- A portfolio that reflects my Christian values? Okay.

This section will get us prepared for the specifics that we will discuss in the next section. Ready? Here we go!

Chapter 13

Debunking Myths

Sometimes when I travel by plane I allow myself the luxury of reading a novel. Some of my favorite authors are Nelson Demille, Tom Clancy, and John Grisham. But every now and then I'll pick up a book by one of these authors and it just never seems to click. I remember reading a Tom Clancy novel that I just couldn't get into. I was about halfway through and committed, so I plodded along, page after page, until I turned to the first line in a new chapter which read, "The sun came up precisely at dawn." Okay. That did it. I threw the book away.

But the worst is where I find holes, statements that I know to be implausible or literally impossible. I was enjoying John Grisham's novel *The Broker* until I came across this line: " . . . mutual fund owned by an international cabal . . ."

Rats! Here we go again, and just when it was getting good, too. Mutual funds are not *owned* by anyone. By definition, the only thing that can be owned relating to a mutual fund are the shares, which are owned by the individual investors. I know, because I have launched mutual funds, hired and fired mutual fund managers, and dealt with every minute aspect of a mutual fund. John Grisham's statement was not accurate.

I realize that Mr. Grisham was not writing a technical manual on "open-ended investment companies regulated by the 1940 Securities Act" (what you know as mutual funds). But I couldn't help but wonder how many millions of readers, who also owned mutual fund shares, actually believed that their fund was *owned* by someone other than the shareholders after they read that sentence in the novel.

Learning the Facts Is Important

There is so much misinformation in our world today that I wonder sometimes how any truth actually gets through at all. We are fed an untruth which, over time, becomes accepted as fact, and then we build on that. I'll have a lot more to say in the section covering values-based investing. But for now, let me give you one example:

The United States is a nation.

Not true. The Founding Fathers went to great lengths to strike that word from any and all founding documents. They realized that what they were constructing was a (voluntary) union of states. You will not find the word nation in any of the formative American documents.

Why is it so important to peel the layers of the onion back until all facts are known? Because without a factual premise, the decisions based on a false premise, by definition, can't be the best. And when making financial decisions, this fundamental is particularly true. Let me take you back to an actual situation that occurred to me where this "false premise" hit me square between the (ethical) eyes.

The relationship between a client and his or her financial advisor can become quite friendly, and that is a good thing. However, if the client does not know the limitations of the advisor, a misassumption can be made by the client that, if not recognized and corrected by the advisor, can adversely impact the client's financial decisions.

Before I became an independent financial advisor, I worked for a highly respected Lutheran financial services company. The company was a wonderful place to work and offered the Lutheran client an environment of shared values within which to purchase a very limited number of proprietary financial products.

In the early 1990s, I began taking courses from the College for Financial Planning and learned a tremendous amount of academic information. The problem was that in many cases, I was literally prohibited from developing financial plans for my clients that utilized this information, because the company did not offer those products. Instruments such as tax credit programs, Intangible Drilling Cost tax deductions, portfolio management methods such as the Nobel Prize-winning Modern Portfolio Theory, and private money management were available to me (and therefore my clients) only in my textbooks.

I remember one Sunday when it hit me. I was an elder in my church, and I was serving communion to members as they knelt at the altar. I remember seeing one of my clients there, kneeling, ready to take communion from me, when I realized that I had not given him my best advice at our most recent meeting. I had not done so because the advice I would have given him came directly from my textbooks, and I was prohibited from talking with him about it because my employer did not offer those financial solutions.

That snapshot image haunted me for weeks until I could not handle it any longer. After praying about it and talking it over with my wife and other close confidants, I contacted my company and told them I would be resigning. They were stunned and asked if I would stay on for a few months, which I did. Finally, the day came for the regional vice president to fly to Nashville and meet with me. We were at an Embassy Suites and met in his room, where we signed all the necessary paperwork. Afterwards, he leaned over and placed everything neatly in his briefcase on the floor, closed the top and locked it, and sat up and looked at me.

"Okay. It's done. Everything is signed. Now, honestly, tell me why you resigned," the perplexed RVP said. I thought hard about how I could explain it succinctly. Then it hit me. *Show him what I could not do for the client kneeling at the altar.*

I got out my notepad and began explaining an Internal Revenue Code Section 42 Tax Credit program and how it worked. I then moved into a description of an investment that produced passive income. With crude drawings on my yellow pad using boxes, numbers, and arrows, I showed him how a client could gain tax credits to pay his tax bill, and then use the depreciation from its passive losses to offset the income generated by the passive income generating investment. (This common tax-advantaged financial planning strategy is referred to as "marrying a PIG with a PAL—passive income generator with a passive activity loss.)

He sat there, stupefied at what I was teaching him. When I was done, he looked up from the paper at me and said, *"You can do that?"* I remember pausing, slowly closing my notebook, and saying back to him, "Now you know why I had to resign."

That same conversation takes place almost daily by our regional vice presidents, except in reverse. Today, they use that product knowledge to educate financial advisors representing many highly respected and visible brokerage houses, insurance companies, and other broker dealers who do not allow their affiliates to sell anything other than stock or bond market products. And guess what the universal response is from these advisors? You guessed it. *"You can do that?"*

The point of this chapter is to make you aware that although there is a wide range of financial strategies and product solutions *potentially* available to you, unless you know for certain that your financial advisor is licensed in those categories and is affiliated with the necessary entities that will allow you to take advantage of them—namely a registered investment advisor, broker dealer, and insurance agency—you may never even know they exist!

Ask your financial advisor the following questions:

- Do you offer stocks, bonds, and mutual funds?
- Can you present me with some investments that offer tax credits and passive income?
- Do I have access to professional third-party money management through you?
- Can you present me with insurance product options such as variable annuities, term life, and variable universal life?

You will most likely not need all of those products, but if any of the financial advisor's answers are "no," then you know that your options will be limited. Some of the options available to you are going to be completely out of your reach. A smaller universe of choices is never better than a larger one.

The Bible Is Not a Financial Textbook

There is another myth out there in the Christian community that needs to be dispelled before we get into the specifics of custom-designing your financial portfolio. The myth, at its core, attempts to use the Bible in a literal sense as a financial textbook. I have real problems with this. I am not saying that the Bible has nothing to say about money—quite the contrary! Without the Bible to give us direction, I think it might be quite literally impossible to please God in the way that we might choose to manage our money. However, to extract from Holy Scripture only those sentences that fit our needs is wrong.

I have a genius friend who is a Ph.D. mathematician and who has authored 184 math textbooks (see what I mean about genius?). He is also a passionate believer. His most recent book is titled *Faith Amidst Reason*, and uses complicated mathematical equations and algorithms to prove the Bible. Marv Bittinger once told me, with great excitement, "The Bible is full of math!" But he would never refer to it as a literal "math textbook."

There are numerous examples of misappropriating God's word for an unintended purpose in our world today. At Christmas, every year, when I see the truncated Scripture, "Peace on earth," my blood boils! God's intent for sending his son Jesus to die for our sins in a most horrible way, and—even more importantly—to take on all of our sin—was to reconcile us back to Him, not so that we would simply have tranquility on earth with each other. A tranquil existence with no war still leads to eternal separation from our Creator and Father, if we are left unredeemed.

Let's take a look at how this kind of out-of-context use of Scripture can also apply to the world of personal finances.

How many times have you heard or read that the Bible says that you should never go into debt? Whole financial philosophies and their collateral multi-million dollar promotional businesses have sprung from this one simple misappropriation of the Word of God. This is a classic example of the simplistic and inappropriate *always* and *never* syndrome.

A Scripture often quoted for developing this theology of money comes from the second part of Proverbs 22:7:

"The rich rule over the poor, and *the borrower is servant to the lender.*"

No news here. Just a prudent reminder. But here's the twist: some people want to suggest that the last part of this text really means,

Since the borrower is the servant of the lender, never, ever get yourself into the position of borrowing, so that you'll never have to be in a servant role.

Okay, maybe. But if we treat the last part of the verse that way, then intellectual honesty requires that we do the same to the first part of that same Proverb which could cause it to mean,

Since the rich rule over the poor, make sure you do everything you can to be rich, so that you are never in the position of being ruled over.

Somehow, I don't think that's what the author of Proverbs actually meant.

Is there a real problem with consumer and credit card debt in America today? You bet there is! It's out of control and needs to be appropriately addressed by every person intending on developing a solid financial plan. But that is an issue that requires an intellectual discussion and review, not a misappropriated and unintended universal scriptural mandate. Without the proper interpretation, certain Scripture can lead to absolutely absurd conclusions. For example, the Bible tells us that

Jesus' first miracle was to turn water into wine, and not only any wine, but the best wine. And this wine was served toward the end of a long wedding feast which likely lasted a couple of days. Should we deduce from this story that Jesus is telling us to:

- Always serve lots of wine at weddings?
- Feast for days?
- Save the best wine for last?

Of course not! The point of this story was much, much bigger than the circumstances within the setting.

Here is one more Scripture to emphasize the danger in pulling phrases out of context to use for unintended purposes. The Bible says:

"If anyone curses his father or mother, he must be put to death."

LEVITICUS 20:9

Ouch! I'm sure glad my parents were not literalists ... I'm not sure that I ever actually cursed them, but I sure can remember being pretty mad at them.

The renowned pastor of Coral Ridge Ministries, Dr. D. James Kennedy, has a very insightful warning that I think should always be applied to lessons from Scripture and the financial world: "Any text, without a proper context, is nothing but a pretext."

Look at the context for any Scripture you hear referenced. Who is the author? Who is he writing or speaking to? What is the context for his message? What is his point?

If I were to misappropriate Scripture this way, I could argue that God calls us to always invest as aggressively as we possibly can. In fact, to the extent that we don't, we'll be thrown into hell. Consider Matthew 25: 14–28, Jesus' parable about the master who leaves and gives each of his three servants money to manage. The first one doubles his money, as does the second one. Both are commended for their efforts and rewarded with being placed in charge of more assets. The third one was afraid of losing the money he had been given, so instead of investing it, he hid it in the ground. When he returns it to the master with no increase, his master is furious and says, "You wicked, lazy servant! . . . Well then, you should have put my money on deposit with the bankers, so that when I returned I would have received it back with interest . . . Throw that worthless servant outside, into the darkness, where there will be weeping and gnashing of teeth." Wow.

So, if I read a literal translation of this parable (without a proper context), I could say that the Bible says we should:

- Always double our money
- Never be conservative
- Use bank savings accounts as a fallback position

Do you see how absurd that is? And if you think it is really a stretch to suggest that any real damage might be done by drawing a completely unintended impression from a verse of Scripture taken completely out of context, consider this. In the February 2006 issue of *Fortune* magazine—read by millions of people—there is an article by Richard McGill Murphy titled "Jesus, Inc." The author uses the fact that Christian businesses are proliferating at an unprecedented rate to question how business and capitalism can square with the Bible. At one point in his rambling, off-target commentary, he refers to the same Scripture I mentioned earlier regarding the servants and their steward-ship of the Master's money: ". . . Jesus seems to use business success as a metaphor for moral virtue."

Of course, we—as believers—know that is not the case. If it were, Paul, Peter, James, John, and Mark would all have been the wealthiest men on the planet! The author then says that Jesus sounds "to modern ears" like a successful entrepreneur. Finally, the author concludes that Christian doctrine simply changes with the culture. "Since then (time of Christ), Christian doctrine has grown more amenable to business," Mr. Murphy surmises. In other words, the Bible is really not the alpha and omega, the unchanging Word of the Almighty God, but rather some sort of philosophical text that is sufficiently flexible to be bended and applied by whichever cultural needs most present themselves from time to time. We risk that interpretation if we do not understand how critical it is to approach the unchanging Word of God with absolutely no preconceived ideas, but rather as completely empty vessels ready to be filled.

Bottom line: the Bible is so much more than a literal financial textbook. It is the very Word of God, the way to redemption and salvation and reunion with our Father! To suggest that it is a simple financial textbook is to trivialize the Word of God and run a very real risk of perverting its intended truth.

Can Money Glorify God?

What is the right biblical context for our decisions about money? Answer—*to glorify God.* Paul says that whatever you do, whether eating or drinking or anything else, do everything to the glory of God. With regard to debt, my friend Ronald Blue wrote a thorough, balanced, intelligent, and biblical book on the subject, called *Master Your Money,* that I highly recommend.

One last story to drive this point home. Jesus says, in Matthew 25:40, that "whatever you do unto the least of these, you do unto me." Medical missionary trips, painting seniors' homes, buying Christmas gifts for those who otherwise would not have that luxury—are all acts that glorify God. I have a friend, Dee Van Tassel from Idaho, who, together with two partners, developed a method for processing soybeans and other grains in such a way that it produces an extraordinarily nutrient-rich food product for humans. It is so efficient that Dee says he can feed a child all the nutrients he needs for about 40 cents a day! Dee's mission is to reach a point where he is feeding 25 million people every day, primarily in famine- and poverty-stricken third world countries. Now, hold that thought.

Let's bring in the question of whether to pay off your mortgage. Let's say that the interest rate (fixed for 30 years) is 6%, but since you are paying an average of 20% in income tax, your true cost after tax is 4.8%. We'll also say that your mortgage is for $300,000.

Now, let's say that you have $300,000 in your bank account and you are looking at making a 30-year investment. You have two choices: either pay off your mortgage and live "debt free," or invest the $300,000 in a well-managed, diversified investment portfolio that we'll say will average a 10% return. Keep in mind that regardless of whether your home is paid off or has a mortgage, it will appreciate (or depreciate) exactly the same. Similarly, in 30 years, either way you go your home will be completely paid for. Now, here are your questions:

1. If you pay off your mortgage with the $300,000, what rate of return will you get on that money over the next 30 years?

   Answer: 6% pre-tax, 4.8% after tax. How satisfied are you with that kind of return? Not very, I'm sure.

2. If you pay off your mortgage, how much of a tithe will you give to God on your home equity?

   Answer: Zero.

3. On the other hand, if you invest the money and achieve a 10% return, how much would you have earned over the next 30 years over and above what it took to pay the monthly mortgage payment?

   Answer: $973,019, or almost a million bucks!

4. How many children could have been fed with just a 10% tithe from your investment portfolio?

   Answer: 665 children could have been fed a full balance of nutrients every day for 30 years if you simply tithed 10% of your earnings.

5. How many children could have been fed each day for 30 years if you gave all of your additional investment earnings for that purpose?

   Answer: 6,665 children would have had the chance to survive, to learn about God, and to build a family that could reflect God's glory.

Now, do you still believe that God has called you to *always* pay off your mortgage? Of course there are any number of factors that must be considered in tandem with the above example, such as the stress of a large mortgage, the risk inherent in the investment, and what might be earned if the mortgage were paid off and the monthly payment free to invest. My interest is in helping to make sure that all of the variables are discussed, and most importantly, that people don't fall into the *always* and *never* trap.

By now you may be having serious questions about where to get quality financial advice. So far, I have railed against self-professed financial gurus on radio and television, and also against the trivialization and misuse of the Bible for unintended purposes. So what's left? How about an entire industry of professional financial advisors who are licensed, educated, and experienced in providing that information to people just like you? They are regulated by extremely tight securities laws that require tremendous disclosure. And a lot of them even share your values.

Chapter 14

From Capitalism to Investment Opportunity

Until now, this book has been rather easy on the technical aspects of money and investing. My intent is to try to keep it as simple as possible, because I know that you are probably reading this in order to make better and more informed decisions about how to invest your IRA, college education savings, or retirement funds. You really don't want to actually *become* a financial advisor, you just want to know what you need to know.

That said, there are two very important points of which I would like you to be aware. Stick with me. I'll do my best to keep it as reader-friendly as possible.

Ultimately, all investments are nothing more than a piece of the capitalism pie. Every investment, whether stock, bond, mutual fund, or partnership, is based on a business model. The model might be something you are somewhat familiar with, such as technology or some form of real estate. However, it may be something you've never even thought of such as credit card debt, equipment leasing, or medical receivables. But they all have two things in common: they all are based on a business model, and they all began with an idea. Let's follow the typical progression of an idea all the way through the investment cycle. Stay with me on this, because it will help your understanding of what investments really are.

When I was running competitively, I had the distinct privilege of being contracted by Nike as one of their elite runners. As a result, I am very familiar with that company, from a runner's point of view. So it is kind of fun for me to use Nike as an example, since I did, in fact, get to watch it grow from literally a garage-based idea to an international economic phenomenon. The following description of Nike's business evolution from idea to end is entirely fictitious. That is, except for the first part. The Bill Bowerman, waffle-iron-in-the-garage story is entirely true. And remarkable. What a great country we live in!

Nike was started by the track coach at the University of Oregon, Bill Bowerman. He was an outstanding coach who was passionate about his runners. He wanted to develop for them a better shoe, one that had superior traction and shock absorption. One day he got an idea. He went into his kitchen, pulled his wife's waffle iron out of the cupboard, and took it to the garage, where he plugged it in. Once heated, he began experimenting with the soles of some running shoes. The waffle iron met its demise and Coach Bowerman came up with what would come to be called the Nike Waffle. It went on to become the most advanced and popular running shoe of its time.

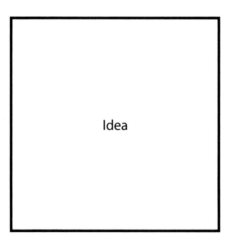

The idea began with a waffle iron, a garage, and a pair of shoes. It worked. But how could the inventor make more shoes and try the idea out for real? He would need money, so he incorporated and went looking for seed capital. This is the initial money that gets an idea off the ground. Let's say he had a brother whom he convinced to join the project for 50% of the profits. All the brother had to do was invest $5,000.

```
┌─────────────────────────┐
│                         │
│                         │
│                         │
│       Seed Capital      │
│                         │
│                         │
│                         │
└─────────────────────────┘
```

The two brothers then "manufactured" the shoes in the garage and gave them to real athletes to try. The athletes loved them and wanted more. Hmmm. More shoes. That meant that the brothers would have to move out of their garage and into a real manufacturing facility. That would require additional machinery and personnel. Maybe even advertising. The brothers scratched their chins and decided to present the company to a wealthy family friend.

This level of investment is referred to as angel financing. No, not the heavenly kind. No wings on these guys, for sure. The angel said he'd invest $1 million for 30% of the company, which the brothers quickly agreed to. After a year of trial and error, the business model was perfected and the shoes were being ordered faster than they could be produced. "Uh oh," the group of three investors said. "Here we go again."

```
┌─────────────────────────┐
│                         │
│                         │
│                         │
│      Angel Financing    │
│                         │
│                         │
└─────────────────────────┘
```

They all scratched their chins again in deep thought. They decided to contact a firm that specialized in new company financing. This level is called vulture capital—I mean venture capital (Freudian slip). These guys play for keeps. The meeting went well, but the VC guys wanted 70% of the company for an investment of $20 million. The brothers and the angel swallowed hard, but agreed. Soon, the company was manufacturing dozens of variations of the waffle shoe and even had designs for its own mass distribution sales force.

```
┌──────────────────────┐
│                      │
│                      │
│                      │
│    Venture Capital    │
│                      │
│                      │
│                      │
└──────────────────────┘
```

It became apparent that to really penetrate every major market in the country, the company would have to invest in both regional production facilities and a national, dedicated sales force. They needed an infusion of about $50 million to pull that off. The VC guys decided that the best way to acquire more financing would be through the sale of private stock. They used a broker dealer to help them put together a stock offering and began a sales effort.

```
┌──────────────────────┐
│                      │
│                      │
│    Private Stock      │
│                      │
└──────────────────────┘
```

Eventually it became apparent that Wall Street would be interested in the company's stock, so an initiative was begun to take the company public. About 14 months and $300,000 later, the company did an IPO (Initial Public Offering) and began selling on a public exchange. The stock was purchased by registered investment advisors, stockbrokers, and institutional investors like pension funds and foundations.

```
┌──────────────┐
│              │
│              │
│     IPO      │
│              │
│              │
└──────────────┘
```

Soon thereafter, the company's stock made it to the last stop in its developmental evolution. Mutual fund managers began buying company shares on behalf of the shareholders of their funds.

```
┌──────────┐
│          │
│  Mutual  │
│   Fund   │
│          │
└──────────┘
```

By now you may be wondering why I illustrated each chronological increment of financing with an ever-smaller box. The decreasing size illustrates the decrease in profit potential that naturally occurs along the evolution of raising capital and building a business. Whoever has the idea and gets it off the ground has the best opportunity to negotiate maximum profit in the event that the idea becomes a profitable business. Next in line is the angel, who has the second opportunity to negotiate a strong profit potential, and so on. In reality, there are innumerable iterations of this evolution, and at each juncture there is opportunity for dilution of the original investors. But the point here is that, generally speaking, the farther you move up the food chain, the better your odds are at a profitable position in the event the business plan succeeds.

One other very interesting illustration needs to be pointed out. Prior to the IPO, the valuation of the business is very straight forward. Basic accounting methods such as a profit & loss statement, cash flow analysis, and balance sheet determine the value of the business and its stock. However, once the company goes public, that valuation methodology is no longer straightforward. Instead, it is substantially affected by the *perception* of those buying and selling the stock.

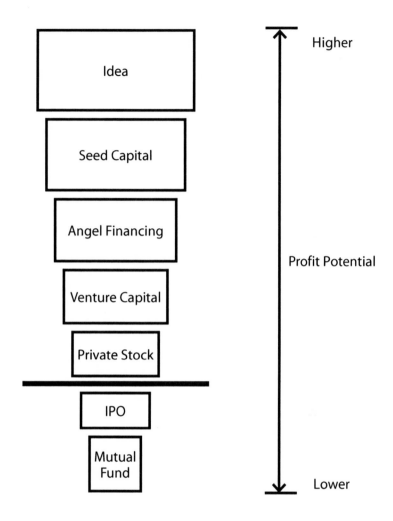

Why is this important? I once had a very, very nice mini-yacht that sat in a slip at a marina right next to a small, old, barnacle-covered sailboat whose sea-worthy days were well in its past. Every time the tide went out, both my beautiful boat and that old ghost of a wreck went down at exactly the same rate. Similarly, when the tide came in, both boats went back up at an exactly equal rate.

A falling tide lowers all boats. A rising tide raises all boats.

The stock market works like that sometimes. The *tide* did not differentiate between my beautiful and expensive yacht and the old, beat-up dingy. So, if you are looking for an investment where you can track a true valuation based on intrinsic business fundamentals, you'll need to buy one that is not publicly traded on an exchange.

Sounds great, but how in the world could I do that? you are probably asking in frustration.

Hey, relax. No problem. That's what much of the rest of this book is all about. Grab a soda and snack and let's find out.

There Are Only Two Places To Invest Money

If you watch political talk shows on television like I do, you are bombarded by advertising that touts it can answer "Your hopes, your dreams . . ." or "At our mutual fund, we care about the investor . . ." or "Our firm believes in the individual investor . . ." And on and on. Or how about all of those online discount brokerage commercials promoting their "advantages"? Faster execution, free trades, and better service. They all purport to have fundamental "differences." But do they really?

Whether it is television advertising, financial news programs, financial sections of newspapers, or financial periodicals, the audience is bombarded with one—and only one—prevailing theme:

> *There are only two places to invest your money:*
> *the stock market and the bank.*

The category we'll refer to as *the stock market* includes such investment instruments as publicly traded stocks, mutual funds, and variable annuities. The category we'll refer to as *the bank* includes such fixed instruments as bonds, bills, CDs, and fixed annuities.

The problem is that this theme—the stock market and the bank—is not true. There are literally hundreds of investments that have nothing to do with the stock market and nothing to do with the bank! They have no stock market risk. None. And they typically offer much higher expected returns than the low- to mid-single digit performance historically associated with the category we are referring to as the bank.

Alternative Investments

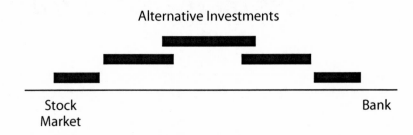

Stock   Bank
Market

We'll get into the specifics of what is referred to as alternative investments in Section VI, but for now just realize that you have substantially more investment options than you ever may have realized.

Tired of the rollercoaster ride of the stock market? Frustrated with the interest yields on bank instruments? You have many, many more choices than you thought. Remember, though, unless the financial advisor you work with is properly licensed and affiliated with a broker dealer who offers alternative investments, you will not be able to access this critically important genre of investments.

Depending on a number of factors such as liquidity needs, age, experience, and net worth, I might recommend that an investor consider as much as 15% to 40% of his or her investment portfolio be comprised of alternative investments.

"Please Pass the Business, but Hold the Stock"

I have no problem with investing in the stock market, and, in fact, I advocate that strategy much of the time. However, I am always uneasy about the unpredictability of the return. There is a fundamental difference between investing in a *business* versus investing in the *stock* of a business.

It is true that sometimes certain stocks will buck a market trend, because of a fundamental dynamic in their favor. However, more times than not, stock valuations are determined in large measure by the *perception* of their intrinsic values, as opposed to simply considering profit and loss of the particular underlying business.

Remember the story of the beautiful mini-yacht I owned? The one that sat in a marina next to an old, run-down, small sailboat. When the tide went *out*, both boats went *down* too. A lowering tide lowers all boats equally, regardless of their intrinsic value.

Given the choice between investing in a business that I can understand (usually packaged as a partnership, or LLC) versus investing in the stock of a business whose valuation can be influenced by factors unrelated to its underlying business model, my preference is for the former. That's not to say that stocks, bonds, and other market-based investments don't play an important role in a properly devised investment portfolio. Rather, many people simply don't think about investments *other* than stocks and bonds.

In the 1992 presidential election campaign, the Clinton War Room held to one simple mantra: "It's the economy, stupid!" It worked. When the dust settled after all the debates about everything from abortion to gun control, THE issue that was left standing was the economy. The Clinton machine—spearheaded by political masters such as Paul Begala and James Carville—was successful in getting voters to believe their negative spin on the economy and focus on it all the way to the voting booth.

Although I am certainly no fan of the Clinton presidency, I will take a page out of their highly successful campaign book to make a point about investing. When considering any investment strategy, let me restate the Clinton mantra this way:

"It's the business model, stupid!"

You wouldn't invest in a company trying to sell flip flops to people in Alaska, or sand to people who live in the desert. Neither would you want to invest in a company that tries to sell air in a jar. Those are ridiculous business models. (On the other hand, there was that pet rock thing . . .)

I have had the privilege of diving deeply into numerous aspects of the financial services industry, including helping to write prospectuses for mutual funds and variable annuities, assisting with the syndication of oil and gas programs, serving as an officer in three private offerings, and being a top-producing financial planner with three different broker dealers. In my 24 years in this industry, one of the key insights I have learned, when considering an investment, is to look hard at the business model underlying the investment.

Entrepreneurs, in particular, lean naturally toward this way of thinking, because they deal with these same issues every moment of every day in their own world.

- Does the business make sense?
- Will it work?
- Has it been tested?
- Is there a track record?
- Where is the money coming from?

So what kinds of businesses are packaged also as investment opportunities? We'll get much more specific in answering that question in Section VI, but just to get you started thinking that way, here are a few:

- National and regional retail restaurants and stores, most of which you probably already patronize
- Office buildings, hotels, and hospitality businesses
- Heavy-duty earth moving equipment, jet engines, ocean liners, medical and general office equipment, and even credit card debt

The list is almost endless. When you drive to work or church, take a good look around you and you'll notice billboards, restaurants, retail stores, railroad cars, airplanes, old and new office buildings, and apartment complexes. Many of these are packaged as investments that have expected returns considerably above what you would earn on a fixed instrument like a bond, CD, or fixed annuity. Yet these investments have no relation to, or correlation with, the stock market.

All investments have risk, including equipment leasing and real estate partnerships. Always read the prospectus carefully, understand the types of risk involved before investing, and talk with a financial advisor who is experienced and licensed in this area.

And remember the first fundamental of considering any investment opportunity ...

"It's the business model, stupid!"

Now, honestly. Is this getting fun, or what?

Chapter 16

Which Package Do You Like?

Okay. With me so far? Here is one more chapter on an important fundamental that you really need to know, but to which you have probably never been exposed. In order to truly have confidence in an investment, you needed to know that the underlying business model makes sense. In Chapter 14, we developed the hypothetical evolution of the waffle shoe that began Nike. Let's use that business again, but this time let's approach it a bit differently.

Let's say that Bill Bowerman and I hooked up. Here's a conversation that might have taken place:

STEPHEN: "Bill, I've run in your waffle shoes, they're great! I think I can beat Steve Prefontaine in these things!"

BILL: "Pure bologna, no chance."

STEPHEN: "Okay, forget that I said that. Let's move on. I also looked over the business model and the numbers look really good. I'd say you have a very predictable cash flow that will allow me to package your business as an investment for my clients."

BILL: "To raise money for the company's operations and growth?"

STEPHEN: "Exactly. Now what we have to do is decide which investment package makes the most sense."

BILL: "What are the options?"

STEPHEN: "Well, there are a lot of them. If you incorporate, you could sell some private stock. If that goes well, you could always do a public offering which would, of course, take about three years and a lot of money in legal and accounting fees, but you'd have unlimited liquidity and an ability to raise money when you needed it."

BILL: "Not sure I want to go through all the scrutiny of a public company, or the hassle of an IPO. What else do you have?"

STEPHEN: "The simplest way to raise money is to do a private offering, which means that you cannot advertise to the general public. Only investors who are accredited ($1 million net worth) can invest. However, I could get a law firm to put that offering together for you in about 45 days, and with not too much expense."

BILL: "Would that be private stock?"

STEPHEN: "Could be, or we could form a partnership with you as the general partner and sell membership units. The other option is to either incorporate or form a partnership, and then sell debentures such as notes or bonds that would pay the investor interest. That way you don't dilute your own equity. You could still own 100% of the company."

I have had these kinds of conversations with dozens of entrepreneurs. One such conversation occurred several years ago with the founder and partner of Collins Financial Services, Inc. This Austin-based company purchases credit card debt from major banks and then either re-sells it in smaller increments with a markup, or works the debt themselves.

We discussed all of the investment packaging I mentioned in my fictional interview with Bill Bowerman, and even talked with a firm that does the back office for a number of mutual funds. I ended up deciding to do what turned out to be a series of three private-placement limited partnerships. Then, with my encouragement, Collins Financial went through the expense and hassle of doing a public registration, so that virtually anyone could invest in their product. I want to publicly thank them for doing so, because I believe the public is attracted to, and entitled to, investments such as this.

As I write this, I'm now going through this exploratory process with a friend of mine who is involved in a company that manufactures a patented "people transport system" for homes that are built on a steep slope above a lake. They have perfected their manufacturing process, hired a sales force, done preliminary advertising, and are now interested in raising additional capital to grow their business.

The reason that having an understanding of the investment *package* is so important is because you want to make sure that you don't ever make the mistake of correlating the investment's business model with the investment's package. I once heard a lady at a seminar say, "I'll never again invest in an IRA. I did that once and I lost money."

That's literally impossible. IRAs (Individual Retirement Accounts) are not investments. If she lost money, it was because of the investment she had her money in *within* the IRA, not the IRA itself. An IRA is simply a part of the tax code that allows for the deductibility of invested dollars under certain conditions. The IRA *investment* could be a mutual fund, stock, bond, partnership, or annuity.

Another one I hear from time to time, just as erroneous, refers to the performance of a variable annuity. A variable annuity does not have any performance. Only its sub-accounts (mutual fund-like investments created exclusively for variable products) have performance. With most variable annuities now offering anywhere between 30 and 90 different sub-accounts, the performance of the overall investment is contingent upon which sub-accounts it is actually invested in.

Limited partnerships have also received a bum rap over the years. My wife and I named our son Reagan after what we think is one of the greatest presidents in history. That said, I was not at all pleased with the treasury secretary in his second term, James Baker, who orchestrated one of the most tumultuous tax reforms of all time. The Tax Reform Act of 1986 had an immediate and devastating impact on limited partnerships in particular. Virtually overnight, millions of investors lost some very serious money simply because of the new way income and losses were to be characterized. Ever since, a lot of uninformed people believe that "partnerships" are a bad or risky investment.

To put that ridiculous statement into proper context, recall the (fictitious) conversation I had with Bill Bowerman. The overwhelming reason why an investment performs, or doesn't, is not because of how it happens to be *packaged*, but rather because the underlying business model either makes sense, or it doesn't.

From a financial planning perspective, I care a great deal about how an investment is packaged. But from a strictly investment performance standpoint, it's all about the viability of the business model (will the waffle shoe sell, or not?), not the way it is packaged.

How are we doing? You still with me? Let's talk about risk now.

Chapter 17

What Risk?

"Daddy, I'm going out to ride my bike with Reagan," my little 5-year-old said to me in her sweet voice as she passed quickly through the kitchen, headed for the front door. Unfortunately, as she said those words looking directly at me, her body moved in the opposite direction. As she finished her sentence and turned her face forward, *BAM!* Her head hit the protruding edge of the counter. Ouch!

How many times have you witnessed children walking, playing, running, skipping right into harm's way, oblivious to the risks that doors, countertops, walls, and other fixed objects present? I've often said to forget helmets for bikers and motorcyclists, kids are the ones that should be required to wear them 24/7 until they are at least ten years old.

Risk comes in all sorts of dimensions. Back to my mini-yacht for a moment. Every time I took it out on the Gulf of Mexico I assessed the risk presented by the weather, my passengers, other boats, time of day, and every other variable I could imagine. In fact, now that I think about it, I never really *enjoyed* taking that boat out, precisely because all I did was worry about risk.

Same thing with my horses, especially if I was playing host to other riders. You can never really know what you'll endure riding a horse.

Those 1000-pound beasts can jump and dance with wild eyes at the simple—but unanticipated—flight of a bird darting out of a bush. (And those deer, with fangs exposed, just lurking behind trees, moving stealthily toward a point of ambush. I can certainly understand why horses would fear deer.)

Health risks, travel risks, relationship risks, business risks. The list of risks is almost endless. The same might be said for investing. But don't let that fact grow fangs and put you in a panic such that you steer clear of investing altogether. Instead, just be armed with knowledge. Here's the context for what we'll learn in this chapter:

The key to minimizing your investment risk is:

1. Know clearly what risks are involved, and
2. Eliminate those risks that you can, mitigate those that you can, and manage the rest.

So, what are the specific risks that you need to be aware of? Let's walk through them.

The risk that most people think of first when they think of investing is stock market risk. Of course, this risk only applies to an investment in the stock market such as a bond, stock, mutual fund, or variable annuity. If you are not investing in the stock market, your money will not be exposed to market risk.

Another risk that a lot of people rightly worry about is liquidity risk. This risk is associated with an inability to get your money out quickly and without penalty. A bank savings account can be said to have no liquidity risk, because you can stop by any branch at any time that the bank is open (which, by the way, is not often enough, in my opinion, but I digress ...). On the other hand, if you were to purchase an interest in an oil drilling program, you would most certainly encounter the full brunt of liquidity risk if you called the issuer and said,

"Hello, my name is John Smith and I invested $25,000 with you eight months ago and I've decided I want my money back. Will you please wire me my money today?"

"You want *what?*" is the response you would hear right before the receptionist's hand went over the phone. She would turn to the office and say,

"Hey, guys, you're not going to believe this! Some investor just called and says he wants us to wire him his money back." (Guffaw, guffaw, guffaw . . .)

Now let me now point out a real risk that we, on our side of the industry, see all the time, but which many investors lull themselves into believing is not of concern to them. Opportunity risk. This one does have fangs.

Let me quantify this for you. Suppose that you are retiring at 65 and want to rely on your 401(k) nest egg to provide a comfortable retirement for you. Further, you have decided that you need $3,000 a month in income from your nest egg. However, you have also decided that, unlike a lot of your friends, you are not going to be so foolish as to invest your money in anything that is risky. Nope. You are smart. It'll be banks and the FDIC insurance they offer for you.

Okay. Here we go. You start with $300,000 in your 401(k), which you transferred to an IRA at your bank and invested at an interest rate of 5%. Heck, you even got a free toaster just for doing the right thing. And wasn't that branch manager a nice fellow, just the kind of professional you knew you deserved.

Your first month goes great. Sure enough, the $3,000 check comes on time, right to your mailbox. Same thing the following month. In fact, you laugh at the headlines of the newspaper when you read six months into your retirement: "Stock Market Loses 500 Points In One Day!"

Ha! Not of any concern to you. You are smart. Life is good. At least until you walk out to your mailbox early in the eleventh year of your dream retirement life. No check. Hmm. That's strange. And last month's check wasn't for the full $3,000, either. A bead of sweat builds on your forehead.

"No, Mr. Smart, there is no error," Mr. Banker says. "We paid your account 5% interest annually and you withdrew $3,000 a month. Now, your account is closed. There is no more money in it."

Sounds implausible, doesn't it? I wish it were, but unfortunately, opportunity risk lulls people into complacency all too often, and many times to a point of no return.

Now Mr. Dummo, on the other hand, decided to split his investments into four different types, each with a different level of overall risk. The first one was a money market fund for $75,000. The second investment achieved a 4% return for 25 months, which produced a little more than $81,000. He turned that into an investment of 6% and used it over the next 29 months to pay his $3,000 monthly retirement income. His third cache of $75,000 he invested for the next 54 months and received a 12% return, which created a balance of $128,355. He then re-invested that amount into another investment that produced 6%, and received his required $3,000 monthly income for the next 48 months until that account was consumed. This left his last investment of $75,000, which he had been able to achieve a 15% return on. After 102 months at a return of 15%, the original $75,000 had grown to $266,289. With this account, he decided to invest in a diversified portfolio that was able to achieve a 12% return each year. With this scenario, Mr. Dummo was able to keep his monthly income of $3,000 a month intact for a total of 321 months, or almost 27 years. Remember, Mr. Smart's $3,000 monthly income stopped after just over 10 years.

Investing in the Stock Market

Chapter 18

What You Can and Cannot Know

It was a cold morning, with frost on the ground that crunched under our feet as we walked in silence out to our "fort." We hoped to get a deer. My four-and-a-half-year-old son's little gloved hand was enveloped in mine. Reagan was so bundled up against the Tennessee winter's chill that he looked like a miniature Michelin Man. I had told him that we couldn't talk if we wanted to see any deer, and—so typical for Reagan, he's such a *boy*—he was following orders.

It had not yet gotten light, and with the sky entirely clear, there were still a lot of stars shining. He pulled me closer with his hand and whispered, "Dad, what's that?" I looked where he was pointing and told him that it was a star. We continued walking in silence for another couple hundred yards and then Reagan, apparently pondering the whole "star thing," leaned in again and said, "If that star fell down here, would you be able to pick it up?" (Did I say how much I cherish my kids?)

When I listen to the frenetic postulating about the stock market, what I really hear is, "If that star falls, can I pick it up?" No! You can't! First of all, that star will never fall, regardless of how much you want it to. And secondly, even if it did, you'd never be able to pick it up! Get real.

There is so much misinformation regarding the stock market to wade through that I feel sorry for the average investor. As I mentioned, I fly a lot, and when I'm between flights I'll find the nearest airline frequent-flier lounge to get caught up on my e-mail. Regardless of the time of day it happens to be, as I walk into the main room I always see an audience glued to a flat screen Television watching some financial news program, eyes focused on whatever talking head happens to be on air at that moment. Of course, there are also the streaming market notes on the bottom and *to-the-second* market updates on the side. I can't help but wonder if any of the people in the room actually believe that by watching these programs, the stars will fall and they'll be able to pick them up, moving quickly enough on some hot tip that they will add substantial value to the performance of their portfolio.

My goal for this chapter is to help you better understand how you can make an informed decision about how to invest in the stock market. I will give you my opinion of what is knowable, applicable and attainable, and also what is not. The stock market is a vast, vitally important part of the global economy, and potentially an important component of your own investment portfolio. But if you are going to invest with naiveté, you run the risk of being overwhelmed and confused at best, or misdirected and financially ruined, at worse. In my 24 years in this industry, I have accumulated enough stories of real-life situations to illustrate both extremes, and they are too numerous to recite in the pages of this book. Nonetheless, there are a few that I will share in the limited space of this chapter that are real and poignant examples of how *not* to engage the stock market.

Modern Portfolio Theory

My philosophy of stock market investing is based on the most widely accepted portfolio management technique that exists, Modern Portfolio Theory (MPT). This body of academic knowledge was developed over about five decades, and has two contributors who were awarded the Nobel Prize in Economic Science. So important is MPT to the world of investing that it is cited in United States law (Section 404© of the Employee Retirement Income Security Act) as a safe harbor for defined contribution plan sponsors. In lay terminology, that means that if an employer meets this definition, it is highly unlikely that any lawsuit filed against him because of "poor investment performance" by a plan participant would succeed.

An element of MPT involves asset class correlation co-efficiencies, which basically means that asset classes such as large company U.S. stocks, emerging country growth stocks, bonds, gold, etc. do not move together. Instead, each will move up, down, or sideways according to its own characteristics. That is why a truly diversified portfolio will have a number of different asset classes strategically selected so as to attempt to reduce overall volatility and improve overall return. This is a very straightforward mathematical calculation.

As basic and understood as this might be in the academic world of portfolio management, it is apparently one of the many casualties of the homespun advice conveniently dispensed by at least one self-promoting "financial guru" who, by his very own words, confirms that he has no such basic knowledge.

Don't Believe Everything You Hear!

While in my car recently, I pushed my radio's "scan" button and picked up a program where Radio Man was passionately dishing out his emotionally-based financial advice. For me, a licensed, experienced, and academically educated financial advisor, listening to him was like listening to someone slowly scraping their fingernails across a blackboard. Nonetheless, I thought I'd force myself, just to see if there was any possibility of coming to a different conclusion about what I thought he represented. But no sooner had I steeled myself to listen than I heard him give a listener a profoundly erroneous piece of advice.

The question had to do with whether the listener should invest some of his portfolio in gold in order to gain further diversification. *Of course he should!* I thought. Every Nobel Prize laureate who contributed to the development of Modern Portfolio Theory, every candidate who passed the exam to become a Certified Financial Planner (CFP) or Certified Financial Analyst (CFA), every trust officer in charge of investing assets, and every money manager in the world knows that gold and other hard assets have certain characteristics that make them uniquely attractive assets to include at times in a well-diversified portfolio.

Instead, though, our Radio Man laughed at the listener's preposterous idea. He stated that gold *had only achieved less than a 5% annualized return* over the last 20 years. What Mr. Radio Man apparently didn't know, because he did not *have* to know it to get a radio gig, was the basic premise upon which the world's most accepted truths for portfolio management rest: asset class correlation co-efficiency. Namely, that adding certain asset classes—which by themselves might not be particularly enticing as a singular investment—to an entire portfolio of strategically selected assets, could certainly produce for the investor not only an enhanced overall return, but also potentially reduce his risk. Gold most assuredly can be an important asset class to consider when an investor is attempting to increase overall return and reduce overall risk.

I could cite literally hundreds of references to the science of portfolio management using negatively correlated asset class combinations to attempt to increase return while also reducing risk. For the sake of brevity, I'll here reference only one such study, "Investing in Global Hard Assets: A Diversification Tool for Portfolios," a report by Ibbotson Associates, March 2005, updated by James St. Aubin, CFA, Senior Analyst. The study concludes,

> "Global hard assets (GHA) offer investors an attractive portfolio diversification option. Portfolios including GHA have been shown to offer better performance than those without GHA. Results suggest that including GHA in a portfolio may increase expected returns and reduce portfolio risk."

The following graph illustrates the potential significant benefits of adding hard assets, of which precious metals/gold is a part, to an investment portfolio.

Efficient Frontier with and without Global Hard Assets

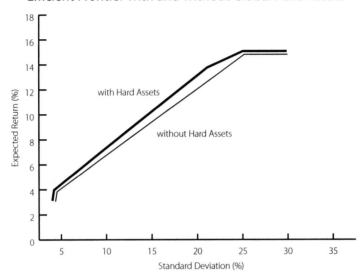

Asset Allocations with and without Global Hard Assets

Asset Class	Low Risk		Medium Risk		High Risk	
	with Global Hard Assets	without Global Hard Assets	with Global Hard Assets	without Global Hard Assets	with Global Hard Assets	without Global Hard Assets
Global Hard Assets	5	0	15	0	25	0
US Large Cap Stocks	15	15	30	30	40	45
US Small Cap Stocks	0	0	10	10	15	15
International Stocks	5	5	10	15	20	25
US Interm Term Bonds	45	50	20	25	0	15
US Treasury Bills	30	30	15	20	0	0
Expected Returns	6.05	5.68	9.75	9.11	13.03	12.09
Standard Deviations	5.66	5.72	12.01	11.82	18.17	17.93
Sharpe Ratio	0.50	0.43	0.54	0.50	0.54	0.49

Note: Sharpe ratios computed using expected returns for the portfolios and Treasury bills (see below) and expected portfolio standard deviations.

Expected Return and Deviations

Asset Class	Expected Return	Standard Deviation
Global Hard Assets	11.75	19.64
US Large Cap Stocks	12.02	20.31
US Small Cap Stocks	15.39	29.68
International Stocks	14.89	26.46
US Interm Term Bonds	4.34	6.68
US Treasury Bills	3.22	2.92

Expected Correlation Coeffients

Asset Class	Global Hard Assets	US Large-Cap Stocks	US Small-Cap Stocks	International Stocks	Interm.-Term Bonds	30 Day Treasury Bill
Global Hard Assets	1	0.29	0.34	0.36	-0.25	-0.08
US Large Cap Stocks	0.29	1	0.86	0.59	0.19	0.03
US Small Cap Stocks	0.34	0.86	1	0.49	0.05	-0.03
International Stocks	0.36	0.59	0.49	1	-0.05	-0.12
US Interm Term Bonds	-0.25	0.19	0.05	-0.05	1	0.28
US Treasury Bills	-0.08	0.03	-0.03	-0.12	0.28	1

The profound disparity between the facts portrayed by the academic science of investing and financial planning on the one hand, and the emotional shoot-from-the-hip rhetoric by people like Mr. Radio Man on the other, is real and can have a damaging impact on people's lives. It is also why I strenuously encourage investors to pay no attention to *marketers* of financial advice, but instead look to those professionals who are licensed, academically trained, and accountable for any advice they offer.

Diversification Is Important

Leaving the contrast between the world of marketing and investment science, I want to expound a bit more on the concept of diversification.

You may have heard of the diversification strategy of *asset allocation,* which is only slightly more intellectually meaningful than the old adage, "Don't put all of your eggs in the same basket." It is important to divide your money between different types of asset classes such as:

- bonds (both government issue and corporate)
- large company stocks (such as Wal-mart)
- small company stocks (such as those you might find on NASDAQ)
- international equities (such as those found in the EAFE Index)
- hard assets (gold, real estate)
- emerging markets (Africa, Southeast Asia, etc.)

This could be considered Modern Portfolio Theory *light*. That said, even these *light* fundamentals of asset allocation are found in the much more comprehensive processes of Modern Portfolio Theory (MPT).

The Three Fundamentals of Modern Portfolio Theory

There are three fundamental premises upon which MPT is based:

1. No one has ever, or can ever, consistently predict the timing and direction of the stock market.
2. There is no such thing as an undervalued security. All buyers and all sellers have the exact same information at exactly the same time. (Well, except for Martha Stewart . . .)
3. Therefore, by a wide margin, the predominant indicator of a portfolio's performance is attributable to the *types of asset classes* in its composition.

Do you realize what you just read? If these premises are true, the ramifications are huge! Because the logical progression leads us to ask—no, yell—

> "If no one can truly consistently predict the direction and timing of the market, and if there are no "gems" out there to be found before everyone else does, why are we paying attention to all of the talking heads?"

The answer is to be found in human nature. Investors *want* to believe that they actually can time the market and find undervalued securities, and that there is a trillion-dollar financial and media behemoth just itching to help nurture that false hope.

Let me give you a parallel example that will help you understand this phenomenon. What is the safest and surest way to lose weight? The answer is simple, timeless, universal, and entirely based on empirically verifiable scientific fact:

Consume fewer calories than you burn: do aerobic exercises and eat multiple, small portions of healthy food throughout the day.

That's it. Period. Works every time it is tried. So why do we still see magazines promoting the latest fad diet? All of these trendy new diets fall into one of two categories. The first one is a variation on eating what you want, and losing weight while you sleep. Yeah, right.

The other category has as its fundamental promise a newly found "miracle" formula that involves a high dose of protein, or carrots, or fish, or the juice of the mystical garbonzo root found in the shallow streams of Nepal. (Okay, I made that last one up, but you know what I mean.)

The same is true with stock market investing. Investors want to believe that from time to time gravity will not apply itself against them. So they subscribe to magazines and newspapers, watch financial programs, and "check in" with their stockbroker for the latest tip. All of this in an endless, fruitless attempt to find predictability and that elusive double-digit annual investment return. And the sad fact of the matter is that economic science suggests that all that effort will be expended in vain. Adding insult to injury, there are at any time hundreds of investments available to investors that offer the predictable, strong returns that they are seeking, and which also have the side benefit of having no stock market risk. More about that later.

The Myth of "Secret" Information

The speed at which information moves across our planet is now virtually instantaneous. This phenomenon, though, is very recent in human history. One hundred and forty-four years ago, when Robert E. Lee was using creative ways of deploying the small Confederate Army in an attempt to defend his beloved Virginia against the much larger invading Union Army, he would use stealth tactics, such as long night marches, to move into strategic position. There were no drones, no satellites, no cell phones or radios. All a general had to do was, as Nathan Bedford Forrest said, "Be there first and with the most." For much of the first two years of the war, that's what happened. Lincoln was furious that a small band of Confederates, without supplies or food and ample munitions, could elude the might of the largest and most heavily armed military machine on earth.

One day, however, a Union infantry soldier, marching through the streets of a small Virginia town twelve hours after Lee's army had walked those very same streets, saw a small piece of paper blowing across his path. He picked it up and was stunned to see that he was looking at a drawing of the very routes Lee was going to take in the next three days! Apparently, this small map had fallen off one of Lee's aides as they had passed through that town hours earlier.[5]

To say that this information was valuable to the pursuing Union Army would be a huge understatement. The Union soldier had found a "gem" of information that no one else had. And his army then made historic use of it.

By contrast, my kids and I were recently in Lieper's Fork, Tennessee, walking up a steep, heavily wooded hill with a realtor. It was a cold, brisk January day, but the kids were ready to be outside and I needed to check out this property to see if it would be suitable as a place to build our new home. Jody, my realtor buddy, as he stepped over logs, pushed briars out of his path, and caught his breath, kept talking back and forth with the owner of the land via cell phone to get instructions as to the boundaries. From time to time, Jody would also pause to look at his phone's screen. He was reading text messages being sent to him from his employees in mainland China whom he had hired to process batches of data for his mortgage company.

Here we were, on top of a hill in the middle of nowhere, and Jody was speaking with a property owner who was checking our location using GPS data via his computer in his home, and at the same time Jody was reviewing text messages sent by employees located on the other side of the planet! Amazing.

Do you think that you are going to be able to find information that no one else has access to that will help you better manage your investments in the stock market? Who are you kidding?

Fifty years ago, in the days that preceded satellite-based communication and the Internet, a stockbroker would learn about various companies, and the valuation of their stock and bonds, from research acquired by the employing broker dealer. If your grandfather wanted information about the stock market, his most accessible and up-to-date source was his stockbroker. Today, that same information is available publicly to everyone and anyone at the same time via the Internet. That's right . . . anyone, anywhere. All buyers and all sellers. Even in China.

Chapter 19

The Role of Stockbrokers

No chapter in this book is going to make more enemies for me than this one. I really would rather skip this topic, but ethically I can't. You need to know. The consequences and implications are too great. Let me just say that my comments are intended as educational and not judgmental. Similarly, while I have serious questions about the business model that promotes the world of stockbrokers, I am not condemning any of the well-intentioned, honest and conscientious individuals that work in that business.

A stockbroker, acting properly, will explain to his client that what he does is only a small part of what needs to be done to optimize an investment and financial plan. If he doesn't say that, then he is not being honest, or—quite possibly—he is ignorant.

Think of some of the big investment firms that advertise on Television. They usually purport to "work harder" for the client, or "to know their clients better" than their competitors. As I see these commercials in my mind, my stomach suggests that I might be sick.

You see, although a properly designed financial plan will likely include some stock market-based investments (stocks, bonds, mutual funds, variable annuities), common sense dictates that it will just as likely include investments that have nothing to do with the stock market. The problem arises when the stockbroker doesn't know that those other investments even exist!

Our firm, Faith Financial Planners, recruits financial advisors from all over the industry. Some come from the independent niche that we represent, but others have most of their experience in the insurance business, or in selling stocks and bonds. All new Faith Financial members, regardless of their career experience, are required to go through extensive training so that they know what we know. One of the most amazing dynamics that happens is when a stockbroker goes through our training. He (or she) is shocked. Stunned. It is as if the proverbial scales fall from their eyes. We hear comments like *"You can do that?"* and *"How long has this been around?"* and *"Why am I just now finding out about this?"* Some, while extremely excited to take their newfound knowledge back to their clients, also become angry that they were not given this information by their former employer.

But criticizing the big investment firms that sell stocks and bonds is really not appropriate. Come on, that's what they do. That's like being critical of the ice cream guy who comes through your neighborhood on hot summer days selling ice cream bars and popsicles. Are you going to be angry that he's not giving your kids a well-balanced meal? *"Get your ice cream here, and we also have broccoli, roast beef, and apples!"* Not going to happen, because that's not what ice cream vendors sell. It would be ridiculous to expect otherwise.

The same is true with stockbrokers. You see, it is not their job to *provide education* about products that they don't sell. It's that simple. If an investment firm is in the business of taking companies public, or underwriting municipal bonds, why should they teach their sales force about Internal Revenue Code Section 42 Tax Credit Programs, real estate partnerships, equipment-leasing programs, or other alternative investments?

Buyer Beware

Buyer beware. That universal principle is also scriptural, applicable to both the spiritual and physical worlds. Do you expect the insurance agent who handles your auto insurance to have a balanced and experienced perspective on your stock portfolio? And if you bought a life insurance policy from an insurance salesman, would you expect him to offer appropriate and competent advice on your investments? Similarly, in general terms you should not expect a stockbroker to give you competent and balanced advice on anything other than your stock portfolio. And never forget that commissions on the sale and purchase of stocks and bonds is generally the primary method by which stockbrokers earn a living. If you don't buy and you don't sell, your stockbroker can't earn a commission. There is absolutely nothing unethical about that model, but you need to remember it.

About ten years ago, my wife and I were in need of a garage addition to our home. We had bought an old farmhouse, north of Nashville, that we renovated to resemble an antebellum home. The only problem was that antebellum homes didn't factor in automobiles. Imagine that. So we had to build a 20th century garage. I can only do that historic thing so far. I was not going to substitute my car for a horse and buggy.

There was an ad in the local newspaper for a company that, among other things, built garages. We called the company with our request, and the next day they sent out a nicely dressed salesman in his mid-thirties. We told him what we were looking for: a two-story, three-stall garage with a big open room upstairs. He indicated that would be no problem, and went about doing all of his measurements. He then told us he would be back the next day with his estimate, and left.

Sure enough, the next day he came back with his clipboard in hand and sales manager holding his hand. Well, not literally holding his hand, but it was obvious that they wanted this sale. The salesman pointed out all of the costs, "tax included." I was somewhat perplexed, though. Something was not right. I went back over the dimensions and—ah ha! There it was. No upstairs. *What were they thinking?* I had specifically requested an upstairs as part of the project. I inquired about this and was told that they didn't do that kind of work. "What?" I said incredulously. "What do you mean you 'don't do that kind of work?'"

After much haggling and gnashing of teeth, it became clear that the reason they "don't do that kind of work" was because the only kind of work they did was *siding!* Give me a break. Siding. Not that there is necessarily anything wrong with siding, but that's not what I was looking for. Good heavens, I wanted a garage!

It is also this way with many stockbrokers and so-called financial advisors. You want to build a retirement plan? College savings plan? Financial plan? "Great, we can help," they say. Yet, what they really mean is that they are selling *siding,* and they think they may be able to make that work in place of what might be considered the better blueprint.

It's not just stockbrokers who we often find ignorant of the need for alternative investments. I had two different conversations in the last six months with the presidents of two well-known broker dealers, employing approximately 800 financial advisors. *Neither firm offered alternative investments, and their advisors were not even allowed to discuss anything specific with their clients beyond stocks, bonds, mutual funds, and other stock market products.* What this means to unsuspecting investors like you is that to the extent you rely entirely on a broker to advise you regarding your investment portfolio, your investment options will be severely limited.

"What exactly is a DPP?" one firm's founder and president asked. Unbelievable. I had to explain to this industry veteran of 20 years, a highly successful stockbroker, what Direct Participation Programs *alternative investments* were and give him examples.

After I explained what they were, one president responded, "Wow, yeah. I can see where those would be helpful in a lot of clients' portfolios." Amazing!

That conversation was no less incredible to me than if I had gone to my doctor and heard him say, *"You said you thought you might need ibuprofen? What exactly is that?"*

When I pressed each of the two firms' leaders on why they had a prohibition against their advisors discussing anything but stock market investments with their clients, they each referred with some exasperation to the additional burdens that would be required in their business model if they were to do so. Said one, "You're talking about having to add more training to our field force, additional supervision and compliance, and purchasing an insurance rider for our E & O policy. It's just not worth it."

Not worth it. Say that to the retiree when his stock portfolio is down by 30% and he can't travel to see his grandkids. *Not worth it.* Say that to the couple struggling with health problems, saving aggressively toward an early retirement to be able to enjoy the few good years of life left, only to watch their unbalanced portfolio suffer under too much stock market risk. *Not worth it.*

Not worth it to whom?

The bottom line here is that every investor needs to know what they are dealing with. Before you take advice from any financial professional, whether a stockbroker, insurance salesman, or independent advisor, ask the following questions:

- Can you explain to me what a Section 42 Tax Credit Program is?
- Are you licensed to sell alternative investments, such as real estate partnerships, that have no stock market risk?
- Do you offer third-party management of mutual fund, variable annuity, and stock/bond portfolios?

If the answer is "no" to any of the three questions, understand that it is—by definition—impossible for this person to give you comprehensive and balanced advice.

Chapter 20

Online Trading

Are you a do-it-yourself type? Tired of paying commissions on trades to stock jockeys who get compensated whether what they advise turns out to be good or not? Do you like watching the stock market? If these questions resonate with you, then more than likely you have an online discount brokerage account.

With few exceptions, I recommend that investors defer most of the decisions regarding how best to invest their retirement savings, college funding, or other significant amount to professionals, such as a proven money manager working in tandem with an independent financial advisor. But there are millions of people who want to try to control their own investing, and who are diligent and disciplined in that endeavor. Then too, I know others who just like to keep a little "play money" in an online discount account and trade from time to time.

So, which trading platform is best? There are a lot of online trading platforms available, and each attempts to out-price and out-dazzle the next with more "streaming charts and graphs" and "independent research." In the final analysis, though, they usually end up offering the same functionality and very close and competitive pricing.

There is one emerging fundamental difference, though, that truly does offer distinction: values-based discount brokerage platforms. This innovation goes well beyond the traditional platform by offering investors the opportunity to reflect their faith and values in their stock purchase decisions. Before purchasing a company's stock, the investor who utilizes a values-based trading platform can find out whether the company is involved in:

- Abortion
- Tobacco
- Gambling
- Alcohol
- Pornography
- Supporting the gay, lesbian, bisexual, and transgender political agenda
- Promoting positive, pro-family values, and philanthropic giving to organizations promoting traditional American values

As an investor of God's money, whether you invest through a financial advisor or trade stocks for your own account, be aware that you have the option of acting in stewardship with the money that God has entrusted to you. For more specific information on available values-based online discount brokerage services, please log on to www.RICAonline.com.

The Mutual Fund Phenomenon

There are over 14,000 mutual funds today. There are A shares, B shares, C shares, T shares, an almost limitless number of ways that funds are priced and can be purchased. There are so many variations on pricing that when I see my kids' bowls of alphabet soup, there isn't a letter that surfaces that doesn't remind me of a mutual fund pricing method!

Exacerbating the pricing dynamics are the various ways of computing breakpoints. The more shares you buy, the less expensive the initial purchase—on some.

And what exactly are these mutual funds investing in? Does a fund that refers to itself as a small cap fund really limit its holdings to just small company stocks? Or does the manager have the authority to buy stocks from other asset classes, such as mid-cap or large cap? The answer is that most likely he does. So why call it a small cap fund if it's not invested only in small company stocks? What if what you really want is a small cap fund?

In addition, how do you know that your fund isn't purchasing stock in a company that is profiting from abortion clinics? How do you know that your daughter's college education fund, which you have invested in mutual funds, isn't holding stocks of companies that make their profit from the pornography industry? How do you know that while you decry the moral collapse of America, your mutual funds aren't investing your money directly into companies who openly promote the advance of the gay, lesbian, bisexual, and transgender agenda?

Of the 14,000 funds available, can you tell me why you own the one(s) that are in your portfolio? Can you tell me how your fund(s) compares to its peers? Can you tell me how long you will own it, how much of your portfolio it should comprise, and why?

Finally, how happy are you when the fund's net asset value loses money, but you still have to pay tax on interest, dividends, and capital gains? Talk about adding insult on top of injury!

What's the solution to this Rubic's Cube? Stay away from mutual funds altogether? Absolutely not. Mutual funds can be an important part of a balanced investment portfolio. The solution involves following a few simple steps:

1. For balances of $25,000 or more, utilize a professional money management firm that will buy true no-load funds and Exchange Traded Funds selected from a platform that offers hundreds or thousands of options. Choose a firm and an investment strategy that meets your risk and performance objectives. Finally, make sure that the firm you utilize also does values-based investing (the vast majority do not).
2. For balances under $25,000, utilize one or two funds that have strong track records, and screen out those companies that do not meet your personal values.
3. Where possible, try to utilize IRA, Section 529, UTMA, or other tax-advantaged plans that offer some tax relief.

But beware. The popularity of mutual funds is such that many fund companies and financial advisors act as if mutual funds are the Holy Grail. They'll suggest mutual funds for this, mutual funds for that, and mutual funds in between. Mutual funds are nothing more than one important part of a balanced investment diet. Overload on them and you'll be mutual-fund obese. Ignore them altogether and you might get mutual-fund rickets.

One last point: performance. As a licensed and experienced financial advisor, I am prohibited by law from giving out false or misleading information. Even if regulations didn't require me to speak the truth, my ethics and experience would dictate such.

However, there are some people who refer to themselves as "experts" in the financial advice industry who are neither licensed nor experienced. They are self-promoters who make their living from selling their books, presenting seminars, and/or having their own radio programs. In many cases, these self-proclaimed investment gurus have never been licensed, never had a real client, never even had any formal education on the subject of which they purport to be an expert. What they do have is a combination of personal opinion and a high degree of marketing ability.

One such person actually wrote, in a syndicated article that appeared in my local newspaper, a response to a question about where to invest money. This person advised putting all of the money into four different asset classes of mutual funds, and that in doing so, a 12% return could be expected. That is a profoundly misleading statement. To put that into perspective, let me explain what would have happened if I, a licensed professional, had written that:

- I would have had to submit the article to my compliance director before it was printed. I guarantee you that neither he, nor anyone in his position with any securities firm in the country, would have approved it.
- He would likely have formally reprimanded me and immediately placed me under heightened supervision.
- If it had been printed anyway, I would likely have been at least censured by the NASD, or had my license suspended.
- My broker dealer would almost certainly have terminated me, and my subsequent ability to find employment in the securities industry would have been severely impaired.

Why all the fuss? Because no one has ever been able to predict the market, and therefore no one can tell anyone what the performance of a mutual fund—or any combination of funds—will be. I can cite any number of years when that statement would have proven profoundly untrue. The performance of such an investment allocation would have been not only under 12%, but even under zero percent.

Imagine the damage that could be done to someone's life if misleading statements were actually acted upon. That's why the securities industry is so heavily regulated, and why no investor should ever take investment advice from anyone who is not licensed, experienced, and academically trained.

Chapter 22

Privately Managed Accounts

"*I sold* my business five years ago and invested $3 million into the stock market. I thought I knew what I was doing, it just didn't look that complicated," he said sadly. "Right now, as of this morning, less than two years later, my stock portfolio is worth less than 50% of what it was when I bought it. I've lost half of the profit from my life's work and I'm just sick of the whole thing."

I was saddened to hear this as I walked out of my hotel into the late morning breeze, cell phone to my ear. Brian Khan was someone referred to me by one of my clients. After asking him a lot of questions involving goals, taxes, liquidity needs, and assessing his risk temperament, one of my primary recommendations was that Brian turn his portfolio over to a professional money management firm that I would introduce to him. He agreed that the challenge of effectively managing his portfolio was way past his ability, and he had the humility and intelligence (I think those words might be redundant!) to acknowledge that fact.

Letting go of the reigns to the management of your investment portfolio to a professional money management firm can be a very smart move. You gain from that firm's expertise, technology, and perspective.

Adding that level of competency to the direction of your portfolio is one reason to employ professional money managers.

Another dynamic that investors gain is customization. Let me explain it this way. Many people live in communities that offer neighborhood swimming pools. I spent much of my high school and early college days as a life guard, manager, and swim coach at these pools. My job was to enforce the rules:

- Only members allowed
- Hours of operation limited
- Seasonal opening and closing
- Appropriate attire
- Chemical standards for pool water
- Water temperature
- Only certain food and beverages allowed

As popular as neighborhood pools are, they are not found in most gated and wealthy communities. Why is that? Because, unlike the community pool, wealthy homeowners who want the pleasures of a pool also want to make all the rules. They build their own pool and control it as they choose.

The differences between mutual funds and privately managed accounts are similar. When an investor hands over his money to a mutual fund, he loses any control. The manager makes all decisions for the benefit of the "community pool": when to buy, when to sell, whether to trigger a taxable event, etc.

By contrast, when an investor opens an account with a money manager, it is the investor who tells the manager what the rules will be, whether he needs tax efficiency, what risk he's willing to take, how much liquidity he needs, etc.

Foundations, high-net worth individuals and families, and people with large sums to invest usually leapfrog the mutual fund option and instead hire a private account manager, or what we refer to as professional money manager. In fact, many mutual fund managers are also private account managers. With few exceptions, it just makes no sense to invest in mutual funds when there is sufficient money to create a fully diversified private account portfolio.

Let me review some of the advantages of private accounts over mutual funds:

- A much higher degree of customization
- Lower fees
- Personalized communication
- Greater flexibility

So why doesn't everybody skip the mutual fund level and go directly to professional money management? The primary reason is that the minimum amount required to open a privately managed account can range from a low of $100,000, and may be as high as $1 million.

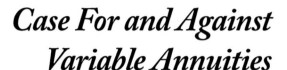

Chapter 23

Case For and Against Variable Annuities

"*I want* to be able to take out about 7% each year. I have a heart condition, and who knows how much longer I'll be around," Jack said. He watched a squirrel jump through their snow-covered back yard and race up a bird feeder to grab his share of the feed that Jack's wife Doris had left for the critters. Looking back at me across his dining room table, he continued, "I've worked hard for my retirement, and now I want to enjoy it. I don't have enough money to just let it sit in the bank. And whether I see another 20 years or not, Doris is going to need the income for a long time."

One of my new advisors at the time, Tom Redmond, had asked me to meet with Jack and Doris the next time I paid a visit to Indianapolis. Tom pulled out the information and account statements that Jack had given us to review and said, "Okay. I see that you have all of your retirement account invested in mutual funds. How do you propose to safeguard your income from this account if you were to die before Doris and the account value was down 10%, 20%, or even 50%?"

Jack's eyebrows went up as his countenance changed to exasperation. "That's just it. I don't know what to do about that. I can't get the kind of income we need from something that's guaranteed like a CD, but I can't get the guarantees I need from mutual funds that are subject to the risks of the stock market." His hands went up in surrender as he said, "Is there anything you can suggest?"

As a matter of fact, there is an investment product that was designed for just this kind of situation. It offers:

- The upside of the stock market
- A death benefit guarantee against loss of income when there is a death and the market value has declined
- A living benefit guarantee when the market value declines and there is a need for income

In fact, this product offers so many different options that an investor can actually custom-build his own according to his very individualized needs and wants.

This interesting and flexible investment is called a variable annuity.

What Is a Variable Annuity?

Although variable annuities have become highly complex financial instruments with an almost never-ending list of options, fundamentally they are quite simple. Forgetting the technical aspects for a moment, just think of stocks and bonds. Now, think of adding a professional manager to decide which ones to buy and sell. That would be a mutual fund. Now, put that mutual fund (and maybe as many as 90 others) inside an annuity, so that there are no taxes due until there is a distribution—maybe years down the road. That's a variable annuity.

Now, I'll add those technical aspects. In actuality, a variable annuity does not have mutual funds as investment options, but rather *separate accounts*, or *sub-accounts*, as they are referred to sometimes. For our purposes, though, think of them as you would mutual funds. There are usually between 50 and 90 different sub-account options, representing all of the major asset classes, and managed by the same managers you recognize as managing mutual funds.

In recent years, variable annuities have run into some serious challenges by the financial media and self-proclaimed financial experts, because of their higher expenses. This criticism is justified if there is no real reason for a financial advisor to recommend a variable annuity instead of mutual funds. Generally, variable annuities carry a "management and expense" charge, ranging anywhere from 6/10ths of one percent to as high as 1.4%. This expense covers a number of items, especially the standard death benefit guarantee. The criticism is based on the presumption that the financial advisor recommends the higher cost product to his client only because he receives a higher commission than he would have had the investor purchased mutual funds.

However, this criticism may boomerang back to point out the ignorance of the accuser. In one situation, a self-proclaimed, book-selling financial expert was on her television program deriding the egregious expenses of variable annuities and admonishing her dutiful listeners never to purchase one. She then took a call from a lady who went on to explain how she was so very thankful that her now deceased husband had the foresight and prudence to invest in a variable annuity. It seems that he had invested an initial sum of $300,000, only to watch the stock market go down and erode his account value to just over $200,000. While the account was down, he passed away. Instead of receiving a check from a mutual fund for the reduced account value, she received a check from the variable annuity insurance company for the full $300,000. At that, the caller hung up and our financial guru was speechless. I love it when that happens!

Let's go back to Jack and Doris. They took our recommendation and did the paperwork required to transfer their retirement account into a variable annuity that offered guarantees on both a death benefit and a living benefit. We then did the paperwork to hire a professional money manager to do the allocation of the money in the retirement plan among the 90 different investment options, so that Jack and Doris would be able to eat well and sleep well. They would be able to eat well because the money manager would follow a specific investment policy that would attempt to minimize risk, while simultaneously attempting to maximize the return. They would be able to sleep well because the manager utilized values-based investing to attempt to reduce Jack's exposure to companies involved in the abortion, pornography, and tobacco industries, and companies that supported the gay and lesbian radical political agenda.

What happened next, though, didn't surprise me. Tom, my new advisor, called me a couple of weeks later all upset. It seems that Jack had called him to say that after discussing the situation with the advisor who had sold him the mutual fund portfolio years earlier, Jack had become convinced that the expenses on the variable annuity were too high. He wanted to just leave the money in the mutual funds. I told Tom not to worry, that I would call Jack and discuss it with him.

When I reached Jack on the phone a day later, I asked Jack if he would explain why he had changed his mind. Sure enough, Jack related the story just as I had heard it from Tom. When he was done I said, "Jack, I guess I misunderstood what you were looking for. If you want low fees, I suggest that you not only forget about the variable annuity, but skip the mutual funds, too. Instead, let me introduce you to some money managers who will develop a customized portfolio for you and will do so with a fee structure that is substantially lower than the fees you are currently paying on your mutual funds." I paused to let Jack think about that idea.

He responded with, "Lower fees than my mutual funds?"

"Yes," I said, "and by a significant margin. But before you get too excited about that option, let me go back and review what I thought it was that you and Doris were looking for. I thought that you were really concerned about taking some of the risk out by putting a safety net underneath your investments. My impression was that the most important concern for you was that regardless of whether you lived 20 years or 2, whether the stock market went up or down, you had the underlying guarantees that would pay you and Doris an income—no matter what."

"Yes! Yes! That's exactly what I want!" he exclaimed.

"You can't get those guarantees in a privately managed account, Jack. And you can't get those guarantees in a mutual fund portfolio either," I said. "You can get them in a variable annuity, just like the one Tom and I recommended. It is true that there are fees and expenses associated with those guarantees—we went over them with you at your dining room table, and they are also listed in both the brochure and prospectus. So, it's all about what's important to you, Jack," I ended.

With that, Jack's mind was made up. He had been misled by the mutual fund salesperson who didn't bother to even ask Jack what was important to him. Instead, he had simply tried to use the scare tactic of "You're going to pay higher fees with a variable annuity." I'd like to take that mutual fund salesman on one of my long runs . . . a particularly hilly route.

Guidelines To Consider

The horrible attack on America on September 11, 2001 changed us in many ways. It led to new measures in airport security, the creation of the Patriot Act, and even changes in investment products. From 1981, when I first entered this industry, until 2001, it was unheard of to be able to offer any investor a combination of the advantages of the stock market coupled with the guarantees and security of income protection. However, since 9/11, variable annuities have added variations of what are referred to as "living benefits" to compliment the traditional death benefit that had been the only guarantee available with that particular investment. This is a remarkable and critically important innovation for retirees who need the upside potential of the stock market, but can't risk losing their retirement income. This option just makes common sense. No one would consider not owning health insurance, or homeowner insurance, or auto insurance. Why should retirees not be given the opportunity to purchase insurance on their retirement income, as well?

As I indicated earlier, there are numerous options available on variable annuity contracts, but all of them are derived from an ironclad guarantee to provide income regardless of how low the account value falls. The living benefit usually will guarantee an increase of between (your choice) 5% and 7%, compounded annually on the initial amount invested. The owner can access this amount at some specified future date as a guaranteed monthly income, or can simply forget about it and withdraw from the account value at will, particularly if that account is higher.

So, instead of just having one value, as in the case with a mutual fund portfolio, a variable annuity has three values:

1. Account value
2. Income guarantee amount
3. Death benefit

Which of the three values he/she utilizes will depend on what happens to the market, and what the investor's needs and life events are. It is important to note that each option (or rider) has a corresponding cost associated with it, so be careful of your total expense on the contract.

Following are my suggested guidelines when considering the purchase of a variable annuity:

- One of the most important considerations is the investment options (sub-accounts). Be sure that they represent all of the major asset classes, and that you do not have substantial restrictions that impede your ability to have a money manager allocate your investment among the various options whenever he feels it necessary to maximize your return.

- Don't purchase a variable annuity without also simultaneously hiring a professional money management firm to manage the specific allocation of your money among the dozens of investment options within your variable annuity. Someone must decide where your money should be allocated, how long it should remain there, and when to make a change. You do not want to try to make those decisions on a daily basis yourself, and the person who sold you the variable annuity does not have the time, expertise, infrastructure, and possibly licensing to manage it, either. Just as in the case of mutual funds, find a firm that meets your risk and performance objectives, and that will apply values-based investing to reflect your values.

- Be aware that you can reflect your values in the way that your variable annuity is managed. If you are pro-life, specify to the money manager that you don't want your money invested in the abortion industry. If you are sickened by the advance of the gay and lesbian political movement, tell your money manager to invest your money away from companies that support their agenda. It's *your money*—shouldn't it reflect *your values?*

- If you do not need a death benefit, or any living benefits, but simply want the tax-deferral feature of a variable annuity, know that there are variable annuity options available for very low cost (such as a total cost of only $20 monthly).

- If you do not need the tax-deferral feature, the living benefit, or the death benefit, a variable annuity likely is not the most appropriate option for you.

SIX

Alternative Investments

Chapter 24

What Alternative Investments Can Mean for You

A few years ago, I was meeting with a wonderful lady outside of Dallas about her financial plan. A very experienced financial advisor in that area, Rick, had recently joined us and asked me to meet with a few of his clients. This lady was actually more a friend than a client, since all of her financial investments had been made through another advisor. Rick and I listened as Wanda told us how frustrated she was with the poor performance of her mutual funds.

"He told me just to wait it out, you know, that they'd come back in time. All I know is that I'm not getting any younger and I need this money to grow!" the 60-year-old lady grumbled. "Here, take a look at these reports," and she slid several statements in front of us. Sure enough, the value of the funds that she owned was quite a bit lower than the original amount invested.

I wanted to get a full picture of her situation, so I asked, "Wanda, do these reports represent all of your investments, other than your home?"

"Actually, no," she responded and then went searching through her briefcase. "Here," she said as she handed another report to me. "That same guy that sold me the mutual funds also sold me this thing, but I don't know what it is, or even how to read the statement."

It turned out to be a real estate partnership and—wow—Wanda had done quite well indeed. When I explained that to her, she was quite pleased, but also bewildered. "How can that be?" she asked. "If these mutual funds have performed so poorly, why would this real estate thing be doing so well?"

Welcome to the world of alternative investments. They are known by that title because they are, in fact, an alternative to the stock market and the bank. Most people buy into the idea that there are only two places to invest money—the stock market and the bank. Not true. In fact, alternative investment business models are all around you everyday, and you probably never even knew.

These partnerships can offer annualized returns in the 6% to 18% range, paying distributions quarterly or monthly. They typically have a holding period of 3 to 10 years. A lot of these investments are appropriate for qualified money such as IRAs. The public programs will have minimal investment requirements, typically in the $1,000—$5,000 range, whereas the private versions will likely be in the $25,000—to $100,000 range.

Each partnership is different, so read each prospectus and brochure carefully. Although there is no stock market risk associated with partnership programs, they do have risks and are certainly not guaranteed. The three most common risks to be aware of in this category are *liquidity, business,* and *financial.* Let me here focus on liquidity risk, because if there's any misunderstanding on this point, it could prove to be a serious problem.

Like most families, we have a routine. I come home around 6:00, and Libby and I spend time with the kids: you know, bathing, wrestling, school work, etc. Then, if we're lucky, Lib and I will have a few minutes to sit and talk before she goes to bed, which leaves me alone to think about what I might want to make myself for supper, read the newspaper, watch the news, and do some work. One night after this routine, the house was quiet and I was standing in the kitchen nibbling on cashews and reading the paper. Out of my peripheral vision I realized that my beautiful, brown-haired, brown-eyed five-year-old daughter, Ann-Rachel, had come sleepily down the stairs and was right next to me. I said, "What's the matter, honey?"

Putting her hand on top of her head she said, "Daddy, I have a headache."

"Okay, I'll get you some medicine." I reached up in the cabinet and pulled out the right prescription, poured it into a medicine spoon, and handed it to her. She took it from me and slurped it all down. With that accomplished, I kissed her, turned her toward the stairs, and went back to the newspaper. Again out of my peripheral vision I noticed that she had stopped at the bottom of the stairs. I turned to her and said softly, "What's the matter?"

With a quizzical expression on her face she said, "Daddy, I *still* have a headache."

Ann-Rachel, at age five, didn't realize that it takes time for the medicine to work. So, too, does it take time for an alternative investment's business model to work. It has to *do* something, and that will take a certain amount of time. Therefore, when you invest in a partnership, you need to understand that you have committed your money to a business model for a specified period of time, so that it can *do* what it *does* to try to make you money.

Understand how and when your money may come back to you from this investment, and how long the anticipated holding period is. Consider the underlying business model to make sure that it makes sense, but even then, know that if that sector of the economy has problems, your investment in that sector through a partnership might, too. Finally, consider the financial vulnerability of the partnership. In many cases, this particular risk can be mitigated when the investors actually own the asset (real estate, equipment, etc.).

Chapter 25

Alternative Investments Are All Around You

Picture yourself getting into your car for a drive. First stop is an International House of Pancakes (IHOP) for breakfast. Satisfied with your meal, you get back into your car for some shopping. You pull up to the Walgreens drive-through to pick up a prescription. Next stop is Home Depot for some materials for a project you're working on. Standing in the check-out line and seeing so many people with credit cards in hand, you wonder how many of those people will have trouble paying their credit card bills. Getting back into your car, you head toward your next destination, but have to stop at a railroad crossing and wait as a train carrying shipping containers slowly passes by. While waiting, you look up to see an airplane heading in toward a landing. Now, with the train passed, you head toward your next destination, Pet Smart, where you'll look over the displays to find the right food for your daughter's fish. Finally, you stop by the office where you need to print some reports that you'll take home to review later that night, when the kids are asleep.

Now, let's go back through that drive and find alternative investments. I see about a dozen business models that fall into three categories:

Real Estate—The IHOP, Walgreens and your office building could be part of a real estate partnership.

Equipment Leasing—The rail cars and the shipping containers they were hauling, the display shelves at Home Depot and Pet Smart, the jet engines on the airplane, and the computer equipment at your office all could be part of equipment-leasing partnerships.

Charged-Off Receivables—Delinquent credit card balances could be part of a charged off receivables partnership.

Let me now walk you through each of these three distinctly different business models that represent investment opportunities for many investors. They have nothing to do with the risk of the stock market, and nothing to do with the interest rate returns on bank instruments.

Chapter 26

Three Business Models

Real Estate

There are any number of real estate partnerships that could be comprised of office buildings, warehouses, retail stores, restaurants, and industrial developments.

Some of the more interesting partnership opportunities for investors are those that involve the retail and restaurant brands that investors are familiar with. Typically, a partnership will purchase a piece of land in an attractive retail area and offer it to a name-brand retail or restaurant establishment, such as those in our story. The financial arrangements are such that the property will be built and then financed for 2–4 years, with annually escalating lease payments which induce the corporate home office to buy it from the partnership. There may be dozens of these properties in any one partnership, which help mitigate risk.

Office buildings are another very popular alternative investment. Each partnership will have its own business model and expertise. For instance, I know of two commercial real estate firms that compete with each other from opposite sides of the spectrum. Firm A purchases office buildings that have fallen on hard times. The building might be 10–15 years old, in need of repairs, and only 60% occupied. Doesn't sound like such a good investment so far, does it? Except now Firm A will buy that building at a steep discount, and come in with their own property management team to give it a complete makeover and begin aggressively leasing it. Additionally, since they were able to buy the building at such a discount, they don't have to borrow any money. This makes this business model a fairly conservative play.

But you won't find these buildings in your first-class corporate locations. So, enter Firm B. This firm builds and buys those beautiful, first-class office buildings that very successful companies lease. These buildings typically offer the best aesthetics, technological innovations, and efficiencies. The lease holders will likely hold their leases for 7 to 15 years, so turnover is not usually a problem. However, to afford the high price tags associated with this business model, typically Firm B will use leverage. In other words, they will borrow money to add to that which they raised from their investor pool (that means people like you). This is not necessarily a bad thing, but it does add an additional element of risk to this business model.

Equipment-Leasing Programs

One day, while sitting on a commercial airplane just over the left wing, waiting to push back from the gate, I started thinking about who exactly owned what on this flying tube. Hanging (precariously, I was thinking) on the wing outside my window was a single jet engine, mirroring the one on the right. It looked like a GE engine, or perhaps a Pratt & Whitney. Because of the kind of work that I do, I knew that each of the two engines that were to propel this plane were owned not by the airline, but by investor groups. Probably different investor groups. I was wondering who owned the fuselage just as I heard the flight attendant say, "We are ready for push back, please take your seats." As we headed down the runway at ever-increasing speed, I found myself just thinking, "I sure do hope all those different investor groups get along!"

Equipment-leasing programs come in all sorts of shapes and sizes. Some do computer and office equipment, others do only large earth-moving trucks and dozers, while others focus on medical technology. Large partnerships will even own offshore drilling platforms, ocean liners, and railroad cars. Virtually anything you can think of that is utilized in business can be included in an equipment-leasing program.

Charged-Off Receivables

A fascinating business model that I have become very familiar with involves the purchase and management of what is referred to as charged-off receivables. This category might include everything from delinquent auto loans to phone bills, medical bills, and credit cards. Since my highest familiarity is with delinquent credit card debt, let me focus on that category.

I don't need to go through all of the statistics regarding the amount of unsecured, revolving credit card debt that exists in this country. Let's just agree that it is staggering, profoundly unhealthy, and out of control. To me, the inappropriate use of credit is not the worst of the problem, as bad as that is. Worse is the fundamental spiritual problem of not being satisfied with what God has given. People misuse credit because they want more and more and more. It is this attempt to live beyond what we are given that is the problem. The Apostle Paul puts it this way:

> "But godliness with contentment is great gain . . . People who want to get rich fall into temptation and a trap and into many foolish and harmful desires that plunge men into ruin and destruction. For the love of money is the root of all kinds of evil."
>
> I Timothy 6:6, 9–10

All that said, the phenomenon of unsecured debt is not going to go away any time soon. And as some of that credit becomes delinquent, it becomes what is referred to in the banking world as a "non-performing asset" which has to be taken off the books. Generally, after six months of "non performing," a bank will sell the debt along with a pool of other non-performing debt to a firm that specializes in managing delinquent accounts. I am sure there are some really ugly people in that industry, but I am not familiar with them. The firm that I am familiar with buys blocks of anywhere from $10 million to $100 million or more from the large banks that issue credit cards. Shockingly, the purchase price on the debt that they buy will range from 2 cents on the dollar to a high of about 4 cents on the dollar. That means if we use an average of 3 cents on the dollar, they would buy a $2000 credit card debt obligation for $60.

There are three ways that this firm can make money on the debt. First, they can turn right around and by carving it up, sell small pieces of it to collection firms that can't afford to buy in such large volumes. Second, they can actually lease it to a national network of collection attorneys. Third, they can keep portions of it for their own in-house collection department. The profit potential on any of these three levels is enormous.

Let me say a word about the collection process that I have witnessed. From what I understand, there are three kinds of people that find themselves in the pool of non-performing credit card debt:

1. **Life Category**—those who have suffered an unfortunate life circumstance such as the death of a spouse, a debilitating illness, a divorce, or a job layoff. These unfortunate people have every intent to pay what they owe, but they need time and they need help. The collection firm I have seen that works with this category is sensitive, flexible, and supportive.

2. **Dumb Category**—usually made up of young people who go to their mailbox one day and find a "free" credit card giving them access to $2000 of immediate credit. Jane and Johnny, both 21, rush out and buy all those beautiful clothes and that plasma TV they have always wanted. They have no job and no clue how they are going to pay the credit card bill. After six months of being harassed by the bank, they get a call from the new owner of their debt.

"I know, I know, I'm supposed to pay you $2000. But I don't have any money, I'm telling you!" Jane exclaims with emotion.

"Okay, if you can't pay the whole amount, what could you pay on a monthly basis, $25?" the collection firm asks.

"Well, yes, I could do that," Jane responds.

"Well then, here's the deal. IF you pay $25 a month and you don't miss any payments, we will eliminate all of the interest charges, all of the penalties, and we'll even reduce your obligation down to $1000," the professional calmly explains.

What do you think Jane's response is? She's practically giddy. And when she makes that last $25 payment, the collection firm notifies the credit bureaus that Jane's account has been satisfied. Her credit score goes up and she can rent that apartment she needs, get the cell phone she needs, and get on with her life, having—hopefully—learned a very important lesson.

3. **Con Category**—the third category of non performers is made up of professional con artists. This group has made a business out of gaining credit lines and then moving on, with absolutely no intent to pay. They change addresses, phones, and are on the run. This category will be hounded by the collection firm with all of the legal prowess it can muster.

Because there is so much inventory coupled with tremendous profit potential, the charged-off receivables asset class has attracted a lot of attention recently. Be careful. There are a lot of people that get into this business who do not know what they are doing and whose business model is suspect, at best. That said, a firm with a solid track record in this industry can offer a very viable investment opportunity for suitable investors.

Taxes?
What Taxes?

Chapter 27

Income Taxes and Investing

One day the Pharisees set out to trap Jesus with a question. They asked, "Tell us then, what is your opinion? Is it right to pay taxes to Caesar or not?" (Matthew 22:17). Jesus took a minute and asked them to show him the coin and tell him whose picture was on the coin. "Caesar's," they replied.

Jesus astounded them with his answer by saying, "Give to Caesar what is Caesar's, and to God what is God's" (Matthew 22:21).

The United States Tax Code places the burden of determining how much is "Caesar's" on each individual citizen. I am distressed to hear naive Christians with good intentions proclaim they gladly pay their taxes. Sometimes this kind of attitude camouflages the fact that too much tax is being paid unnecessarily.

How much tax is enough is a philosophical issue. It came before the courts in 1947 in *Commissioner v. Newman*, when Justice Learned Hand wrote, "Over and over again courts have said that there is nothing sinister in so arranging one's affairs as to keep taxes as low as possible. Everyone does so, rich or poor, and all do right, for nobody owes any public duty to pay more than the law demands: Taxes are enforced extractions, not voluntary contributions. To demand more in the name of morals is mere cant." So from both the words of Jesus and the tax court, we can proceed to review the U.S. income tax system and hold the philosophical premise that while we should pay our taxes, we should not pay any more tax than required.

There are few absolutes in the world of investment planning. There is one axiom, however, that comes pretty close to an absolute: Never make an investment exclusively on the basis of tax implications. There are few exceptions to this rule. One exception might be IRC Section 42 (affordable housing program) and the tax credits it offers. Other possible exceptions might be certain types of qualified energy programs. But as an operating rule of thumb, investments should be made for their economic potential, with income tax considerations as an ancillary part of the decision process.

Another helpful general rule is that there is usually a corollary between tax benefits and loss of liquidity. For example, an investment in an annuity usually enjoys tax-deferred status on any subsequent gain. However, any distribution from that annuity prior to age fifty-nine-and-a-half will be treated as earnings-out-first, and the gain will be subject to a 10% tax penalty. So much for liquidity.

Numerous investments offer enticing income tax advantages. When properly arranged, for example, annuities and life insurance encounter no income tax on the gain in the contract cash value until there is a distribution. This tax advantage is referred to as tax deferral. Municipal bonds are generally free of federal income tax, and may also be free of state income tax. The dividends on these investments are then said to be tax exempt. As pointed out earlier, an investment in a properly managed Section 42 affordable-housing program may offer tax credits. Tax credits are the most powerful tax advantage, since each dollar of credit reduces by one dollar your tax liability.

One of the most common mistakes in this area is to equate a tax benefit with the underlying investment. For example, I've heard people say they would not invest in an IRA again, because it had a poor rate of return. In fact, the portion of the tax code that authorizes Individual Retirement Accounts (IRAs) distinctly lists the types of investments that may qualify for this special tax advantage. A mutual fund might be categorized as tax exposed (meaning any dividends, interest, or capital gains would be taxable in the year they are earned), or tax deferred, in the case of an IRA. It might even be offered as a "separate account" in a variable annuity or a variable universal life contract, and qualify as tax deferred as a result. Be careful that you don't mistakenly assume that any special tax advantage that an investment receives is synonymous with the underlying investment itself.

There are any number of legitimate ways to mitigate, defer, or even eliminate taxes. Congress continuously engages in "social engineering," attempting to get the country to behave one way or another by giving certain investment strategies distinct tax advantages. In my (now) 25 years in the industry, I can't even count the number of changes that have been made to the Individual Retirement Account (IRA). So, in this section, I'm not going to commit any energy to the IRA, Section 529 College Savings Plans, UTMA, UGMA, or other tax-driven programs that change as often as the political landscape. Just check with your accountant, or go online and obtain the current limits and guidelines.

Instead, I want to talk about two programs that are not well known, have not changed much in recent history, and which can have an enormous impact on a financial plan in very specific circumstances.

Chapter I. U.S. Code Section 42

My all-time favorite hymn is Martin Luther's "A Mighty Fortress Is Our God." My favorite car (right now) is the Chrysler SRT8. My favorite contemporary Christian group is "Third Day." My favorite recreation is deer hunting. And, after all these years and all that I have experienced in this industry, my all-time single, most favorite investment instrument is . . . (drum roll, please) the Section 42 Tax Credit Program.

The most powerful tax advantage is not deferral, such as what annuities offer. Neither is it a deduction, such as what an IRA or 401(k) offer. Rather, the most powerful tax advantage you can access is a tax credit.

A tax credit is like a coupon for paying part of your tax bill. For example, if you owe $10,000 in federal income taxes and you have

$4,000 in tax credits, you simply subtract the credits from what you owe. Interested? It gets even better.

In the late 1980s, Congress enacted legislation that provided tax credits for each state in the country to use to help build "affordable housing" in communities where the median income had skyrocketed and a lot of the service sector could no longer afford to live there. For example, teachers, firemen, and policemen live on moderate incomes. If the median income of the area was to rise dramatically, these important elements of the community could no longer afford to live in the areas that they served. This is also true for senior citizens living on a fixed income.

In short, the Section 42 Low-Income Housing Program was created and has been very successful. It is a wonderful example of how the federal and state governments can work with the private sector to solve a real social problem.

The housing itself must meet very strict guidelines, and therefore is a very attractive addition to any community. Generally, these units are garden-style apartments. It is likely that you have driven by a Section 42 qualifying complex and not even known that is what it was.

Investors can generally invest as little as $1,000, and up to a maximum of about $80,000. The return to the investor is not in the form of a cash distribution, but rather tax credits. These will range from about 9%—11% per year over a ten-year period, with expected total yields of around 105%. Although the credits should be the primary reason to invest, these programs also offer a return of capital in the form of a pro-rata share for each investor when the properties are sold, somewhere between the 11th and 15th years. Obviously, no one can tell you on the front end when you invest whether you will make a profit on the sale of the investment, so you'll need to do your own due diligence on that end and come to your own conclusion.

Keep in mind that the tax credits have very substantial and different advantages from what you might otherwise expect. For example, the credit is a tax-free yield, unlike a distribution from a corporate bond, CD, or mutual fund. Additionally, they tend to be fairly secure investments, since the credits are pre-funded in the year the program is organized and then distributed over the next ten years. This means that if Congress, always trying to find ways to wreck something that works, decides to cancel the Section 42 Program, it will not affect the distribution of credits in future years from programs already allocated.

Also, this is not exactly like taking advantage of a tax "loophole." Hardly. The credits are authorized and distributed by the U.S. Treasury Department—you know, the same guys that run the IRS.

Finally, to really get the maximum benefit from this investment, you might want to "marry" it to a partnership such as one of the alternative investments discussed earlier. That's because by doing so, it might allow the distribution you receive from your otherwise taxable partnership to be tax free!

Since the Section 42 Program involves real estate as the underlying asset, and since investors are "limited members" of that partnership, the depreciation each year is passed on to the investors (along with the credits). This is considered a "passive loss" which you can only use to offset "passive income," such as that which is developed by so many of the alternative investments.

So, picture me driving in a brand new Chrysler SRT8 toward my hunting property while singing "A Mighty Fortress Is Our God," simultaneously listening to "Third Day" on my radio. I'm also on the cell phone telling my accountant that I received $6,000 in tax credits for this year, and you can imagine one very happy guy!

Chapter 28

Oil & Gas

One of my favorite pastimes is keeping up with the Tennessee Titans. I know way too much about them. I read everything, listen to the sports shows, and have met several of the players. What a frivolous way to spend my energy. On the other hand, I think that's why I enjoy it so much. *They do the work, go through all the pain, and take the risks.* I get enough of that in my real life!

At games, during the television time-outs, there are always commercials playing on the jumbotron. There's this one particular one which advertises one of those steak restaurants where you can eat the peanuts and throw the shells on the floor (or at the guy in the next booth when he's not looking). The ad shows an animated version of three Titans helmets with a single peanut under one of them. Then the helmets begin circulating faster and faster, until you're dizzy, and then they abruptly stop. The objective is to try to follow the helmet with the peanut underneath and know which one that is when they stop moving.

Out of the 69,000 fans in that stadium, I guarantee you that I am the only one who watches that little peanut game and thinks of oil and gas drilling programs. That's because of all of the different investments I have seen or been involved in, following the money in one of these programs can be just as complicated and frustrating. On the other hand, I'm writing about them in this book because, done properly, they offer phenomenal tax incentives. How about a 95% deduction—of virtually any amount—in the year you invest?

Remember that scene in one of the *Crocodile Dundee* movies where he's in New York and some punk comes up to him with a knife and demands Dundee's money? Dundee just smiles, reaches down, and pulls out a huge knife of his own. Then he says in his Down Under accent, "You call *that* a knife? Nah, *this* here's a knife!"

I can just hear Dundee, as a financial advisor, talking with a client who is proud of his IRA deduction: "You call *that* a deduction? Nah, here fellah, now this here oil and gas program, now *that's* what I call a deduction."

Some of the programs are publicly registered, and therefore offer almost any investor the opportunity to participate with as little as a $5,000 investment. Others have minimums in the $100,000 range.

Oil and gas drilling programs are not for most investors. However, you should definitely take a serious look at an oil and gas program if you have:

- won the lottery
- received an NFL signing bonus
- sold your business for a substantial profit
- sold property, stock, or other investments for a large gain.

One of my all-time favorite intellectual heroes is William F. Buckley. I framed something I heard him say one time and put it in the Faith Financial offices. It reads:

"It may be true that reason will not save us; but it is also certainly true that the lack of reason will not save us."

In oil and gas terms it would go something like this:

"It may be true that you won't get a great return on the money you invest in an oil and gas program, but it is also certainly true that not investing in one and sending all of your money to the IRS instead will be a guaranteed zero-percent return on that money."

Your choice.

Advice for Retirees

Chapter 29

Good News

His assets totaled almost $1 million. On top of that, he had a pension of almost $3,000 a month, Social Security, and rental property income. However, he and his wife were about seventy years old and not in the best of health. As we talked during an annual review, I looked at Jack McGrueger and said, "Jack, in reviewing your financial plan, I have uncovered a real problem."

Jack's face took on a grim look. "Oh, what's that?" he said.

"You don't spend enough money!"

Retirees, in general, do have a problem. They tend to not spend enough money—which is really counterintuitive. Individuals in this age category many times live like paupers. In the financial planning process, there are two distinct dimensions—accumulation and distribution. One is used while you are a wage earner, and the other is used as you move into retirement. There is a tendency at every age to focus on the accumulation phase—where the objective is to save, earn higher returns on your investments, and pay fewer taxes. Throughout life, people apply so much effort toward the goal of accumulation that, typically, when it comes time in life to change to distribution, they struggle and almost feel as if they are violating some ethical principle. This phase gets so ingrained in people—in particular, those individuals who grew up during the Great Depression—that accumulation ends up becoming the goal for life!

Retirees who have a hard time moving to the distribution phase of financial planning fail to appreciate that money is only a facility for supporting life goals. Prudent financial planning is not just about accumulating money. By now, you know that this book is an effort to help people understand that money is nothing more than sustenance for life. Think of money in terms of the air you breathe: You need it to sustain you throughout life. If you were, say, playing basketball, you'd find that your body would require substantially more, sometimes in gasps. But while sleeping, you don't require tremendous volumes, since your system is relaxed. So it is also with money. Whatever amount you need better be there when you need it, or your life goals will suffer. The problem with many retirees is that over the years they become so fixated on the need to accumulate money that the idea of accumulation ends up becoming the goal itself. Instead of using their hard-earned accumulation to sustain a life of purpose during retirement, they continue to sock away more money into their savings. In the context of our metaphor, that is like having enough air to play basketball, but being afraid to use it. As a result, many retirees end up sleeping through their retirement.

Seniors tend to guard their wealth because of an underlying fear that if they are not careful, their resources will disappear. Yet if these retirees were simply to use the same prudent financial planning principles that permitted their financial success in the first place, they would realize that they could also successfully manage the distribution. Through prudent management, they will be able to have their money work for them in retirement just as it did in prior years. Although successfully mastering this dimension requires a different strategy, the principle is exactly the same in effect—determine what you want for your life and develop the appropriate financial retirement plan to support it.

As I challenge retirees to commit to an appropriate distribution plan, I use a type of code language that means "live life." I don't mean that the retiree should live a narcissistic, self-consumed lifestyle. Rather, I want them to think creatively. For example, when their local church presents a major $10,000 mission project to the congregation and asks for help with the funding, many retirees automatically and immediately remove themselves from consideration. They listen to the presentation, but in their mind they've already decided, "This does not apply to me." They don't respond in this manner because they lack spiritual commitment. Rather, they respond this way because they have a financial mind-set that doesn't acknowledge that they have adequate financial resources. They protect their capital at all costs. In actuality, statistics show that many of these seniors do have the money for their church—and for a great deal of other beneficiaries, as well.

Whether you are a retiree or a young twenty-five-year-old, the same prudent financial principles apply. There are powerful, life-changing lessons in these principles for any age group. Fundamentally, the question remains the same: What is your life plan? Both ends of the age spectrum must continuously address this question.

Chapter 30

Multidimensional Thinking for Retirees

Interestingly, for all the obvious differences between age groups, retirees tend to make the same mistake as their young counterparts when it comes to planning their financial resources. Specifically, they buy CDs, invest in bonds, amass large amounts of equity in their home, and then look around to see what that produces for income. In essence, they allow their financial plan to dictate their life plan. They've put their (financial planning) cart before the (life) horse.

If retirees would first consider their life goals and then develop a financial plan to support that life (put the horse before the cart), they would feel much more in control and find that life becomes ever more fulfilling.

The majority of financial planners take a fairly remedial risk-averse approach when it comes to investment recommendations for retirees. They fall into the same trap as their clients—they propose the overriding goal of protecting the nest egg at all costs.

Let me be clear that I am not suggesting that anyone jeopardize his nest egg. Rather, my suggestion is to first consider the retiree's dreams for life—almost as if money were no object—before committing to a particular financial strategy. For example, if everything in life were free, what would the retiree do with his next twenty-five years—from age sixty-five to age ninety? If you can get the retiree to dig deep and to answer this question honestly, then the financial plan will begin to take shape. The point of the exercise is to suspend thoughts about money and instead focus on what he wants to do with his life.

This thought process takes time—sometimes days, weeks, or months. What does he want to do with his life for the next twenty-five years? The financial planner must wait until the retiree answers this question. Then and only then will the planner be able to help arrange the retiree's financial portfolio to accomplish support for this life plan.

For example, suppose a retiree is successful and has accumulated $750,000 by age seventy for a nest egg. At this point, his home is completely paid for (or almost paid for) and only requires a low monthly maintenance. Between his pension and Social Security, he is able to pay his monthly expenses.

If the $750,000 were invested in bank instruments (certificates of deposit) earning 4.5%, interest earnings would equal $33,750 a year. Instead of bank instruments, what if he used the same approach that created the $750,000—or an appropriate asset allocation using a combination of mutual funds and variable annuities? If he were able to get a 12% return, his income would jump to $90,000 a year, or a difference of $56,250 a year. Without adjusting for inflation, that's a difference of $1,406,250 over 25 years—almost $1.5 million—and the principal investment of $750,000 is not touched. Would this person make different life choices if he knew, at the conclusion of the financial planning process, that somebody would walk in the door and hand him a check for $1.4 million? You lose opportunity and money if you create your financial plan without a life plan and instead allow the financial plan to dictate your life choices.

About six years ago, Mary Adams came into my office with a hodgepodge of a financial plan—really no plan at all. Two years before our meeting, her husband had died. She had some mutual funds with a stockbroker in Chicago, a couple of annuities, some CDs, and a large amount of money in her checking account. When we started the process, her goal was to organize her financial junk drawer into a cohesive plan. As we went through the financial planning process, eventually we managed to double what she had anticipated her monthly income to be. As we rearranged her investment allocation, she was astounded that her income could be that high. She could not fathom that her income could increase from $2,000 a month to $4,000 a month simply through rearranging her assets into a coordinated portfolio.

During the first year of this new plan, Mary maintained her same spending habits. The additional income accumulated in her investment portfolio so that it grew at an even faster rate. In the second year of the program, Mary could see the reality of her increased income, because it was accounted for on confirmation statements and annual reports.

One day I was in a staff meeting and my assistant interrupted. "Mary is on the phone, and it is fairly urgent that she talk with you right now if you can make it." I left the meeting and thought something serious might have happened to Mary.

On the phone, Mary explained, "I'm visiting my grandchildren in a city about two hours away. This past week, I've had a difficult time squeezing my grandchildren into my small car." On a whim, Mary had stopped at a car dealership and fallen in love with a van. "Right now, Stephen, my five grandchildren are climbing all over this van. The salesman says this van is a great vehicle for a grandmother. You told me that I could spend more money, and I want to buy this van. Do I have enough money?"

Her enthusiasm dripped through the phone, and I laughed with her. "Absolutely, Mary. Buy the van."

An Effective Retirement Portfolio

I don't want to give the impression that everyone can always raise his standard of living simply by rearranging an investment portfolio. That's foolish. Rather, my point is that for the most part, retirees tend to use outdated financial strategies that may have worked well in the 1930s, 1940s, 1950s, and even the 1960s. But today, the financial landscape looks entirely different from what it did back then. Just as technology, improvements in health services, transportation, and a host of other areas of life have benefited retirees, so, too, can state-of-the-art portfolio management.

One of the easiest ways to move toward this improvement, without taking on substantial risk, is to consider moving from bonds and CDs to a combination of alternative investments that offer higher expected returns, a variable annuity that offers the upside of the market and guarantees on retirement income coupled with professional money management, and maybe a privately managed account. All of these, incidentally, can be values-based. If your financial planner doesn't have these kinds of options, I recommend you change financial planners. But it's your choice. Just like our earlier example, you, too, can choose to have either $33,000 a year or $90,000 a year. It's a free country.

One final thought about arranging an effective retirement portfolio. This has not so much to do with the individual choice of investments, but rather the convenience of managing the resulting income. I usually recommend that retirees have three separate dimensions of their financial portfolio:

1. A financial engine which consists of all of the alternative investments, variable annuities, mutual funds, stocks and bonds that produce the income
2. A holding account consisting of a high-yielding money market that also offers free unlimited checking
3. A simple bank checking account

The idea is to have all of the earnings, or what you need of them, taken from your financial engine and deposited into your holding account, which is comprised of a money market fund. You can also direct your Social Security and pension into this holding account. That way, you always know exactly what your income is, where it came from, and when it was deposited. Then, just as if you were still receiving a paycheck from an employer, once each month you write yourself one check consisting of all the money you need to cover your living expenses. That money gets deposited into your checking account to pay your tithe, the utility bill,

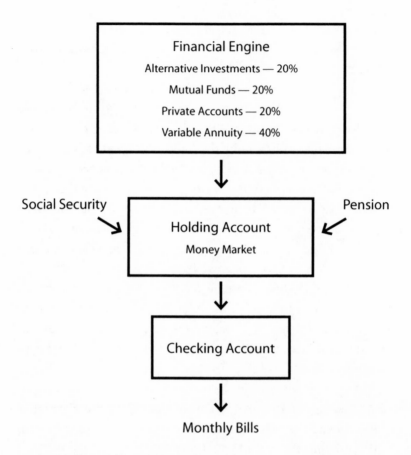

medical bills, etc. You should always leave plenty of extra money in your holding account for emergencies and opportunities, too.

Each quarter you should review the activity in your holding account to make sure that there are no surprises. Then, each year, you should meet with your financial advisor to review your financial engine to see if it needs any tuning, and also to make any changes in your distribution. Sometimes, you might find that you can actually move money back into your financial engine if it is not needed in the holding account.

For more information, please see www.financialstewardshipkit.com.

Chapter 31

The Trust Factor in Estate Management

One of the saddest facts about dealing with retirees—particularly those individuals in their seventies, eighties, and nineties—is the inherent lack of trust they generally have. Many people who fall into this age bracket absolutely refuse to share anything about their financial situation with the family. The consequences of this lack of financial information for the family are multiple, and go beyond just financial issues.

If you don't inform your family about your financial matters, when you die they won't have a clue whether you even had any financial resources, where to find those financial resources, how they were titled, and how to process them. Many times people find out this information in probate court. This lack of information creates all sorts of problems and difficulties that transcend the financial.

When I was in Colorado, I went to see a young family on a ranch. I was working for a Lutheran financial services company, and this family had a file with the company, so I decided to meet them. From the files, I saw a number of people—in fact, four different families—in this region with the last name of Krueger. So I asked, "Are you related to the other Kruegers?" It was a pretty safe guess—they lived in the same county, they were members of the same church, and their last name was the same.

After a long pause, the thirty-five-year-old farmer sat down with a deep sigh and said, "Yes, they are my siblings. I have three brothers who are married and have children." He had no smile on his face; rather, he was frowning. He continued, "But we don't talk with them."

I wasn't sure what to do with that information and didn't ask for elaboration. Over the ensuing months I got to know the Kevin Kruegers as I helped them with their financial and estate planning. I learned they owned a fourth of a previously undivided, large, original family farm. Kevin Krueger wanted to pass this land along to his children, a son and three girls. The children were too young at that point to appreciate the estate planning elements or to know if they would want to be farmers. Because of Kevin Krueger's experience with dividing an estate, he wanted his children's inheritance to be handled in a more efficient manner than his inheritance from his parents had been.

Kevin Krueger's motivation came from a family fiasco about five years previously. His parents, who were in their late seventies, had died suddenly in an automobile accident. These parents had not done any estate planning. In a simple will, the parents left the entire 35,000 acres on an undivided basis to the four sons who helped work the farm. Now they had a new problem—how would four families work the same farm? Who would divide it? Who would divide it with the greatest degree of fairness?

Because they were members of the same family and were all Christians, they decided to have a big family meeting. Kevin Krueger was the estate executor, so he prepared the details for the meeting. He came with a recommendation of how to divide the farm. He based his recommendation on land utilization, water rights, and those types of considerations. Everyone was in agreement that his plan made the most sense.

The next question to be determined was more specific. Which person should own which portion of the estate? Kevin had a recommendation about this, as well. Everyone at the meeting agreed his suggestion made a lot of sense. His recommendation catered to the specific interests of each sibling.

Within a week, however, Kevin got a letter from one brother's attorney. The letter stated the brother had decided against accepting that parcel and instead wanted a different parcel. In the interest of accommodating the family, Kevin said okay, but the other brother involved in the exchange did not agree with the change. This type of swapping and disagreement went on until an attorney represented every sibling. Everyone was threatening everyone else with a lawsuit.

Over the years, the courts finally settled the entire estate. In the end, no one got what he thought should have been his portion—and no one was speaking to the others. Sadly, this is a true story.

How can you prevent such a situation from happening in your family? As uncomfortable as it may be for the children, I recommend that the children approach the parents. Be blunt and say things like, "We need to talk about how you are going to transfer your estate upon your death. You need to tell me your wishes so I can make sure those wishes are honored."

"A good man leaves an inheritance for his children's children, but a sinner's wealth is stored up for the righteous" (Proverbs 13:22). *Strong's Concordance of the Bible* lists 237 verses of Scripture that contain the word inheritance. In comparison, only 96 verses have the word forgiven or forgive in them. This comparison provides insight into God's concept of inheritance.

The material that we accumulate on this earth will only be used to glorify God in the next generation if we protect it through developing an appropriate estate-transfer program. There are almost countless ways your estate may be eroded after your death, most especially through taxes. Most often, this situation can be mitigated with an effective transfer process—which is put in place before death.

The most popular means to transfer wealth through inheritance is through a will. In its most basic form, a will is a letter of instructions, which is usually administered through the state probate court system. Although many states have improved on this process, making it less time-consuming and expensive, still the time and expense can add a great deal to the survivors' stress and frustration. However, the situation is even worse when the deceased fails to leave a will. In these situations, the probate court administers something called the laws of intestacy. If you die without a will, then the state uses a statute to dictate the distribution of your possessions. The survivors' grief and frustration is compounded through intestacy, which could have been avoided entirely with proper planning.

One way people are addressing the concerns of cost, time, and lack of privacy in the management and transfer of an estate is through a living trust. This process begins the estate management process while the parties are still alive. Their assets are transferred to the trust. When compared to making a simple will, establishing a living trust often involves some additional effort, time, and expense. Yet at the time of death or of cognitive disability, there will be considerably less hassle, cost, and frustration because a trust is not subject to the probate court process. My suggestion is to consult with a financial planner and attorney to determine whether a will or a living trust would be most appropriate for your particular situation.

Another item you should address is a living will. This document establishes your wishes regarding life support systems. Before signing such a document, you will want to consult family and your pastor for proper counsel.

It's Your Money, But Whose Values?

Chapter 32

The Value of Virtue

Recently while driving, I was listening to the radio and heard Rush Limbaugh respond to a caller who was lamenting the moral decay of the country. The caller was obviously agitated and asked Rush what he, as an ordinary citizen, could do to make a difference. Rush's response reflected what is being said more and more these days:

> "Live in such a way that your personal values are reflected in everything that you do."
>
> Rush Limbaugh radio program 1/24/06

This section will, no doubt, be the most controversial, but in my opinion, it is also the most important section of *Money on Loan from God*. Before I delve into the specifics of how to use values-based investing not only to reach your financial goals, but also to make a positive difference in the cultural war we are engaged in, we need to first identify the problem. It is important to step back and look at our culture, both Christian and secular, to see where exactly we are on a historical continuum, and how far we have strayed from our Judeo-Christian foundation. Without that perspective, we are left to determine "how we're doing" based solely on our own current cultural experience. With only our individual subjective perspective as a context, we might simply say, "What's the big deal?" Why waste so much energy trying to invest our money in a way that protects our values?

The big deal is that anything that is sinful, and distracts us from pursuing an ever-increasing, intimate relationship with our redemptive Savior, is of paramount significance to our earthly and eternal life! Greed, lust, jealousy, envy, pride, or any other sin is an abomination to God, and a roadblock to our ability to become more Christ-like. Therefore, to the extent that our culture reduces the significance of faith and values and elevates such sinful attractions as hedonism, pride, and self-gratification, it becomes that much more difficult to nurture our relationship with our Creator and Redeemer individually, within our families, and in our country.

The desire to resurrect traditional American cultural values is not to be misinterpreted as a desire to replace our constitutional government with a theocracy, which is a combination of law and religion that has the effect of perverting both parts equally. That said, no country in the history of this planet has been given the blessings and success of the United States of America. It can easily be argued that there has been a "cause-and-effect" between America's foundation of faith and values and its unprecedented success. For over two hundred years the United States, like no other country in history, has balanced the ideals of a rock-solid foundation upon God Almighty as the supreme and sovereign authority on the one hand, with freedom and liberty for each individual, regardless of religion, on the other.

Without the appropriate respect and commitment to those foundational principles, this country will drift evermore into the black hole of *license instead of freedom, entitlement instead of personal responsibility, and hedonism instead of virtue.* The result of that drift is a culture that codifies into law, and institutionalizes into culture, Satan's real and eternal attempt to destroy God's creation. It marginalizes our imperative need for God's redemption individually, and for God's guidance politically and culturally.

We are exhorted by the Apostle Paul to rise above our carnal desires:

> "Whatever is true, whatever is noble, whatever is right, whatever is pure, whatever is lovely, whatever is admirable—if anything is excellent, or praiseworthy—think about such things."
>
> PHILIPPIANS 4:8

So, to the extent that we have the opportunity as American citizens to construct and maintain a government and culture that values the "higher things," as Paul says, then we have the privileged obligation to do so.

On the other hand, we must also guard against self-righteousness, which leads to bigotry, discrimination, and pride. One need only look at the cancer of segregation and the tumult of the civil rights movement to see the devastation that comes from bigotry and hate. Like slavery in the 18th and 19th centuries, and indentured servitude even into the 20th century, man's pride and greed has placed ugly stains on the beauty that is otherwise the tapestry of American history.

Jesus admonishes us to love all, even to the point of praying for our enemies. We are to respect everyone, regardless of race, gender, sexual orientation, religion, or financial status. As the ultimate example, Jesus even went so far as to pray that his Father would forgive the very soldiers who were striking the hammer against the nail that was piercing his hand. No, we are not called to condemn this world, or to pull away from it and head to isolation where we can have our Christian family living in a Christian house, surrounded by a Christian fence, where we get Christian milk from our Christian cows.

Rather, we are called to be "light" and "salt" to a sinful world, leading by example to help those who are lost and in need of salvation:

> "You are the salt of the earth. But if the salt loses its saltiness, how can it be made salty again? It is no longer good for anything, except to be thrown out and trampled by men. You are the

light of the world. A city on a hill cannot be hidden. Neither do people light a lamp and put it under a bowl. Instead, they put it on its stand, and it gives light to everyone in the house. In the same way, let your light shine before men, that they may see your good deeds and praise your Father in heaven."

MATTHEW 5:13–16

As for the culture that we are to inculcate in our society, Paul says the following:

"You must teach what is in accord with sound doctrine. Teach the older men to be temperate, worthy of respect, self-controlled, and sound in faith, in love, and in endurance. Likewise, teach the older women to be reverent in the way they live, not to be slanderers, or addicted to much wine, but to teach what is good. Then they can train the younger women to love their husbands and children, to be self-controlled and pure, to be busy at home, to be kind, and to be subject to their husbands, so that no one will malign the word of God.

"Similarly, encourage the young men to be self-controlled. In everything set them an example by doing what is good. In your teaching show integrity, seriousness and soundness of speech that cannot be condemned, so that those who oppose you may be ashamed because they have nothing bad to say about us.

"For the grace of God that brings salvation has appeared to all men. It teaches us to say 'No' to ungodliness and worldly passions, and to live self-controlled, upright and Godly lives in this present age, while we wait for the blessed hope—the glorious appearing of our great God and Savior, Jesus Christ, who gave himself for us to redeem us from all wickedness and *to purify for himself a people that are his very own, eager to do what is good.*"

TITUS 2:2–8, 11–14

So, there you go. God gives us His blueprint for a life plan, a family model, and a culture pleasing to him. In that regard, let me ask you a poignant question.

How do you think we're doing?

Chapter 33

Whoever Wins the War
Gets To Write the History

I was driving home late one night after a meeting in Atlanta with Ron Blue, now the President of the Christian Financial Professionals Network. It was about a five-hour drive back to Nashville and I was bored, so I turned on my satellite radio and began flipping through the one hundred and forty different radio stations. I would pause at each station to hear the programming, and at one point I was shocked to hear some extremely foul language on the radio. I looked at the digital read-out and the name of the station appeared as "Out." It took me a couple of seconds to put the name of the station with the program that was being aired. Two lesbians were doing a call-in show and discussing their sexual escapades in as lewd and crude ways as anyone could imagine.

It seems only yesterday, but it is now a full ten years since I read a *USA Today* article about Ellen Degeneres about to make history by "coming out" that night on her prime-time show. What was so unprecedented as to be history-making ten years ago is now in full bloom on radio, television and throughout the tapestry of our culture. If it were not for the effectiveness of a handful of conservative watchdog organizations, such as American Family Association (www.AFA.net), today there would be even more cultural damage.

Tim Wildmon, President of AFA, recently shared with us his concern that our children today may be growing up in a world in which there no longer exists the Christian benchmarks of right versus wrong, benchmarks that generations of Americans had previously embraced as traditional American values.

The question has to be considered. *Do we even care anymore what becomes of our culture?* It takes serious money to maintain the momentum of cultural decay that exists in our present world, and by paying attention to how we invest our money, we *can* stem that tide. But my concern is that since the *act* of investing with values must first be preceded by the conviction to hold tight to what is right, I sincerely wonder if we still have the fundamental interest to do so.

Consider this allegory that has been made popular by George Barna in his book, *The Frog and the Kettle,* and see if it doesn't fit our present situation. How do you boil a frog? Very, very slowly. So slowly, in fact, that it never realizes the temperature is creeping up until it is too late.

In 2006, I can assure you that we in the United States are seeping in a very warm caldron. In fact, the temperature is almost to the boiling point. What we are engaged in is nothing short of a literal war for the soul of this country. And if we do not win this war, future generations will be left to fend for themselves in a world where up has become down and down has become up. Because whoever wins *this* war, as in all victories throughout history, will then establish the *new truths upon which future generations derive their cultural, political, and religious pathways.*

Listen to conversations going on at any time in a Starbucks. Sit in on any number of college liberal arts lectures. Read popular periodicals such as *GQ, Esquire, Madamoiselle, Cosmopolitan,* or *People Magazine.* Watch MTV, VH1, the Logo Network, *Will & Grace,* or any number of prime-time TV shows. Listen to any number of church sermons, or political speeches, and you *will* hear evidences of these *new truths,* including:

- There is no value in maintaining the nuclear family. To each his or her own.
- What is so wrong with gay marriage? Marriage is all about love and relationship.

- Why not offer on-demand porn on cell phones? Pursuing personal gratification in all forms is the ultimate life goal.
- The Founding Fathers believed in freedom from religion and gave us a Constitution which promotes our right to do as we please.
- No God, or state law, or parent, or husband, or boyfriend should have a right to tell a woman, or girl, whether she may have an abortion, because that is a right protected by federal law, just as the Founding Fathers intended.

Put another way, Will Rogers said that the problem in America isn't so much what people don't know; the problem is what people think they know that just ain't so. If we allow those people who don't know the foundational truth, and *don't want* to know it, to write our new history, from where shall future generations find their right bearings?

Example: The Civil War

Forgive me for taking you on a somewhat long digression at this point, but I believe that an historical example will help illustrate how great the impact will be if we lose this present cultural war. To help you understand the impact of how historical perspective is secured, can you imagine how history would read today had England won in 1776? Instead of George Washington, John Adams, Thomas Jefferson, and the rest of our Founding Fathers being presented in glowing terms as we know them today, those rebels would likely have been hanged for treason (each had death warrants issued by the British government). That is how our textbooks would read today, since we would still be loyal British citizens.

If you think that is far-fetched, consider what actually did happen in America in 1861–1865. Today, few Americans understand what truly occurred in the American Civil War, or the War Between the States. The predominant history books only tell one side, that which is today politically correct. We are told that the righteous northern states, led by a champion of anti-slavery, put down a rebellion of states trying desperately to continue slavery. This understanding of what really happened is a classic example of *whoever wins the war gets to write the history.*

Being born outside of Chicago in northern Indiana, and with all of my relatives on both sides of the family living in that area, I learned about the Civil War from a northern perspective. Throughout my life, everything I read in my school textbooks, saw on television, or read in the media was consistent with my understanding of events. Then in 1987, while living in Tennessee, I visited a museum located on the place where the Battle of Franklin had been fought on November 30, 1864. What I saw there stunned me: blood-soaked wooden floors where surgeons had amputated wounded soldiers' arms and legs, photographs of malnourished and shoeless sixteen-year-old Confederate soldiers fighting alongside their grandfathers.

This was the place where it had actually happened. I was so troubled, and my paradigm of that war was so shaken, that I just had to learn more. I began accumulating a small library of historical books, memoirs of soldiers, Pulitzer-Prize winning biographies of leaders, as well as magazines on the subject. What soon emerged was a history of that period far different from the one that appears today in our politically correct culture. For example, my history never taught me that:

- There were tens of thousands of African-American soldiers in the Confederate Army, many of whom fought valiantly.[6]

- The Emancipation Proclamation did not precede the war, but actually came after two years of war and was intended only for political gain. It specifically did not apply to any states that were not "currently in rebellion," meaning that all slaves held in northern (Union) states were NOT freed.

- The entire fortifications of the Union Army, erected in 1862 in Nashville, were built with forced black labor, by either slaves or runaway slaves, and it is estimated that 300–800 workers died during construction.[7]

- The Union so obviously recognized that the war had so little to do with slavery, and so much to do with the Constitutional struggle of states' rights versus a much more powerful federal government, that Ulysses S. Grant said, "If I thought this war was to abolish slavery, I would resign my commission and offer my sword to the other side." Grant held slaves until the 13th Amendment was ratified after the war.[8]

- Slave trading had already been outlawed by most southern states by the time of the war, and less than 5% of southerners owned slaves.[9]

- The Union Army regularly disregarded the accepted military code of conduct, at times using both civilian and military southerners as "human shields." In at least one case, it authorized rape on a grand scale, and utterly destroyed entire cities, including churches, schools, homes, and hospitals.[10]

- This same great Union Army that was supposedly sent south to free the black man was then redirected westward, where it was used to destroy the entire Indian race. Same generals, same cannons, same government.

The point is not that one side was entirely right and one side was entirely wrong. Rather, my point is that today, some 145 years later, *only one side is even told*, and that is the one that the *victors* tell. To find the historical facts I cite above and thousands of others equally as shocking and illuminating, you have to do a primary record search of memoirs, biographies, and war records at the Library of Congress. The history books that our generation studied, and the books our children are studying now, do not provide a balanced and accurate portrayal of a war that many historians now believe was unnecessary, beyond horrible, and which forever changed the power of American federal government in a way that our founding fathers desperately tried to keep from ever occurring.[11]

In another country and a later time, the same phenomenon held true. When the Bolsheviks gained control of Russia in October 1917 and formed the Union of Soviet Socialist Republics, they completely changed the history books. For the next 74 years, children were taught a history of the world that was full of lies, distortions, and half truths.

Can you imagine how history would read today had Hitler succeeded?

Values in Today's Culture

Now, in our present time, the powerful Internet search engine Google has decided to partner with the communist government of China in censoring their citizens from reading anything about faith in God, the Christian religion, anything that is pro-democracy or liberty, and, of course, a twisted version of the truth of what actually happened in 1989 in Tiananmen Square. Can you imagine putting the word *Christian* in your "search" box and have nothing come up? And then, unknowingly, sending a "cookie" back to the oppressive government informing them of your anti-government behavior?

It is with the precedent of human history that I ask, What will future generations of Americans read about *their* history? What culture will we leave for our offspring? What will be born out of the cultural war that we are engaged in today? The stakes could not be higher, because if we don't win this war, history tells us that our children's children will have lost their historical Judeo-Christian cultural anchor. A quick look around the world we live in today provides all the evidence needed to verify that we are, in fact, on a slippery slope.

My wife, Libby, and I finally gave in and bought a DVD player with our new car. We had been concerned that it might be too much of the focus of the kids every time they got in "Mom's taxi." On the other hand, the hair pulling, biting, name calling, and screeching that sometimes occurs when four siblings, ages 3–9, are together in the small quarters of a vehicle can be a real safety hazard for the driver. Having thus justified the DVD player for the new van, Libby and I purchased a number of old television reruns and new movies for the kids to watch. To our amazement and relief, the kids' favorites turned out to be none other than *F Troop, Gilligan's Island, Petticoat Junction,* and *Leave It to Beaver.* In this

day and age of senseless violence and gratuitous sex in virtually all programming, listening to those replays from the past just plain feels good!

Today, instead of *F Troop* and *Gilligan's Island*, two of the most popular prime-time shows on television are *Sex in the City* and *Desperate
Housewives*. Their audiences of predominantly women are huge, and the
shows have influenced our entire culture. *Sex in the City* is about four
women in their never-ending rush to find the next hedonistic pleasure,
which generally involves recreational sex. *Desperate Housewives* is more
of a spoof, but still portrays the objective of life as a continuous attempt
at pleasing self, especially with sex. No matter that one of the starlet's sex
toys is an underage boy. Is this what will be playing in the next generation of "Mom's taxis" for children to watch?

Alan Bostick, a journalist writing in our local paper about the historical impact of the gay cowboy movie *Brokeback Mountain*, asked the
question, "Can one film help change the course of American social history?"

"Yes," answers David Taylor, owner of a nightclub and rank-
ing member of the radical gay political organization Human Rights
Campaign. "The more people that have exposure to gay and lesbian
people, the more they tend to accept them into the greater society," Mr.
Taylor says.[12]

Let me end this section with an example of the how the *new truth*
seeds itself into the fabric of our culture when there is too little concern for *foundational truth*. The University of California at Los Angeles
(UCLA), a bellweather of cultural evolution, has recently changed its
history curriculum to include a history of the Civil War as seen by some
of its important constituents, including a history of the Civil War from
the point of view of lesbians.[13]

Chapter 34

The Feminization of Our Christian Culture

This slow but continuous erosion of values in our culture is evident everywhere, and is generally pointed out by our Christian community—that is, with one conspicuous exception. I am continuously stunned at the lack of any outcry by our pastors, teachers, authors, and even moms and dads at what current culture is passing off to women and girls as fun, harmless, and normal. The effects are anything but harmless, as new statistics reveal. Yet this culture's influence is everywhere and almost entirely unchecked.

For example, while waiting in line at the local grocery store, shoppers' eyes—including those of my young daughters—naturally roam the magazine racks located at the checkout counter. Without exception, many of the women's magazines feature blatant elements of soft porn, including suggested techniques for enjoying casual sex, at least one headline about sex toys, and articles on "getting the next guy." Recently, at the checkout counter at a Kroger grocery store, the cover of *Cosmopolitan* (Feb. 2006) was positioned just where the shopper's eyes could read:

- How To Snag Any Man You Want
- Letting Go In Bed

- 60 Sex Skills
- Never Lose Your Orgasm Again
- 10 Times It's OK To Be A Bitch

Now, let me assure you that I believe God made us to be very sexual beings, and, if anything, I think there is not enough emphasis on good sex, intimacy, and even partying between a husband and wife. In fact, I keep trying to get Libby to join me in teaching a class on that subject. We'll title it, "Why Stop Enjoying Your Spouse Just Because You Got Married?"

The other night we were at one of our favorite "date night" locales, having great conversation, laughing, and enjoying ourselves. I had earlier noticed that there were three guys sitting together not far from us. When they got up to leave, one of them paused as he passed by our chairs and said, "I just have to tell you something. You guys seem to be a great couple. How long have you been married?"

Libby replied with a beautiful smile, "Eight years." With that, he shook his head and put on his coat and said, "I just want to congratulate you. It is really nice to see two married people having so much fun together."

But *husband and wife* is not the idea behind any of the magazines at the grocery store checkout counter. Instead of husband or wife, reference is made to the all-inclusive term *partner*. And that term is nothing less than poison.

What used to be considered seamy and inappropriate even in private is now an accepted and even promoted part of our culture. It's not enough that *Cosmopolitan* zeros in on promoting hedonism for adult women: now there's *CosmoGIRL!* so that our young daughters can get an early start.

What is so sad is that all of this has happened while the Christian community has given the phenomenon not even a glance. A couple of years ago, I met with a group of about six people who represented a national Christian women's group and a huge Christian book publisher. We were discussing the idea of values-based investing and how well that message resonated with the men of Promise Keepers. The question for our meeting was whether the idea of values-based investing would simi-larly fit with the message to women. Finally, one of the men spoke up and said, "I don't think it will fit. Promise Keepers is all about telling men how they can do better. Our message is about how women need to hear that they are already good enough."

I couldn't believe my ears! I thought Jesus had to suffer and die on the cross to redeem ALL people of both genders, specifically because none of us can ever be, on our own, "good enough." No doubt, the statement was made to emphasize what he saw as an endemic lack of self-esteem among women. As well-intentioned as his motives might have been, I fear that with the focus on the well-being of the person and not on the redemptive power of Christ, it becomes a very small step to then justify the pursuit of self-gratification, carnal pleasure and all of the other sinful distractions that marginalize our life without Christ.

Are shows like *Sex in the City*, women's magazines that promote recreational sex, and new attitudes about relationships just fun and harmless? No, they are not. And the evidence is mounting. Consider this startling report by the National Center for Health Statistics, released on September 15, 2005:

> "The report . . . offers one more sign that young women are more sexually confident than they used to be."

It went on to say that "slightly *more girls* than boys have had inter-course before age 20." And finally, "the same proportion of high school girls and boys have had sex only one time with a particular person or have relationships with others that they are not romantically involved with."

"This is a point of major social transition," James Wagoner, President of Advocates for Youth, a Washington-based reproductive health orga-nization said. "The data are now coming out and roiling the idea that boys are the hunters and young girls are the prey. It absolutely defies the stereotype."

This report, and others released within the last year, also shows that as many as 50% of teens have had oral sex, with the percentage for giving and receiving the same between both boys and girls. The reports' find-

ings conclude that oral sex is not considered in the same intimate sexual
context as intercourse by teens.

Finally, a recent report from the Center For Disease Control (CDC)
found that although same-sex experimentation has been steady for boys
and men at about 6%, it has risen dramatically in girls and women, particularly in the late teens and 20s, to a new high of 14%.

To add to this historic of change in sexual mores, a major *USA Today*
article recently explored the phenomenon of the dramatic rise of female
teachers sexually preying on their young male students. The day I wrote
this, I took a break for supper and opened up the local newspaper to find
the following feature article:

> FRANKLIN, TN—A 37-year-old woman who admitted to having
> sex with the 16-year-old son of friends was sentenced yesterday
> to 117 days in jail and a year of probation.
>
> Her case, experts say, is part of a rising trend of women being
> charged with and convicted of statutory rape. The sentence was
> reached as an agreement between Williamson County prosecu-
> tors and Gwendolyn "Lea" Stevens, who pleaded guilty in May
> to statutory rape and drug charges in a case involving a boy who
> had turned 16 just two days before.
>
> "She felt it was in her best interest to accept this agreement
> and is glad it's over," said Mark Puryear, Stevens' lawyer. "She's
> remorseful it happened."
>
> Donna Moore, a psychologist and coordinator of sex
> offender services at the behavioral health clinic Centerstone,
> conducted a psychosexual evaluation of Stevens and testified at
> a hearing in December. Moore has treated sex offenders since
> 1993 and said she has seen an increase in cases of women having
> sex with teenage boys.
>
> The increase is small, Moore said, "because there were so
> few females prosecuted before. The difficulty is in the perception
> society has with cases like this." Moore went on to say, "Women
> tend to get lighter sentences and do not get the same treatment
> as male offenders."

Last August, Pamela Rogers, a former Warren County elementary school teacher and coach, was sentenced to nine months in jail for having sex with a 13-year-old boy. The then–28-year-old admitted guilt on four counts of sexual battery by an authority figure.

The Spiritual Nurture of Women and Girls

I am the father of three beautiful young girls with whom I am madly in love. I am sickened at what I see being paraded before them as harmless and "just fun," on television, in music, in magazines, and in fashion. I am also sick at how Christian culture is absolutely silent on this critically important cultural phenomenon. Instead, stuck with an outdated gender stereotype and infected by the influx of feminism, churches and ministry continue their age-old focus on the much more socially acceptable crusade against the shortcomings of boys and men. Promise Keepers does a superb job of convincing men and helping them find strength, self-worth, and direction in the person of Jesus Christ. You can be sure that my son and I will be at Promise Keepers when he reaches an appropriate age! But where will I take my girls? Who will help Libby and me hold them accountable and give them conviction that develops character and self-worth in Christ?

As a father, I take my responsibility of spiritual leadership profoundly seriously. My now ten-year-old daughter, Ruby, who is very bright and full of the Holy Spirit, was recently wrestling with a particularly tough issue. I wanted to find the right time and way to let her know that she is not alone in this struggle, that God has placed me in the family to be the spiritual head of the household, and that I take that responsibility with extreme seriousness and humility.

One night, I was in her room and we were both on her floor petting our dog Betty, who is part beagle, part basset, and—in my opinion—a lot of pig. We were talking about her day, and I thought this might be a good time to have that more serious conversation.

"Hey, Ruby," I said, letting her know I was changing the subject. "You know, about that problem you are really concerned with? Let me tell you something that I want you to never forget. God has made me the spiritual head of this household. He expects me to deliver to Him a family that loves Him. The way I look at it, there are three primary places where that nurturing best takes place: here at home, at church, and at school. I will never, ever allow any one of those to be taken away from you. That is my responsibility and I have to answer to God one day for that. Do you understand what I mean?" I asked.

Ruby looked at me with a very intense countenance, and eyes that revealed a lot going on inside her pretty little head. Still, I wanted to really drive home the point that the battle is my responsibility, as her father.

"Do you remember that scene in the movie *The Chronicles of Narnia: The Lion, the Witch and the Wardrobe*, where the White Witch (Satan) leaves Aslan (God) after meeting him in his tent? Just before she is carried away by her guards, she turns to Aslan and says, 'How do I know that you'll keep your word?'" Ruby nodded that she remembered. "Do you remember what happened next? The lion Aslan roared so loud at her that the whole earth shook, and the witch and her guards quickly scampered away. Well, one day, I am going to stand in front of that lion and I don't want to hear his thunderous roar exclaiming, 'Why didn't you take spiritual care of the family that I gave to you?'" As I mouthed those words, I tried to sound like a roaring lion. Ruby literally fell back as I did this. She got the point. Her eyes sparkled, she smiled broadly, and she looked as if a thousand-pound weight had been lifted from her shoulders.

God will hold every father accountable for his spiritual leadership. What an incredibly joyous burden that is! And that job is made so much more joyous when there is the presence of a Christ-centered, loving, supportive wife. What a difference she can make with her support!

Yet there remains the head-in-the-sand Christian community which defies both Scripture and current American culture. A couple of Sundays ago, I almost fell out of my pew at the conspicuous omission I heard from a pastor preaching the sermon. He was challenging us to higher ground, better vessels for God's glory. He then went into a dramatic application of this principle everywhere he thought it applied. Men were to be better husbands, children were to honor their parents, friends were to be sacrificial in their love for one another, and so on. The only constituent group he passed over was . . . you guessed it, women.

This "double standard", of course, began years ago and continues unchallenged today in the secular media. Recently, Dr. James Dobson of Focus on the Family presented evidence of how far reaching the feminization of our culture has become. In a recent online column for its Focus On Your Child web page[14], the question of the day was,

"Is Your Son Glad to Be a Boy?"

The article went on to point out how the mass media portrays men:

1. "Disrespect for men pervades the entertainment industry, including many television commercials. One formula involves a beautiful woman (or a bevy of them) who is intelligent, sexy, admirable, and self-assured. She encounters a slob of a man, usually in a bar, who is braggadocio, ignorant, balding, and overweight. The 'stupid guy', as I will call him, quickly disgraces himself on screen, at which point the woman sneers or walks away." Furthermore, "the polarity of the stupid guy ads is *never* reversed."

2. "In Hollywood, traditional masculine roles 'gave way in the seventies and eighties to the man-hating diatribes in *Thelma and Louise* and *Nine to Five*' and 'to aggressive and masculine women such as those depicted in *Charlie's Angels* or the latest remake of *Joan of Arc.* . . .' Maleness in such movies is almost always depicted in subservient and weak roles."

3. "Television sitcoms also blast away at traditional masculinity, much like a wrecking ball crashing into a building. After enough direct hits, the structure begins to crumble. There is not a single example, as I write, of a healthy family depicted on network programming that includes a masculine guy who loves his kids and is respected by his wife. None!"

4. "We also see examples of the 'men are fools' idea expressed in contemporary greeting cards. Although it is politically incorrect

to ridicule women, homosexuals, or minorities, white male bashing—at least the heterosexual variety—is fair game. Visit a Hallmark store or other retail outlet sometime and you'll notice it has become a very lucrative business. Women purchase these humiliating cards by the millions. It is interesting, however, that cards intended for sale to men do not carry the same tone. Their messages are typically gentle and loving toward wives or sweethearts. The difference … is striking."

5. Other examples of man-bashing in our culture include:

- the textbooks for university women's study programs
- "the feminization of the workplace" (Dr. Tim Irwin, business consultant)
- the anti-masculine agenda in public schools
- the prevalence of sexual harassment charges for innocent remarks
- the movement to remove urinals and force men to sit down while urinating
- the attacks by homosexual activists against the Boy Scouts of America
- the gender bias of the Take Our Daughters to Work Day initiative.

It is profoundly sad that the Christian community has simply slept while this snake of feminism has nibbled away at vulnerable soft tissue with its potent venom. In one of the most glaring examples of the feminization of the Christian culture imaginable, I was horrified to hear what happened to a good friend of mine, someone whom I have been blessed to receive Christian instruction from, and who has been a phenomenally successful Sunday School teacher. Apparently, he was publicly rebuked and humiliated in front of his church for his part of what was a strained marriage. John had struggled with his marriage for years. His wife and he had not been intimate in any sense for some time. His wife found all the fulfillment that she needed in her work at church, and in relationship with her female friends. John and his wife finally went to counseling to try to reconcile. He repented for his part in the estrangement, including at a private meeting with the elders of his church. She did not. Instead, she wanted nothing more to do with the marriage and even quit the counseling. John was subsequently served with divorce papers.

So, how did the local church help this struggling couple? Unimaginably, their church not only *accepted the wife divorcing her husband*, but then in one of the worst examples of church authority gone awry, it actually publicly rebuked the husband! That's right. During a Sunday morning worship service, right after the children's choir sang, and with the wife sitting comfortably in her pew among her friends, the pastor launched into "church discipline" that needed to be applied toward John. And all this happened not at some tiny church hidden back in the remote mountains of Appalachia, but rather at one of the largest churches in Indianapolis.

I was having dinner with a few Christian businessmen and we were discussing my book, and this incident in particular. One of the men said, "Hey, that's nothing. In my church there have been three wives who have divorced their husbands for what they called 'emotional abandonment'."

Much of the Church, I fear, has become infected with a combination of feminism and considerably outdated gender stereotypes. Again, another example of what can happen when the other side wins the war and *new truths* replace foundational truths.

In Ephesians, does the Apostle <u>Paul</u> write that "... husbands are to love their wives, provide for them, give them security and help their self-esteem, and above all, make them feel good?" Is there any evidence to suggest that Peter, or James, or John curtailed their preaching in order to make their wives happier?

Obviously, nothing could be farther from the truth. Instead, Paul takes the issue of spousal love much, much higher and directs that husbands are to love their wives, *just as Christ loves His church*, but—and this is the point that our culture is missing today—not for the wives' subjective, emotional, carnal pleasure! Rather, "to make her holy, cleansing by the washing with water through the word, and to present her to himself as a radiant church, without stain, or wrinkle, or any other blemish, but holy and blameless."

In other words, the end point to the love that a husband is to show his wife is her holiness and purity in God's eyes! How different this is than the truncated, out-of-context admonishment so often heard today which implies that the objective of loving a wife is only for *her happiness.* What a terrible, ungodly, and destructive distortion.

There is no greater job that I can have as a husband and father than the incredible honor of helping my wife (and children) be that "holy" gift to God, a part of his "radiant church." It is with profound humility and joy that I gratefully accept this responsibility given to me as head of the household. *And I know that I will be held accountable, by God Almighty, for my performance.*

Fallout in the Church

The symptoms of the fallout from this feminization of the Christian culture are measurable and even staggering. According to reports on www.churchformen.com,

- More than 90% of men believe in God, and five out of six call themselves Christians. But only two out of six attend church on a given Sunday.
- Relatively few churches are able to establish or maintain a vibrant men's ministry.
- The typical U.S. church draws an adult crowd that is 61% female and 39% male.
- Midweek activities often draw 70–80% female participation.

On the back of a Promise Keepers' brochure titled, "Where Are the Men?" are two important questions:

1. What is it about modern Christianity that is driving men away?
2. Jesus was a magnet for men, but our churches repel them. What has changed?

The same brochure goes on to say,

"Churches around the world are short of men. No other major religion suffers such a large, chronic shortage of males. . . . Jesus had no trouble captivating men. Fishermen dropped their nets full of fish to follow Him. . . ."

Finally, the fallout does not only affect men. God knows that both men and women are sinners, equally convicted and equally in need of the redemptive power of Jesus Christ and the healing balm of the Holy Spirit. So imagine how alienated and frustrated it is to a woman who—like her husband—is dealing with her own sin, whether that be past or present, and manifested as lust, adultery, greed, envy, pride, jealousy, or any other abomination to God and impediment to spiritual peace and blessing. Where can a woman go for spiritual help, accountability, and direction if the presumption of her church is that women are not really sinners?

My wife has experienced this very phenomenon, having her own real issues to work through. She found that the various women's groups she explored spent more time complaining about their husbands than dealing with the raw and present pain of their own members. Recently, I was talking about this phenomenon with a good friend of mine, a fellow entrepreneur and a man of great passion for Christ. When I mentioned that my wife simply cannot find the spiritual sustenance that she needs (as a fellow sinner and child of God) from any women's groups, I was surprised at how quickly and abruptly he said, "Add my wife to that list, too." In fact, he went on to say that he and his wife are close friends with three other couples, and each of the wives has expressed the same frustration.

Let me end this subject with a comment from my wife, Libby, who, from time to time, has been exasperated in her attempts to find intimate spiritual sustenance and accountability within the church.

"I long for a safe, soft place to land among female friends and fellow Christians who recognize me without my makeup and don't task me to 'bring the juiceboxes.' Rather, I long for women

who also care so much for my own salvation that they are willing to risk asking, 'How's it really going?' and then listen to my
answer and challenge me with 'Okay, let's talk about your sin.'
The image of an untouchable, asexual, smiling, patient, and
sweet 'Stepford Sister' would not survive a mile in my mini-
van. Sometimes my throat actually hurts from yelling above the
din of four young, healthy, and noisy children competing for my
attention on the ride home after school. Our house is in con-
stant disarray, there's no milk in the fridge and again, I can't find
my keys (or cell phone).

"Although the group study situations I have found may
include accepting our shortcomings (codeword for sins), very
little accountability, if any, exists. Instead the agenda tends
toward blaming others, often husbands, for whatever painful
experience is the topic of discussion (a fight that morning, no
money in the account, little help with the household/kids, etc.).
It is a common theme to discuss the husband who is: absent,
Type A, insensitive, emotionally unavailable, critical, at the
office, distracted, etc. Now, I am well aware we can all present
a scenario to appear pretty much how we want to be perceived,
but I am disappointed that this game of good wife/bad husband
or 'blame the spouse' is not only accepted, but perpetuated. It is
critically important to recognize that we, remaining unaccount-
able and therefore unforgiven and unchanged, also remain in
our sin. So this idea that somehow another is responsible for
our sinful behavior (or response) actually keeps us in that sin,
by preventing honest introspection, confession, and subsequent
behavior change.

"My desire is not for a group wherein the participants pull
up a chair every meeting to 'dump their trucks' and collectively
despair over their misfortunes. On the contrary, I seek a group
where we are encouraged to embrace our (forgiven!) pasts, sinful
as they may be, and use our own experiences and empathy to
reach out to those who are hurting—and make no mistake,
we are all hurting—and in need of the balm of Jesus Christ's

redemptive grace and the love of the body of Christ (that's us). We are not only our pasts and our mistakes, but a composite of all, bad and good, that brought us to this place. As a precious friend said during prayer, 'It is all level ground at the base of the cross.' This is true, but not because we are all level! Let us admire God's awesome tapestry with its rich texture of knots and tangles and indescribable colors that represent our flaw-filled and forgiven lives. This is what I long for, but this can never be so long as there is a presumption in the church that when it comes to the Christian woman, there really is no sin."

There are currently two separate and distinct battles of historic proportion raging involving our precious Christian faith. Both battles have profound and lasting implications for our church and our country. One of the battles is being fought *within the church* over the truth and relevance of the message of Jesus Christ. This chapter is indicative of this conflict. More comprehensive and empirical evidence is masterfully researched and presented by the acclaimed survey research scientist George Barna in his seminal book, *Revolution.* I strongly encourage every Christian to read this important treatise on the historic change that is occurring in American Christendom.

The other battle is being waged predominantly outside the church, in corporate America. However, its impact on the effectiveness and integrity of the church cannot be overstated. In my opinion, it is only because we have paid so little attention to the battle *outside* the church that we now find ourselves engaged in the battle *within* the church. In the seminar titled "Lead Like Jesus," Bishop George McKinney, Ph.D., of the California Graduate School of Theology, articulates a crisp message on this subject. He eloquently styles the impact of the moral decay of the outside culture on our church today with the phrase, "*worldly stinkin' thinkin'.*"

We are stewards of the money God has given us to manage and invest. Unfortunately, we only considered investment performance and turned a blind eye to who was using our money. We could have eliminated funding to the pornography industry, to Planned Parenthood, and to the politicians and political action committees that advocate abortion on demand. We could have sent a weighty message to the media who fill our broadcasts and periodicals with their soft porn, while advancing the political agenda of the gay and lesbian community. We could have stopped the advance of this *worldly stinkin' thinkin'* when it first appeared. Unfortunately, since we were not good stewards, the losses we have suffered in the war for secular America have now evolved into a malignant mass that impacts the very essence of our beloved church.

It is time we said, "Enough!" It is time we took control of the stewardship of our money, pulling it out of those stocks, bonds, mutual funds, and retirement plans that invest in the moral decay of our culture. We must re-direct our money on loan from God toward those companies that reflect the values of the steward who is entrusted with its management.

Chapter 35

The New (Gay) Economy[15]

This chapter of *Money on Loan from God* will help you understand how important it is that the money you invest be done in accordance with your values. Why is that important? Because, as I stated earlier, it is really not *your* money. It is God's. We are just the managers—on behalf of God. And Scripture makes it clear that He will hold us accountable for our stewardship of His resources. God and the application of all of His resources are about perfecting His creation. To the extent that we become lazy and allow our history, politics, and culture to stray from truth and God's purposes, we no longer honor God in our communal lives.

Chapter 33 dealt with how those that win the war get the privilege of writing history, and how rancid that history might be if we lose this real and current cultural war. Chapter 34 dealt with the feminization of the Christian culture. This phenomenon has occurred precisely because we paid too little attention to the war for America's secular soul, to the point where its effect is now manifest in our churches. Now let me show you an even clearer example of where moral decay has become institutionalized, and show you how our own money has been used to make this happen.

It is often said, by those who do not truly understand, that there is no difference between the sin of homosexuality and any other sin. On one level—sin versus sin—that is absolutely true. However, on another level—the attempt at institutionalizing the sin as an accepted part of our cultural, political, and economic fabric, the differences could not be more significant. Let me give you an example.

Some people are just plain *greedy*. I don't know if they are born that way, or if they learn that behavior. Either way, it sure seems to be a growing trend.

You see it in our culture, our economy, and our politics. Hollywood glorifies it with movies, including the hit movie *Wall Street* in which Michael Douglas infamously said "Greed is Right. Greed is Good." You see it in the way drivers will not hesitate to cut you off on the interstate, or in the soccer mom who forces her child into the best position on the team. You see it in politics, where so many candidates are greedy for power. Greed is ubiquitous, and though always a part of human nature, it has recently taken on a new dimension: institutionalization.

Greed has become a movement with an agenda that has already succeeded in forever changing American culture and economics. Propped up by philanthropy, hiring practices, and policies of most of the Fortune 500 corporations, there is now an aggressive attempt by the greed community to force traditional America to accept it as simply another alternative lifestyle. They have already succeeded in our economy, and are making strong inroads into our politics, educational systems, and—yes—even the Christian Church.

So what? Greed is just another sin, and we all sin. Right? Why not accept peaceful coexistence, if not open integration, between the two Americas?

Okay, far enough. Forgive me for my allegory of what might appear to be nothing more than intellectual recreation. It is not. My purpose is to objectify the issue in order to appropriately identify its fundamental components. This is a critical increment in the scientific method applied to theological thinking. Without this process, we are left to our own interpretations (that's scary!). Let me give you an example.

I have a wonderful friend who is always challenging me with some theological/intellectual question such as, "Can God build a rock so heavy that he can't lift it?" One day, I was walking into my favorite grocery store when I crossed her path. She almost gasped when she saw me, because she had a question that had been on her mind for some time that she wanted to ask me. I forget what the question was, but I remember that I paused only about a nanosecond before I answered. She stood in bewilderment at the juxtaposition between the intellectual trauma she had endured incubating the question, and the speed and confidence with which I delivered a response. That spawned a more poignant question from her: "How can you be so certain? How can you *know?*"

I explained to her that by dissolving every question down to its ultimate fundamentals, most every question can be fairly easily answered. It's all about principle. The problem today, according to George Barna in his book, *Revolution,* is that less than 10% of born-again believers have a biblical, absolute, values-based worldview from which to make principle-driven choices. This is precisely why the new Truth Project, offered by Dr. Del Tachett with *Focus on the Family,* is so important. More information can be found at www.thetruthproject.org.

For example: What is it to be gay or lesbian? An ethnicity? No. A gender? No. Being gay is not about any outward identifiable characteristic, but rather about a *behavior.* And what is that behavior? *A sexual relationship between two members of the same gender.*

On the question of whether or not the act of being gay is sinful, there really is no intelligent debate. Whereas there are numerous references to homosexuality as sin throughout both the Old and New Testaments, sometimes including extreme adverse consequences, both immediate and eternal, from God, there is not one reference to that behavior that does not treat it as being a sin.

Is It Personal, Or Institutional?

If being gay (i.e., sinful) ended at this point, it would simply be one more personal human sin. Unfortunately, today that is only the beginning. Unlike virtually every other sin one can think of (murder, theft, incest, lying, etc.), the gay community has an agenda with historic political, cultural, and economic ramifications. I don't care about what someone does behind closed doors. That's a *personal* issue between them and God. But I care a great deal about an attempt to *institutionalize* a sin as part of the fabric of my country.

Picture watching *The Simpsons* with your children when one of the characters "comes out" as gay or lesbian. Stay tuned—that is exactly what we are told will happen this season.[16] Here are more examples:

- A Volvo commercial showing a gay couple with a baby and a pregnant lesbian with her partner, and the slogan, "*Whether you're starting a family or creating one as you go. . . Volvo. For Life.*"This ad has run in both the print and online media, though not (yet) on television.
- IBM ran a print ad in publications like the same-sex parenting magazine *And Baby* that shows several of its own gay employees, including a pregnant woman.
- Financial services companies such as John Hancock Financial Services, Prudential Financial, Merrill Lynch, Washington Mutual, Chase Home Finance, Citigroup, and JP Morgan Brown Co., a brokerage service of JP Morgan, have taken out ads featuring gay and lesbian couples, developed marketing campaigns specifically directed to that group, and/or provided substantial financial support to gay and lesbian political organizations.
- Subaru sold a total of 89,607 vehicles in the U.S. in 1993 when it began targeting the same-sex segment, according to Tim Bennett, Director of Marketing Programs at Subaru of America. Last year, 186,819 Subarus were sold in this country. "Can I say it helped? Not definitely, but our sales have increased over the last nine years," Bennett said. "Our purchase consideration within that group has risen."[17]

From a purely economic point of view, it's no wonder corporate America is chasing after the gay community. According to the article "The Gay Consumer—How To Tap This Market," appearing in *BCBusiness*, gays and lesbians are more likely to earn higher wages, spend discretionary dollars, and patronize those businesses that show a true effort to be gay friendly.[18]

A major U.S. university-backed study found gay couples reported a household income 60% higher than the U.S. average. Says DeTracy of Buzz Marketing, "The average gay male couple doesn't have kids. There is more income, there is more money to spend on cars and furniture."[19]

My wife and I rented a home in Breckenridge, Colorado, last September to celebrate our anniversary. Imagine my surprise as I plopped myself on the cozy couch, began thumbing through a travel magazine on the coffee table, and saw ads with (obviously) gay men, such as the ones for Wyndham El Conquistador and Atlantis Cruise Lines. Others were more subtle, but included Bridgestone Tires, Delta Airlines, and two women advertising Olivia Travel. I quickly turned back to the cover to see the name of the publication. What should I have expected from a magazine with a name like *Outtraveler?*[20]

The now famous prime-time kiss between Madonna and Christina Aguilera and Britney Spears was just an "event." How about Showtime's popular new lesbian series, *The L Word?* I didn't even know it existed until I was purchasing a Christmas CD last year at a music store in the mall and saw a prominent display of recent episodes available on DVD. *The L Word,* I thought. Hmm. Could be a reference to lesbian. Pink package and all. I did some investigation. Man, am I smart, or what?

Of course, *The L Word,* like *Will & Grace* and *Queer Eye for the Straight Guy* are just examples of the inevitable next step: a series about gays. How about the introduction of an entire broadcasting channel entirely devoted to gays and lesbians? MTV and DirecTV both have plans for exactly such a channel. Now appearing on DirecTV: Logos, the all-gay channel. It's located right next to one of my favorite channels that showcases family-friendly programs.

Lobbying for Legal Advantage

Okay, the economy has gone to gay marketing along with entertainment, too. Surely we can rely on our laws to protect us. You know, the 86% who consider themselves Christians, versus the 4% considered to be gay/lesbian?[21] Not so fast.

Consider the new law just enacted in Illinois with tremendous fanfare and reported by WorldNetDaily on January 22, 2005. The headlines read, "Churches Barred from 'Gay' Discrimination. New Measure Requires Religious Groups To Hire Homosexuals."

State Sen. Carol Ronen, D-Chicago, is on record stating it should be applied to churches, meaning they would not be allowed, for example, to reject a job applicant who practices homosexual behavior.

Ronen said: "If that is their goal, to discriminate against gay people, this law wouldn't allow them to do that. But I don't believe that's what the Catholic Church wants or stands for."

The most insidious example of how far the gay movement has come can be found by logging on to www.HRC.org, the web site for The Human Rights Campaign. This organization is the largest lobbying initiative on behalf of the gay, lesbian, bisexual, and transgender (GLBT) community. What you will find on that site will make the scales fall from your eyes, if they are still there.

- Lists of hundreds of American companies graded on their gay-friendliness. The section "Worklife" also features a report on which companies were downgraded for having made contributions to *Focus on the Family* and the Traditional Values Coalition.
- Information on how to "come out."
- Solicitation for donations to help defeat the Marriage Amendment.
- GLBT resources for your community, your schools, and your workplace.
- Other headings include Domestic Partner Benefits, Sexual Orientation Non-discrimination, Transgender, Laws/Legal Resources, Documenting Discrimination, Finding Employers' Policies, GLBT Marketing.

Obviously, organizations have a right in our free society to promote whatever policies they wish. However, what you need to know,

Mr. and Ms. Christian investor, is that The Human Rights Campaign gets substantial money from corporate America to further their radical agenda. Take a look at their "Sponsors & Foundation Support" page. Contributors who have also agreed to offer domestic partner benefits and mandate employee "diversity" training, and who proudly announce their support of this radical political group, include:

- Volvo
- CitiGroup
- IBM
- Prudential Financial
- Washington Mutual Home Loans
- American Airlines
- Cingular
- Nike

Today, nearly half of Fortune 500 companies offer domestic partner health benefits. But many are going beyond the basics. Of the companies that provide such benefits, 90% cover a domestic partner's dependent children; 60% extend adoption assistance to the domestic partner; and 72% also allow employees to take extended family leave to care for a domestic partner or their dependents.[22]

Said Daryl Herrschaft, who runs the HRC workplace advocacy project, "Companies are changing their policies to support gay, lesbian, bisexual, and transgender employees because it gives them a competitive advantage in recruitment, retention and productivity which translates into a better bottom line."[23]

Hawaii or Bust

I remember going to Hawaii for the first time, years ago, and hearing the captain come on the intercom and announce that we had reached that point on our flight where there was no turning back. If there was a problem, it was on to Hawaii for a solution. So, *where's "Hawaii" on this issue?* Faced with potential discrimination lawsuits, coupled with loss of economic opportunity, should the Christian businessman seek the remedy of reaching out to the gay community, or at least a kind of détente?

I guess that depends on who you are serving, and whether you see your income as yours only, or rather as an integral part of the resources God has given you to manage on his behalf.

Did Jesus eat with prostitutes and scumbags? Yes, he certainly did. From what we know, he did so that he could *teach* them! Please hear this: *Teach* them. Not *be like* them, but *teach* them. Did he distinguish between the sin and the sinner? Yes, he certainly did. Did Jesus do business intentionally with any form of institutionalized sin such as the Jerusalem Mafia, prostitution, or the drug trade? Certainly not!

Let me remind you of the point I tried to make earlier: distinguishing between *personal sin* and the attempt to *institutionalize sin*.

With regard to the former, by all means we should reach out to the gay community! Not because we want to take advantage of their economic prowess, but rather to *minister* to them. This is best done through our churches and ministries, though we, as the Church, are woefully lacking in that regard. This is Jesus' model and command. Remember Jesus and the woman at the well, or the adulteress about to be stoned? That is taking on the personal sinner, separating the person (redeemed) from the sin (condemned).

On the other hand, Jesus gave us a stark, if surprising example of what he thinks of the institutionalization of sin. Remember what he did when he found greedy "money changers" in the temple? He didn't counsel them, or buy from them to win them over. No, he used brute force to overturn their tables and a whip to send them fleeing while he yelled against their crime. Personal sin and institutionalized sin call for different responses.

Where would we be today had Martin Luther not stood alone, and I mean alone, in front of the awesome power of the world and declared—knowing full well the consequence would be his life—that he could not renounce Christ in favor of a corrupt church? Will we, 500 years later, as a community of believers, be any less fervent?

What Will You Risk?

Faced with a gay economy seemingly here to stay (and growing), let me pose as THE question, the title of one of Charles Colson's great books: *How Now Shall We Live?*

There was an exceedingly poignant moment in the movie *Luther* between Luther and Prince Frederick. Luther was stating his position regarding how God's word alone must govern the acts of man. The poor prince was about to jeopardize his entire kingdom, his life, and his place in history in order to give protection to his favorite student, Luther. Seeking anything that might help his cause he asks, "Trust Christ alone *with no compromises?*" At the moment I heard this I burst out laughing at the preposterous notion of hedging your spiritual bet on Christ with earthly compromises. In Frederick's words the question is blatantly absurd, but in practical reality (which Frederick was facing), we do it all the time.

Your money to invest has been given to you by God and therefore it should never benefit from, or help promote, the institutionalization of any sin. Period.

As George Barna, prolific author and survey research scientist, says on page 24 of his seminal book, *Revolution,*

> "Because we own nothing in this life, it is best to wisely invest the resources we manage for the One who is the true owner of all things."

Can You Help Stem the Tide?

Are there steps that you can take to make sure that you are being faithful with your stewardship on this issue? Yes. Begin by cutting the money off. *Care enough to make sure that money you have invested in mutual funds, your retirement plan, and other investments is not being invested in companies whose policies, practices, and philanthropy further the advancement of the institutionalization of same-sex lifestyles.* For this information you will need the help of technology and counsel—both of which are available free. For more information, go to www.RICAonline.com, or call Faith Financial Planners, Inc. at 877–697–9139.

Many investment companies have recognized the need for investment products designed with Christian values in mind. Whether you have variable annuities, a 401(k) plan, 403(b), TSA, mutual funds, or other investments, you now have the awesome privilege of monitoring what values are supported with your money. Remember, it is all simply money on loan from God. Where are you investing *His* money?

Our Fundamental Motivation

Every sinner needs Christ—*now*. Don't you just feel the wellspring of overflowing and unspeakable joy that is your core life source—Christ, the Redeemer, in you? Isn't that what brings so much to your life and makes everything better and worthwhile? Don't you want everyone to have that, including your fellow sinners who happen to be gay? We want them to have the joy, the peace, and the salvation that Christ has given us.

Hate the sin, but love the sinner. Thank God that's what Jesus does. And, ultimately, we are to be "little Christs," carrying His message to his creation. Hate the sin—say NO to anything that helps advance or institutionalize the gay movement. *For it is sin,* and is a part of the force that is set against God's creation.

On the other hand, love the sinner. Take advantage of every opportunity to show Christ's love for someone who is in a gay lifestyle, no less than you would someone who is in any other sin-filled life, like yours and mine. Because until we know *that* love, redemptive love, we are all but walking dead.

Chapter 36

Male, Female, or Other: The Transgender Movement

Just when you thought you had a good grasp of what was causing the decay of our moral fabric, here comes a new one. Interestingly, the transgender movement didn't even exist when I began researching the values-based investing process about ten years ago. On the other hand, once morals are stripped from a society, quite literally anything goes. Why not? Life then becomes a matter of personal preference and imagination. Take, for example, what is now happening in the movement to institutionalize "transgenders."

A *USA Today* article on June 10, 2005, covers the issue with the headline, "When an Employee Switches Gender, What's a Company To Do?" The article begins with a story about David Rosen, who becomes Donna Rose. We are invited to feel sorry for him—I mean her—because he—I mean she—was kicked out of the "football pool," and no one comes by his—I mean her—cubicle anymore to grab a handful of M&M's. David-to-Donna said, "Everyone wanted my M&M's until I transitioned, and then I had to dust them. They kicked me out of the football pool because the guys felt uncomfortable." Imagine that.

The article barely mentions that Dave—now Donna—then got a divorce and now has a son. Good Lord, how grotesque that a little child must grow up in this environment. No one bothers to consider the impact on the lives of the innocent children—you know, those creations of God that He knew before they were even born, given to their parents to be cared for and nurtured and brought back to a redemptive relationship with their Creator. *USA Today* certainly didn't spend any time on how Dave-to-Donna impacted his/her son.

Jesus said, ""Things that cause people to sin are bound to come, but woe to that person through whom they come. It would be better for him to be thrown into the sea with a millstone tied around his neck than for him to cause one of these little ones to sin. So watch yourselves." (Luke 17:1–3). Powerful stuff from the Creator of the universe.

I truly feel sorry for the Dave-to-Donnas, and the Donna-to-Daves. I mean that in the most serious way. The agonizing they must go through, the questions, the issues—most people can't even imagine the profound complexity of it for them. I want to hug them and tell them how much Jesus loves them, regardless of their gender or circumstances. But what I will never, ever do is support the institutionalization of the transgender movement so that it becomes an accepted part of our societal fabric.

The *USA Today* article goes on to point out,

> "Transgender is a broad term that refers to people who don't conform to traditional gender. It includes transsexuals, who transition from male to female, or female to male, as well as people who dress in another gender's clothing."

Do you really think it will all stop there? Already there is a well-financed campaign to institutionalize same-sex marriage. Next will be polygamy, and ultimately bestiality. Why not? Who writes the rules? If it's not going to be God, then I can guarantee you it will be a combination of sin and Satan.

This is not a new problem. In Leviticus 20:6–27, God sets out the punishment for various sins, most of them ending with death. This includes homosexuality, adultery, and bestiality committed by either a woman or a man. Thank God Jesus came to redeem us from such sin and punishment. But never did he change the law, or accept the sin.

To the adulteress that the crowd had assembled to stone, Jesus said, "Go, and sin no more" (John 8:11). The Apostle Paul writes to Timothy and the new churches about times like those we face:

"But mark this: There will be terrible times in the last days. People will be lovers of themselves, lovers of money, boastful, proud, abusive, disobedient to their parents, ungrateful, unholy, without love, unforgiving, slanderous, without self-control, brutal, not lovers of the good, treacherous, rash, conceited, lovers of pleasure rather than God, having a form of godliness, but denying its power. Have nothing to do with them. They are the kind who worm their way into homes and gain control over weak-willed women, who are loaded down with sins and are swayed by all kinds of evil desires, always learning but never able to acknowledge the truth."

2 TIMOTHY 3:1–7

Regardless of whether you or I support the institutionalization of the transgender movement, corporate America is rapidly making up its mind in favor of the transgender political initiative. According to the Human Rights Campaign (HRC.org), the number of major companies that formally ban any restrictions, or questions regarding transgenders, has grown from 1 in 1997, to over 20 in 2004.

"Where is your mother?" the Reverend Tim Kane painfully asked his nine-year-old daughter who was on the phone, crying, 800 miles away.

"She left yesterday with her friend and said that these two men who are dressed up like girls would take care of us," said the sweet young daughter. "Daddy, I'm scared. Can you come and get us?"

This is a true story of a pastor friend of mine who recently died. His wife left him for another woman and although—thank God—he ended up with custody of the children in Tennessee, his wife had their nine-year-old and seven-year-old daughters a few times a year at her home in Ohio. This is madness!

Yet corporate America is following right along with the political agenda of the gay, lesbian, bisexual, and transgender movement, cowered by their threats of economic sanction. Can someone please tell me where the Christian counterbalance is? And the sick part of all of this is that corporate America is funding this movement while we continue to buy their stock in *our IRAs, our mutual funds, and even our church retirement plans!*

Chapter 37

Diagnosis and Solution

So, what can *you* do? For starters, you have to care! Care that our beloved country, the greatest, most free Christian country to ever exist on this planet, is in rapid moral decay, the end of which will consume all that makes it great. Begin thinking about your investment dollars in three-dimensional terms, not just one-dimensional. For example, if you are going to invest toward your retirement, consider not only what investment strategy you'll use to accomplish that objective, but also recognize that others will benefit from your invested dollars. Who are the beneficiaries of the investment you make in your retirement plan, your IRA, your mutual funds, your variable annuity, your stock and bond portfolio? What will those corporations do with the money? Do they deserve your investing God's money in them? Will they reflect your values, or take your money and use it to crusade against them? This is real stuff that goes on with trillions of dollars every day.

Someone once said, "The only thing that needs to happen for evil to prevail is for good people to do nothing." Don't "do nothing." The stakes are too high.

A lot of financial advisors and money managers dismiss the idea of integrating values into investment management as being a challenge too difficult to achieve. Let me point out something that I read recently that puts that kind of lazy thinking into perspective:

"After flying 2.9 billion miles and seven years, NASA's Stardust space capsule parachuted gently to the floor of Utah's high desert yesterday, carrying dust collected nearly two years ago from a comet orbiting the sun beyond Mars." (Article by Guy Gugliotta, *The Washington Post,* January 16, 2006)

Do you realize what you just read? We (in this case NASA specifically) decided that there was a need to acquire actual particles from a comet that was over a billion miles from earth. So we built a space craft and set it off toward that end and it came back seven years later with what we wanted: particles from a comet named "Wild 2."

Now, are you going to really believe that developing an investment portfolio that can attempt to achieve both your financial objectives and reflect your personal core values is *is just too complicated?* Or is it that your financial advisor is lazy, or just doesn't care?

In order to develop a comprehensive, accurate and timely data base of exactly what companies are doing on culturally and morally significant issues, we formed the Research Institute for Corporate Accountability (RICA). Today, RICA data is utilized by money managers, financial advisors, and institutions to help them align their (or their clients') money with their values. The specific issues researched by RICA include:

- Abortion
- Pornography
- The gay, lesbian, bisexual, and transgender political movement
- Gambling
- Tobacco products
- Alcoholic beverages
- Positive values

You, as an investor, have access to this information in many forms. Log on to www.RICAonline.com as a place to start. Your financial advisor can have access, through a state-of-the-art software screening program, to information that will help you see whether your current investments are promoting someone else's values. Your church, school, and foundation can also access this information, so that the money they are given to invest reflects the Provider's (God's) values.

There really is no excuse anymore to not invest your money according to the stewardship principles established by the God who gave it to you in the first place. Whether you own mutual funds, variable annuities, stocks, or bonds, the RICA research can be applied in such a way as to help you reflect your values in the way your money is invested.

For complete information on how you can turn your investment dollars into a reflection of your faith and values while maintaining your attempt at achieving all of your investment goals, log onto www.FAMPonline.com.

Frogs on a Log

By now you may be really concerned about who is using your IRA, mutual funds, college savings money, and retirement plan to advance their values. I certainly hope you are! Now, the question is what are you going to do about it?

Let me give you a little riddle. There were *five* frogs sitting on a log. They were looking at a lily pad a foot away and considering jumping over to it. *Three* of the frogs decided to jump.

How many frogs were left on the log?

No one knows. The difference between *deciding* to do something and actually doing it is substantial.

Now that you have decided that values-based investing is an important element of your financial stewardship, are you going to actually do something about it, or just sit on the log?

Section

TEN

Victory,
At Last!

Chapter 38

The Importance of Faith

As I sat next to her bed, holding her frail hand and listening to the oxygen pump cycle, I looked at my mom's beautiful face. Her eyes were closed, but they were moving in REM sleep. Was she watching a video in her mind's eye, a replay of her childhood in northern Indiana? Maybe seeing her hard-working, quiet father, or her diligent, loyal mother? Maybe she was seeing her two sisters and the brother she loved so much.

During her cancer treatment a few weeks earlier, when she was still able to physically move to a sofa, she would sometimes slip into hallucinations. Always when that happened, the visions she would articulate involved "the children." Whether she was referring to her six children that she cared for so deeply, and which were so much of her life, or rather all of the many children in preschool that she taught as a teacher and day-care director for so many years, we never knew.

Mom loved her family. And she especially loved her husband of 53 years. They were inseparable. They were the quintessential role models. Although I can recall many stormy arguments, they never surrendered to divorce. What a testament! Instead, they practiced what they taught us: Faith. Always faith. God is omnipotent and He is to be trusted to get us through a tough time. Faith.

Only six months earlier I had watched, with joy overflowing, as my mom jumped on the trampoline in my backyard with my children, ages 3, 4, 6, and 9. They had laughed and jumped and yelled and fell and bounced and played. What joy I had felt as I watched that heavenly scene! Now I held my precious mother's bony hand in a death watch. My little mother, always petite, but now so frail I was afraid that she might break just by her labored breathing.

I had buried my first child eight years earlier, a stillborn beautiful, perfect little boy. Nothing I had ever gone through had prepared me for that. His precious little body in that tiny white casket. Nothing in my life had ever hurt so bad, or been so all-consuming. Yet God had given me otherworldly joy in a revelation to sustain and pull me through. God knows his sheep and He cares for them. Know that. In time of need, He will be there for you. That is His solemn promise. He is nothing if He is not both incredibly personal and the fountainhead of love and joy and peace.

Yet, now I was going to have to sit by helplessly as my sweet, warm, loving, little mother, the cherished grandmother of my children, died.

As I sat there in that quiet room, so close to the person who had bore me, the one who had so many times loved me unconditionally as my world fell apart, I wondered if tonight would be the night that she would finally be united with her Father, the true love of her life, the foundation upon which she had built her life and therefore ours.

Suddenly, Mom opened her eyes. With her hand in mine, she turned her head toward me and saw my sad countenance. After a couple of minutes, she whispered, "Don't feel so bad."

Then, after about a minute, she said the last words I would ever hear her say to me. With a twinkle in her drawn eyes, she said, "Enjoy what you have."

Don't feel so bad? What? *Are you kidding?* Here was death right in front of me. My poor father, the strong, intelligent provider, the leader and rock of our family, was in the other room, sobbing on the couch. Are you kidding, Mom? *Don't feel so bad?*

Enjoy what I have? How am I to enjoy *anything?* I am losing a cornerstone of the building that is my life! Fifty years of a continuous deep relationship, some of the most intimate memories of my life. How can I enjoy anything?

It has now been four months since Mom died. Although she was able to read a few chapters of the first draft of this book before she was diagnosed with cancer, she died before I finished. In those four months, I have very often reflected on those last two admonishments that my mom gave to me. Not surprisingly, they are entirely consistent with her faith in her savior Jesus Christ.

"Don't feel so bad," Jesus told his bewildered disciples who were reeling after hearing that He would no longer be with them physically.

> "Do not let your hearts be troubled. Trust in God; trust also in me. In my Father's house are many rooms; if it were not so, I would have told you. And if I go and prepare a place for you, I will come back and take you to be with me that you also may be where I am. You know the way to the place where I am going."

> JOHN 14:2–4

My mom knew where she was going. She had been preparing all her life. There was not a shred of doubt in her. She knew, too, that the Comforter would be with me until I joined her in eternity.

"Enjoy what you have." My mother had watched me go through the trials of life. She knew that what I had in my faith, my wonderful wife, and my beautiful children was worth it all. She knew that there was nothing else that could surpass the bounty that I already had. All I needed to do was simply "enjoy" it.

> "Even though I walk through the valley of the shadow of death, I will fear no evil. For you are with me; your rod and your staff, they comfort me. You prepare a table before me in the presence of my enemies. You anoint my head with oil; my cup overflows. Surely goodness and love will follow me all the days of my life, and I will dwell in the house of the Lord forever."

> PSALM 23:4–6

Mom fought the good fight, and ran her race with faith. I watched as she was carefully placed on a gurney and carried out, never to return to me in the flesh. It was wrenching.

Fight the Good Fight

As a world-class runner for two decades, I suffered through many injuries. None was more painful than the one I sustained when I thought that I could successfully jump a rain-swollen creek. By just touching the tip of a rock that was midway across, I thought I could land successfully on the other side. Though I did, in fact, hit that rock with the appropriate speed and touch of my right foot, I landed not on the sole of my foot, but rather on the left side of my ankle. I tumbled to the ground in excruciating pain. Unlike so many other injuries, the pain associated with torn ligaments does not abate. I was shaking, teeth gritted, all of my body writhing in pain. I finally found a branch within reach and used it as a staff to help me get back home, where I collapsed on my bed in exactly the same pain that I felt the moment my ankle twisted.

So it is with the death of a loved one. The pain does not abate. It does not go away. And yet there is another dimension that we can tap into, and that is our faith: the profound joy that we have in Christ's victory over Satan and his continuous attempts at destroying God's beautiful creation. Ah, what salve that is for the grieving spirit! Thanks be to God, all praise and glory and honor to our Redeemer!

So, fight the good fight. Focus on Christ alone, and let that prism direct all that you do. Yes, by all means, use money wisely, but not in a vacuum. Money is meaningless, or worse, if it is not used for the glory of God. Do all that you can to invest it in a way that nurtures God's creation and keeps it from being used by Satan to destroy all that is good, and all that is hope.

Be strong in your faith and in your convictions. Don't abdicate your responsibility to be vigilant. Don't cede ground in this eternal battle. We are at risk of losing the generational benchmarks that have so timelessly brought every wayward generation back to a godly foundation. My mother and father have been that benchmark for me, and my wife and I will be that for our children. If we are not that, then from whom will the next generation learn standards? MTV?

"Finally, be strong in the Lord and in his mighty power. Put on the full armor of God so that you can take your stand against the devil's schemes. For our struggle is not against flesh and blood, but against the rulers, against the authorities, against the powers of this dark world, and against the spiritual forces of evil in the heavenly realms. Therefore, put on the full armor of God, so that when the day of evil comes, you will be able to stand your ground, and after you have done everything, to stand. Stand firm then with the belt of truth buckled around your waist, with the breastplate of righteousness in place, and with your feet fitted with the readiness that comes from the gospel of peace. In addition to all this, take up the shield of faith, with which you can extinguish all the flaming arrows of the evil one. Take the helmet of salvation and the sword of the Spirit, which is the word of God."

EPHESIANS 6:10–18

Thank you for this opportunity to share with you. My prayer is that you have gleaned something from these pages that will bring you closer to the God of your creation and salvation, and that wherever I might have offended anyone, I be forgiven.

Personal Information Questionnaire

The title of our financial planning process was created to help people arrange their priorities in a way that produces a biblically-based life plan: **Life. Purpose. Plan. Money.**

First, by understanding and appreciating who we are as redeemed children of God, we find our purpose for life. From that context, we are free to joyfully and confidently actualize that purpose by developing a plan. Once we have a plan, we can then go about the business of determining the proper arrangement of financial resources in order to implement and sustain that life plan.

Before you provide the numbers, data, and information that will allow us to help you develop a financial plan, it is critically important that we know what your life plan is all about. In these first pages, please tell us about your plan. There are no right or wrong approaches to this. Anything you choose to tell us about your goals and dreams will be treated with respect, and will help us to better help you realize your life plan.

CHECKLIST

Checklist of information you might need to review in order to complete this form:

- ❑ Insurance contracts—life, health, disability, long term care
- ❑ Group employee booklet
- ❑ Retirement plan statements/projections
- ❑ Investment account statements
- ❑ Most recent tax return
- ❑ Monthly living expenses (budget)

ABOUT THIS FORM

The Personal Information Questionnaire you are about to complete is a very important part of the financial planning process. The accuracy of this report will determine the value of the output—*Money For Life* Financial Plan. However, if you do not know the exact answer to a question, remember that it is more important to make an educated guess and complete this part of the process than it is to delay further action until you are certain—and run the risk that it simply never gets completed.

* Please be assured that the information you provide will be kept in strict confidence.

PERSONAL INFORMATION

	NAMES	BIRTHDATE	SOCIAL SECURITY #	GRADE LEVEL*	RELATIONSHIP & GENDER
Client	_____	_____	_____		_____
Spouse	_____	_____	_____		_____
Children	_____	_____	_____	_____	_____
	_____	_____	_____	_____	_____
	_____	_____	_____	_____	_____

* Use current grade level if within school year. If this time is in between school years, use the grade the child will be starting.

Current Residence _____ Phone _____ # Years _____

_____ Email _____ Fax _____

Client Employer _____ Phone _____ # Years _____

Address _____ Position _____

Spouse Employer _____ Phone _____ # Years _____

Address _____ Position _____

PERSONAL ☒ALUES PROFILE

Personal values are a reflection of an individual's belief system. Who a person votes for, how a person worships, and what parents teach their children are all obvious reflections of a person's values. How a person invests their money, is just as reflective of that same values system.

Below is a list of issues that reflect certain values. You have the opportunity and responsibility to indicate to your financial advisor which values, if any, you wish to be considered in your investment portfolio. By placing a check in the box next to any of the below issues, you are indicating that you would like your advisor to consider that issue when recommending any investment.

❏ ABORTION—This screen considers companies that manufacture or distribute abortion-causing drugs or contraceptives which can function as an abortion agent, hospitals that perform elective abortions and/or health care plans which cover abortions. Other abortion issues considered include corporate contributions to organizations that perform or promote abortions and distributors of contraceptives which can function as an abortion-causing agent.

❏ ALCOHOL—This screen considers alcohol producers and wholesale distributors.

❏ PORNOGRAPHY—This screen considers companies that manufacture pornography in any format and/or operate adult cabarets. Other pornography issues that may cause a company to be excluded include pornography distribution, hosting of pornographic web sites, profiting from the sale of pornographic banner ads, and advertisers in pornographic magazines.

❏ GAMBLING—This screen considers companies that operate casinos, lotteries and/or manufacture commercial gaming equipment.

❏ TOBACCO—This screen considers companies who grow, process and manufacture tobacco products, as well as companies that distribute tobacco products wholesale.

❏ GAY, LESBIAN, BISEXUAL, TRANSGENDER (GLBT) AD☒OCACY—This screen considers companies whose philanthropy, corporate practices, and/or products and services support the advance of the GLBT political agenda. Examples would include companies who provide substantial financial support to radical GLBT political organizations such as GLAAD, or Human Rights Campaign, or which provide employee benefits to homosexual partners of employees when not required to do so by law, or which target advertising specifically to the gay/lesbian media.

OBJECTIXES

RETIREMENT PLANNING

If you retired today, what monthly income would you want? $ _____
                                                                    (in today's dollars)

Age when YOU desire to retire _____

% of maximum Social Security benefits   (i.e. 80%, 100%) or actual benefit you expect _____

Age when SPOUSE desires to retire _____

% of maximum Social Security benefits   (i.e. 80%, 100%) or actual benefit SPOUSE expects _____

If your goals are currently out of reach, what alternatives do you want us to examine?
Retire later? Live on less money? Use a higher rate of return? _____

COLLEGE FUNDING

Would you like to project the cost of any particular college?   Yes ☐ _____

NAME (CHILD OR DEPENDENT)	COST OF ONE YR UNDER-GRAD	YRS UNDER-GRAD	COST OF ONE YR GRAD	YRS GRAD	% INCREASE IN COST	AMOUNT SAVED	RETURN ON AMT. SAVED
	$		$		%	$	%
	$		$		%	$	%
	$		$		%	$	%

Meeting the costs of your children's college education can be among the most substantial expenditures you will ever face. Please enter all amounts in today's dollars.   Our report can illustrate for you the effects of different after-tax rates of return on invested funds. You may enter one or two, or even up to 4 different after-tax rates of return.

_____% _____% _____% _____%

ACCUMULATION GOALS

Do you have any specific accumulation goals? (vacation home, time off for ministry, etc.)

Please list:	GOAL	AMT NEEDED	YRS UNTIL NEEDED	# YRS NEEDED

INCOME & TAX INFORMATION

Use this sheet to enter totals of earned income (such as Salaries, Self-Employment Income) that are NOT related to assets and liabilities. Fill out the annual number in the year column and an inflation percentage (such as 3%). Tell us how many years to inflate this figure.

What is your filing status: ❑ SINGLE   ❑ MARRIED-JOINT   ❑ MARRIED-SEPARATE   ❑ HEAD OF HOUSEHOLD

DESCRIPTION	ANNUAL AMOUNT	INSTRUCTIONS FOR NEXT YEAR UNTIL...
Number of Exemptions on 1040 form		
Salary—First Client	$	Inflate at ___ % until retirement?
Salary—Second Client	$	Inflate at ___ % until retirement?
Self-Employment Income—First Client	$	Inflate at ___ % until retirement?
Self-Employment Income—Second Client	$	Inflate at ___ % until retirement?

If you know your Social Security Benefit, enter it below.

Social Security Income—First Client	$	Or starting at age ___	inflate at ___ %
Social Security Income—Second Client	$	Or starting at age ___	inflate at ___ %

ANY CARRY-FORWARD CAPITAL LOSSES OR ANY CAPITAL GAINS FOR THIS YEAR? (OPTIONAL)

Additional Source?	$
Short-Term Capital Gains (Loss)	$
Long-Term Capital Gains (Loss)	$

ANY MISCELLANEOUS INCOME & CREDIT ITEMS? (OPTIONAL)

Deferral Preference Income	$
Exclusion Preference Income	$
Foreign Tax Credits	$
Child Care/Earned Income Credit	$
Rehab/Low Income Housing Credit	$
Allowable Investment Tax Credits	$

Note: If we are not going to do a detailed budget for you, then enter your annual discretionary living expenses here. These should not include taxes nor expenses related to your assets (such as your home) and loans.

AND/OR

CASH FLOW	THIS YEAR	INSTRUCTIONS FOR NEXT YEAR UNTIL LIFE EXPECTANCY
Living Expenses*	$	Inflate at ___ % until
Extraordinary Living Expenses	$	Inflate at ___ % until
Itemized Deductions		
Business Expenses		
Charitable Contributions		
Local Income (City) Taxes		
Medical, Dental & Prescription Drugs		

DETAILED BUDGET INFORMATION

If you would like us to do a detailed budget for you, please fill out the information requested below. We have divided many of these expenses into categories. For those items that apply to you, please fill in either an annual or monthly amount. If the expense occurs only in one month, please indicate that month also.

> Examples.   ①If you spend $100 per month on gas, you may enter either $1200 in Column 1 or $100 in Column 2.
>   ②If you spend $3000 for an August vacation, put "August - $3000" in Column 3.

DESCRIPTION	ANNUAL AMOUNT	OR MONTHLY AMOUNT	COMMENTS/DEDUCTIBLE
AUTO AND TRAVEL			
Car Registration			
Gas, Maintenance, etc.			
Vacations			
HOUSEHOLD			
Gas & Electric			
Telephone & Cell Phone			
Misc. Utilities such as Cable TV			
MISCELLANEOUS			
Accounting/Tax Preparation			
Alimony Payments			
Books			
Education			
Entertainment, Clubs			
Financial Planning Services			
Gifts, Flowers			
Hobbies (Golf, etc.)			
Home Computer			
Insurance			
Legal Fees			
Non-Ded. Business Expense			
Safe Deposit Box			
Tithe			
CHILDREN			
Allowances			
Child Support Payments			
PERSONAL			
Clothing			
Eating Out			
Entertainment			
Groceries			
Laundry, Dry Cleaning			
Personal Care (Barber, Beauty)			
OTHER EXPENSES			
1			
2			
EXPENSES FOR RENTERS			
Rent			

LIFE INSURANCE

	1	2	3	4
Policy Name				
Policy Number				
Who owns it?				
Policy Date				
Company Name (if different)				
Who is the beneficiary of this policy?				
Who is the person insured by this policy?				

What is the annual premium? Paid by: ❏ you OR ❏ your employer?	$	$	$	$
CASH VALUE: What is the cash value of the policy as of this date?	$	$	$	$
Death Benefit	$	$	$	$
Do you know the TOTAL amount of money you have invested in this policy?	$	$	$	$
Circle (W) for Whole Life, (F) for Fixed Universal Life, (V) Variable Universal Life, or (T) for Term	W F V T	W F V T	W F V T	W F V T
Current Amount of any loan on this policy?				

Do you want us to determine how much life insurance (or capital) the family would need if you (or your spouse) were to die today? We should perform this analysis approximately every year as your needs change. If so, we will ask you to answer questions in four main areas.

1. How much cash would be available if death were to occur, given your current resources?

2. How much cash would the family need immediately?

3. We will divide the survivor's life into five different periods, such as when more than one child is living at home. We need to know how much money the family would need in each period, including taxes.

4. How much income would be available in today's dollars from various sources such as earned income and Social Security?

HOW MUCH LIFE INSURANCE DO YOU NEED?

BASIC QUESTIONS

- Liquidated Assets: How much money will be available from assets you are willing to sell immediately?

  _____

- What would you like to estimate for final expenses? _____

- Would you want your real estate loans to be paid off? _____

- Do you have a Will? ❏ Yes ❏ No

- Do you have a Living Trust? ❏ Yes ❏ No

SURVIVOR NEEDS: HOW MUCH MONEY WILL THE FAMILY NEED?

We need to analyze the financial needs of the survivor from now until life expectancy and compare the needs with the amount of money that will be available.

Fill out the monthly needs during all periods that apply and the age of the survivor after the last year of that period. If you are single, fill out the periods that apply to your children based upon your age. For example, if you are 48 and your only child would be at home for four more years, fill out "Until Survivor is 52 Years of Age."

FIRST CLIENT'S Death Today					SECOND CLIENT'S Death Today			
PERIOD (Ignore those that don't apply)	AMOUNT NEEDED	SURVIVOR'S STARTING AGE	SURVIVOR'S ENDING AGE		PERIOD (Ignore those that don't apply)	AMOUNT NEEDED	SURVIVOR'S STARTING AGE	SURVIVOR'S ENDING AGE
Two or More Children are at Home					Two or More Children are at Home			
One Child Only is at Home					One Child Only is at Home			
Social Security Pays No Benefits (Blackout)*					Social Security Pays No Benefits (Blackout)*			
Pre-retirement (Widower's Benefit)					Pre-retirement (Widower's Benefit)			
Retirement Until Life Expectancy					Retirement Until Life Expectancy			

* This is the number of years during which the survivor is not entitled to any monthly income from Social Security. It generally begins when the youngest child reaches age 16 and extends until the survivor reaches age 60, when he or she may be eligible for widow's or widower's benefits.

LONG⊠TERM CARE INSURANCE

	1	2	3	4
Policy Name				
Number				
Insured				
Owner				
Daily Benefit				
Annual Premium				
Elimination Period (days)				
Benefit Period (years)				

DISABILITY INSURANCE

	1	2	3	4
Policy Name				
Policy Number				
Owner				
Type				
Insured				
Annual Premium				
% Increase in Premium				
Monthly Benefit				
Benefit at Age 65				
Benefit Duration (months)				
Waiting Period (months)				
Definition of Disability				

WHAT HAPPENS IF YOU BECOME DISABLED?

Your ability to earn an income protects your family's standard of living. This ability can be considered your most important asset. Your family's financial well-being could be drastically affected if you were to become disabled for a long period of time—or even for a short period of time.

Even though you may receive benefits paid by Social Security, by your state, and by your employer, together they may be inadequate to care for your family. If that is the case, then you will want to provide sufficient additional income protection for all members of your family who contribute to the family's finances.

HOW MUCH ANNUAL INCOME DO YOU NEED IF DISABLED?

	First Year	Second Year	Third Year	Fourth Year	Fifth Year
Living Expenses (incl taxes)					
Extraordinary Living Expenses					
Loan, Property & Other Expenses					

If we have entered all your assets, liabilities, and tax form information, we will calculate the amount of annual income you will need, if disabled, from information on our database. We can also automatically include the funding necessary to send your dependent children to college, if we have analyzed their education expenses. However, you may want to adjust the amounts downward, if you plan to decrease your standard of living.

GENERAL INSURANCE

TYPE	POLICY NAME	POLICY BENEFIT	ANNUAL PREMIUM
Medical			
Liability			
Homeowner's			
Auto Values $			

ASSETS & LIABILITIES

QUALIFIED RETIREMENT PLANS

Name of Plan

Account #

Owner

Acct Balance

Interest Rate

Contributed(/year)?

% you pay?

Plan Type

Start withdrawing at age

Comments

Note: You may select from these plan types: 401K, College IRA, Deferred Compensation, IRA, Keogh, Pension or Profit Sharing, Roth IRA, Salary Savings, SEP, Simple IRA, TSA

STOCKS

Name of Stock

Current Value $

Account #

Owner

If want to sell, what's the basis? (Tax Cost/Share) $

Additional Annual Investment $

Comments

MUTUAL FUNDS

Name of Mutual Fund

Current Value $

Account #

Owner

Year Acquired

If want to sell, what's the basis? (Tax Cost) $

Additional Annual Investment $

Comments

ASSETS & LIABILITIES

BONDS

	1	2	3
Name of Bond			
Face Value	$	$	$
Market Value	$	$	$
Interest Rate			
Date of Maturity (MM/YY)			
Bond Type	CORP GOV MUNI	CORP GOV MUNI	CORP GOV MUNI
State of Issue			
% Taxable			
Number of Bonds			
Account #			
Owner			
Year & Month Acquired			
If want to sell, what's the basis? (Tax Cost)	$	$	$
Comments:			

VARIABLE ANNUITIES

Name of Variable Annuity			
Account Balance	$	$	$
Death Benefit			
Surrender Charge			
Account #			
Owner			
Year & Month Acquired			
If want to sell, what's the basis? (Tax Cost)	$	$	$
Additional Annual Investment	$	$	$
Comments			

CASH ACCOUNTS

Name of Cash Asset			
Type of Cash Asset: Checking, Savings, Money Market, CD, Fixed Annuity			
Interest Rate			
% Taxable			
If a CD of Fixed Annuity, Term in Months			
If CD, interest taxable now?			
Account Balance	$	$	$
Surrender Penalty			
Account #			
Owner			
Year & Month Acquired			
Additional Annual Investment	$	$	$
Comments			

ASSETS & LIABILITIES

PERSONAL RESIDENCE

Month & Year Acquired _____   Sell Cost % _____

Owner _____   Property Tax _____

Address _____   Annual % Property Tax will increase _____

Liquidate at Death(Yes/No) _____

Home Worth? _____   Annual Insurance Premium
for homeowner's policy? _____

% Appreciation _____   Other Annual Expenses _____
(Amt expected to appreciate until sale)   (including lawn & pool care, maintenance, landscaping, repairs, etc.)

Purchase Price + the cost of   Expense Escalation Percentage: _____
any major improvements? _____   What is the % increase expected for these other expenses each year?

CURRENT LOANS ON RESIDENCE

Name of Loan or Lender			
Owner			
Type of Loan	MORT BANK PERS INV	MORT BANK PERS INV	MORT BANK PERS INV
Original Amt of Loan			
Interest Rate			
Term to Balloon (if any)			
Year & Month Started			
Term of Loan (months)			
Monthly Payment			

OTHER SUBSTANTIAL PROPERTY (VALUABLE COLLECTIONS, JEWELRY, VEHICLES, ETC.)

Item			
Year & Month Acquired			
Owner			
Liquidate at Death?			
Current Value			
Purchase Price			
% Appreciation			
Investment Asset			
Tax (annually)			
Insurance (annually)			

LIABILITIES

Name of Loan or Lender			
Owner			
Loan Type (see below)			
Original Amt of Loan			
Interest Rate			
Term to Balloon (if any)			
Year & Month Acquired			
Term on Loan (Months)			
Monthly Payment			

RISK TOLERANCE QUESTIONNAIRE

1. I do not need to withdraw funds from my investments for:
   - ❑ Less than 2 years (1)
   - ❑ 2-5 years (3)
   - ❑ 6-10 years (8)
   - ❑ More than 10 years (12)

2. Generally, I prefer an investment with little or no ups or downs in value, and I am willing to accept lower returns these investments may make.
   - ❑ I strongly agree (1)
   - ❑ I agree (3)
   - ❑ I disagree (8)
   - ❑ I strongly disagree (12)

3. This graph below shows the range of possible returns of f our different investments of $10,000 over a one-year period. For example, if you invest in Investment C, you will earn an amount somewhere with the return bar, between a loss of $2,000 and a gain of $5,200.

   Assuming this is the only information you have, which investment would you choose? Circle one of the letters below.

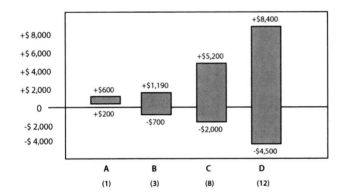

4. In this question, a stock mutual fund you own has experienced a loss of 25% of its value in one month. The stock market has experienced the same loss. What is the action you would like to take?
   - ❑ Sell. You are afraid the stock market is in a downturn and you can't afford more losses. (1)
   - ❑ Sell half. You think the market may rebound, but you only want to expose half of your investment to further losses. (3)
   - ❑ Hold. You understand your investment may be subject to short-term fluctuation (8)
   - ❑ Buy More. You are comfortable with fluctuation and assume the market will regain its previous value and increase. (12)

5. In this question, a substantial part of your assets are in a stock mutual fund that has gradually been decreasing 2% a month. The stock market and your fund have lost 22% from a year ago. What action would you take?
   - ❑ Sell. You now believe that after a year they will not regain their value. (1)
   - ❑ Sell half. You are not willing to leave your entire investment exposed to further loss. (3)
   - ❑ Hold. You are comfortable waiting for the market and fund to regain their value. (8)
   - ❑ Buy More. You believe the market and your fund will regain their value and more. (12)

6. How stable are your current and future income sources (salary, Social Security, pension)?

    ❑ Very unstable (1)
    ❑ Unstable (3)
    ❑ Stable (8)
    ❑ Very Stable (12)

7. How would you describe your investment expertise and the time you spend on investments?

    ❑ You need professional guidance. (1)
    ❑ You have other priorities, but will stay informed. (3)
    ❑ You view investments as an area of interest. (8)
    ❑ You spend time daily or weekly on your investments. (12)

Score: [   ]

Draw a line up from where you scored. This will tell you the portfolio that will be suited for your Investment Profile. If your total score is less than 9 then none of our managed objectives may be suitable for you.

Client Name: _____

Client Signature: _____

Date: _____

If you elect a management style that varies from your score, please initial belo- V

_____. My Registered Representative has explained to me and I fully understand my score on the Risk Tolerance Questionnaire. I am electing to place this account into _____ instead of _____, which is the management style my score shows I would best tolerate. I understand that in the higher risk option, I have accepted the higher volatility within my investment and cannot hold Capital Financial Services, Inc. or the Faith Asset Management Program and its Affiliates liable of any possible losses.

Rep Name: _____

ENDNOTES

1. On April 18, 1521, at the Diet of Worms, Martin Luther was asked, "Do you or do you not recant your books and the errors in them?

   Martin Luther responded, "Since your Majesty and your lordships want a simple, clear, and true answer, I will give it. Unless I am convinced by the teachings of Holy Scripture or by sound reasoning—for I do not believe either the pope or councils alone, since they have often made mistakes and have even said the exact opposite about the same point—I am tied by the Scriptures I have quoted and by my conscience. I cannot and will not recant anything, for to go against conscience is neither safe nor right. Here I stand. God help me! Amen."

2. His letter to Philip Melanchthon of August 1, 1521, as recorded in *Luther's Works*, American Edition, Vol. 48, pgs. 282–282.

   Luther wrote:

   > "If you are a preacher of grace, then preach a true and not a fictitious grace; if grace is true, you must bear a true and not a fictitious sin. God does not save people who are only fictitious sinners. Be a sinner and sin boldly, but believe and rejoice in Christ even more boldly, for he is victorious over sin, death, and the world. As long as we are here [in this world] we have to sin. This life is not the dwelling place of righteousness, but, as Peter says, we look for new heavens and a new earth in which righteousness dwells. It is enough that by the riches of God's glory we have come to know the Lamb, even though we commit fornication and murder a thousand times a day. Do you think that the purchase price that was paid for the redemption of our sins by so great a Lamb is too small? Pray boldly—you too are a mighty sinner."

3. This story is written with the permission of Mr. Gruba.

4. Nathan Bedford Forrest is a hero to some and a villain to others. This book is not intended to be part of that on-going debate, but I invite all who wish to know more to read Robert Selph Henry's biography, *First with the Most*.

5. *Lee*, by Douglas Southall Freeman.

6. There were more blacks in the Confederate Army by 1864 than in the Union Army. There are even monuments to their courage and valiant fighting scattered throughout the states of the Confederacy. Agnes Corbett, Director of Camden, South Carolina Archives said, "That is a part of our history that has not been brought to the surface." At least two black Confederate monuments exist in South Carolina, and several others can be found in other states.

According to John Danylchuk, Captain of the 34th Texas Cavalry Unit in Killeen, Texas, there was on incident in which is unit was asked to reenact a battle for a television miniseries. After he and two other men—one of whom was black—went to meet with the casting director, Danylchuk got a strange phone call. The director said, "Yeah, we'd like to have all you guys—but not the black guy," Danylchuck recalled. "I know why," he continued. "They don't want to see black people wearing gray."

Historians estimate the total number of black men who sided with the Confederacy, either as laborers or soldiers, as anywhere from 60,000 to 90,000. James Eaton, a professor at Florida A&M University who studies black confederates, explained, "Black men did fight on both sides. There's been a whole lot of credible work done about the side of the Union, but they have not given any scholarly research to the Confederate side." ("Monuments Honor the Blacks Who Wore Gray," by Lisa Hofbauer, February 2, 1997, *The Post & Courier*, Charleston, South Carolina.)

From an article by Charles Rice, "America's Civil War," November 1995:

> "Private R.M. Doswell was hastening back to his unit after carrying an order when something attracted his attention. The young Virginian had just spotted one of the new Confederate companies of black soldiers, "a novel sight to me." The black Confederates were guarding a wagon train near Amelia Court House on the retreat from Richmond. Doswell reined in about 100 yards to the rear of the wagon train and watched in fascination as a Union cavalry regiment formed up to charge. The black Confederates fired their weapons like veterans and drove back the overconfident Federals. The horse soldiers re-formed for another charge. This time they broke up the wagon train and scattered the defenders. The black soldiers were captured and disarmed. Doswell suddenly realized his own danger and rode away without being noticed. The date was April 4, 1865. Five days later, Lee would surrender his Army of Northern Virginia at Appomattox Court House."

7. Battle of Nashville Preservation Society, Inc., December 10, 2004.

8. *Politically Incorrect Guide to American History* by Thomas E. Woods, Ph.D., Regnery Publishing, Inc., 2004. By contrast, in an 1865 letter to his wife, Mary Custis Lee, the eventual leader of the Confederate Army, Robert E. Lee, called slavery "a moral and political evil."

9. *Rise and Fall of the Confederate Government* by Jefferson Davis, D. Appleton & Co., New York, NY: 1881.

Slavery was a horrible blight that infected America. But few people realize that the Constitution of the Confederacy outlawed the importation of slaves from abroad, thereby eliminating the slave trade industry. Although slavery, itself, was still protected, the institution and its culture were in a state of fundamental and organic change which, argued by many historians, would have resulted in the eradication of slavery of its own momentum without the collateral damage of the massive loss of life manifested by the war.

10. The North and its Union Army were notorious for their disdain of the South and its people. There are too many examples to list in this book, but to make the point, I'll enumerate three.

   (1) The commander of Union forces occupying Memphis in 1863 became so frustrated at the supply trains being shot at by southerners as the trains left Memphis station and went into the countryside, he issued a formal command that all trains had to have "men and women" who were "southern sympathizers" tied to the outside of the engine on both sides, so that if any train was targeted, the bullet might strike one of their own.

   (2) Similarly, Federal Major John G. Foster, in 1864, positioned 600 Confederate prisoners so that they would be in the line of fire in the event that the Confederates decided to shell Union Army positions.

   (3) While occupying New Orleans, Gen. Benjamin Butler became so infuriated at the recalcitrant attitude of the women of that city that he issued Order Number 28, which authorized "that after when any female shall by word, gesture, or movement insult or show contempt" for any Union soldier, she was to be considered as a prostitute and treated that way. Historian Thomas E. Woods, Ph.D., writes, "This 'right to rape' order horrified the civilized states of Europe and immediate protests were issued from Britain and France." (*Death Before Dishonor, the Immortal 600 Human Shields 130 Years Before Saddam Hussein,* by George W. Contant, 1997; *Captives Immortal: The Story of Six Hundred Confederate Officers and the United States Prisoner of War Policy,* by Mauriel Phillip Joslyn. White Mane Publishing, Shippensburg, PA: 1996; *Politically Incorrect Guide to American History,* by Thomas E. Woods, Jr., Ph.D. Regnery Publishing, Inc.: 2004.)

11. *The Federalist Papers,* by Hamilton, Madison, and Jay. New York: The New American Library. Also, *John Adams,* by David McCulough. New York: Simon & Schuster, 2001.

12. "What 'Brokeback' Win Might Mean," *The Tennessean,* March 5, 2006.

13. Bruin Alumni Association, 2005.

14. Focus on Your Child, 3/10/06, www.focusonyourchild.com.

15. "God, Gays and the Economy," by Stephen Bolt, *Business Reform* magazine.

16. HRC.org website home page, January 24, 2005.

17. FoxNews.com report, May 26, 2004.

18. "The Gay Consumer," *BCBusiness,* October 2004.

19. "The Gay Consumer," *BCBusiness*, October 2004.

20. *Outtraveler*, Fall 2004.

21. HRC.org website, January 24, 2005.

22. HRC.org website, January 24, 2005.

23. HRC.org website, January 24, 2005.

INDEX

Printed in the United States
61075LVS00003B/28-75